DARD LOAN

ADHD IN ADULTS

£26.99

ADHD IN ADULTS

A PSYCHOLOGICAL GUIDE TO PRACTICE

Susan Young
Institute of Psychiatry, UK

Jessica Bramham
Institute of Psychiatry, UK

John Wiley & Sons, Ltd

Copyright © 2007   John Wiley & Sons Ltd, The Atrium, Southern Gate, Chichester,
West Sussex PO19 8SQ, England

Telephone (+44) 1243 779777

Email (for orders and customer service enquiries): cs-books@wiley.co.uk
Visit our Home Page on www.wiley.com

Clipart in Chapter 9 © 2006 Microsoft Corporation. All rights reserved.

Other Wiley Editorial Offices

John Wiley & Sons Inc., 111 River Street, Hoboken, NJ 07030, USA

Jossey-Bass, 989 Market Street, San Francisco, CA 94103-1741, USA

Wiley-VCH Verlag GmbH, Boschstr. 12, D-69469 Weinheim, Germany

John Wiley & Sons Australia Ltd, 42 McDougall Street, Milton, Queensland 4064, Australia

John Wiley & Sons (Asia) Pte Ltd, 2 Clementi Loop #02-01, Jin Xing Distripark, Singapore 129809

John Wiley & Sons Canada Ltd, 6045 Freemont Blvd, Mississauga, ONT, L5R 4J3

Wiley also publishes its books in a variety of electronic formats. Some content that appears in print
may not be available in electronic books.

Library of Congress Cataloging-in-Publication Data

Young, Susan, 1957-
    ADHD in adults : a psychological guide to practice / Susan Young,
Jessica Bramham.
        p. ; cm.
    Includes bibliographical references and index.
    ISBN-13: 978-0-470-01231-4 (hbk : alk. paper)
    ISBN-10: 0-470-01231-5 (hbk : alk. paper)
    ISBN-13: 978-0-470-01232-1 (pbk. : alk. paper)
    ISBN-10: 0-470-01232-3 (pbk. : alk. paper)
    1. Attention-deficit disorder in adults.   2. Attention-deficit-disordered adults.
I. Bramham, Jessica.   II. Title.
    [DNLM: 1. Attention Deficit Disorder with Hyperactivity.   2. Adult.   3. Attention Deficit
Disorder with Hyperactivity–complications. WM 190 Y76a 2007]
    RC394.A85A344 2007
    616.85'89--dc22   2006026962

British Library Cataloguing in Publication Data

A catalogue record for this book is available from the British Library

ISBN-13 978-0-470-01231-4 (hbk) 978-0-470-01232-1 (hbk)
ISBN-10 0-470-01231-5 (hbk) 0-470-01232-3 (pbk)

Typeset in 10/12 pt Times by Thomson Digital, Noida, India
Printed and bound in Great Britain by TJ International Ltd, Padstow, Cornwall
This book is printed on acid-free paper responsibly manufactured from sustainable forestry in which at
least two trees are planted for each one used for paper production.

CONTENTS

LIST OF FIGURES AND TABLES

Figures

Tables

ABOUT THE AUTHORS

Dr Susan Young is a Senior Lecturer at the Institute of Psychiatry, King's College, London. She is a Chartered Clinical and Forensic Psychologist, and a Clinical Neuropsychologist. Dr Young has a Doctorate in Clinical Psychology from University College London and a PhD from King's College London, University of London. She has many years experience working at the renowned Maudsley Hospital in the UK where she developed and set up the neuropsychology service for the UK's first National Adult ADHD service. Dr Young has extensive experience in the assessment and psychological treatment of young people and adults with ADHD, both males and females. She has published widely on the subject, in particular on epidemiology, neuropsychological functioning, psychosocial functioning, comorbidity and psychological treatment.

Dr Jessica Bramham is a Clinical Lecturer at the Institute of Psychiatry, King's College London. She has a Doctorate in Clinical Psychology from the Institute of Psychiatry and an MA from Cambridge University. She is a Chartered Clinical Psychologist and Clinical Neuropsychologist. Dr Bramham was Dr Young's successor at the Adult ADHD Service at the Maudsley Hospital and is currently lead Clinical Psychologist for the service. She has been involved in expanding service in order to meet the growing needs of the adult ADHD population in the UK. Neuropsychological assessment is a particular interest of Dr Bramham. She is involved in researching cognitive functioning in adulthood ADHD, the implementation and evaluation of group and individual psychological interventions.

FOREWORD

For many years it was reassuring for professionals and parents to believe that the problems caused by ADHD simply represented a poor fit between some children and their environments. It was comforting to reassure parents that the problem would be outgrown and with patience and treatment, ADHD was not likely to cause children significant life time adversity. Over the past fifteen years, the belief that ADHD is just a childhood condition quickly outgrown by late adolescence has been increasingly tested. A significant number of individuals, male and female alike, suffering with ADHD in their childhood, continue to suffer and lead lives less than they are capable of often into their geriatric years. Though a number of early pioneers advised professionals to consider the plight of many adults with histories of ADHD, it was not until the concept of ADHD was popularized in the lay press and media that serious attention began to be paid to the condition. Though some would argue the condition and its treatments are controversial, within the scientific and mental health community little controversy remains. The body of literature attesting to the emotional, cognitive, vocational, academic, substance use and criminal risks of the condition is growing. As Editor-in-Chief of the Journal of Attention Disorders I have observed that in each of the past two years we have received an increasing number of articles researching adult ADHD issues and in fact are devoting an increasing number of our journal pages to the condition during these years.

Though one third of adults with ADHD may progress satisfactorily into their adult years, another one third continues to experience some level of problems while the final third continues to experience and often develops significant problems related to ADHD and other comorbid conditions. By combining a number of outcome studies, it is reasonable to conclude that 10% to 20% of adults with histories of ADHD experience few problems. Sixty percent continue to demonstrate symptoms of ADHD and experience social, academic and emotional problems to at least a mild to moderate degree and 10% to 30% develop antisocial problems in addition to their continued difficulty with ADHD and other comorbidities. Many of these negative outcomes are linked to the continuity, severity and persistence of ADHD symptoms. Though males may experience more problems with disruptive and aggressive behavior, females with ADHD appear to suffer equally in all other arenas of life.

In 2002, Dr. Ann Teeter-Ellison and I had the pleasure to edit the first comprehensive clinical volume addressing adult ADHD, *Clinician's Guide to Adult ADHD: Assessment and Intervention* (Goldstein and Teeter-Ellison, 2002). At the time, there were a limited number of peer reviewed research studies dealing with adults and even fewer research tested methods for evaluating and most importantly treating adults with ADHD through combined medical and psychological interventions. It was our intent in this volume to begin aggressively addressing this issue and to offer authors with promising though untested ideas, particularly in regards to psychological and psychosocial treatment, the opportunity to contribute to our volume. A number of years earlier I had the opportunity to meet and spend time with Susan Young in London. Susan was focusing her treatment efforts on developing a model of psychotherapy for adults with ADHD. Susan agreed to author a contribution to our text. Her chapter (Young, 2002) provided one of the first published comprehensive approaches to treating adult ADHD through a cognitive behavioral therapy model. In this chapter, Susan reviewed the typical impairments confronting adults with ADHD, provided four extensive case examples and then set out to outline a cognitive behavioral therapy approach for treating adults with ADHD based on her work. One of the aspects that appealed to me about Susan's approach was that she emphasized that psychotherapists and mental health professionals should seek out and help adults with ADHD take advantage of their strengths as a means of creating balance in their lives and learning to cope with their symptoms and impairments. She noted at the conclusion of her chapter that with the help of caring professionals adults with ADHD "have choice and opportunity to develop these talents and adapt the environment to suit their personal needs. What they often lack is the vision and courage to do so" (pg. 158).

In the following years, Susan and Jessica Bramham joined forces. Together they have worked diligently to create a psychosocial model to treat adult ADHD utilizing a cognitive behavioral framework. This volume is a ground-breaking first step in standardizing the psychosocial treatment of adults with ADHD. Though the Young-Bramham program has yet to be empirically validated, the work of American researchers Safren, Otto, Sprich, Perlman, Wilens and Biederman (in press) and Safren, Perlman, Sprich and Otto (2005), has begun the important process of validating cognitive behavioral approach to treating adults with ADHD. This approach has been found to not only offer personal insight and psychological relief but also the reduction of symptom severity and daily impairment.

The hypothesis that ADHD represents a lifetime condition has been tested and verified. Current theory for the etiology of ADHD is consistent with a lifetime presentation reflecting developmental rather than pathological differences between affected individuals and the general population. The consequences of living with the burden of a significantly disabling condition, one that leads to impaired self-discipline, has resulted in demonstrated problems across all arenas of life for adults with ADHD. The condition serves as a risk factor limiting potential for academic and vocational achievement as well as acting as a catalyst for comorbid psychiatric and life problems.

Though much work remains to be done to understand the developmental course, risk, and protective factors involved in the adult outcome of ADHD, the present volume will serve as a bright beacon guiding professionals in their care of adults with ADHD in what has been an often dark and murky journey.

Sam Goldstein, PhD

Salt Lake City, Utah

REFERENCES

Goldstein, S., & Teeter-Ellison, P.A. (Eds.) (2002). *Clinician's Guide to Adult ADHD: Assessment and Intervention.* New York, NY: Academic Press.

Safren, S.A., Otto, M.W., Sprich, S., Perlman, C.L., Wilens, T.E., & Biederman, J. (in press). Cognitive behavioral therapy for ADHD in medication-treated adults with continued symptoms. *Behavior Research and Therapy.*

Safren, S.A., Perlman, C.A., Sprich, S., & Otto M.W. (2005) *Mastering your adult ADHD: A cognitive-behavioral treatment program.* New York: Oxford University Press.

Young, S.J. (2002). A model of psychotherapy for adults with ADHD. In S. Goldstein and R. Brooks (Eds.). *A Clinician's Guide to Adult ADHD: Assessment and Intervention.* New York, NY: Academic Press.

FOREWORD

"The journey probably started with the words "You have ADHD." To the client these words were not just a diagnosis, but framework for self-understanding." These words taken from the authors' module on termination are a statement of the central thesis of this book. This is a clinically driven manual for understanding and helping adults with ADHD. The strength of this manual is that it is clinically driven. The authors are not constrained by a particular view of how change occurs, the structures of the DSM or ICD, the ideology of a particular method of therapy, or a narrow arena of functional impairment.

Young and Bramham define three ways in which change may occur. Biological change may occur either through maturation or as a result of taking medication, in which case one observes a direct improvement in symptoms *per se*. Environmental change can occur when the client's milieu is modified in such a way as to minimise the impact of symptoms or optimise the visibility of strengths. Psychological change occurs through the use of cognitive, behavioural, psychoeducational and interpersonal techniques that provide a scaffolding for building skills that were not previously present. The authors further simplify this schema for understanding change by noting that it can occur from the outside in, as well as from the inside out.

Psychiatrists who prescribe medication and CBT therapists are most interested in change from the inside out. The focus of these authors is not on any one direction of change. Instead they have focused on the dialectic between symptoms and functioning that is unique to this particular group of clients. This is a book by clinicians who have learned about ADHD from their clients. The result is a practical manual that can be as easily referenced in individual, group or workshop formats. The instrumental tools that accompany each module are made available to the reader on a web site for ease of presentation.

What emerges from this perspective is clinical wisdom. One can see and feel both the client and the therapy. Sometimes the authors sound almost simplistic in stating the obvious. "Achievement is a strong reinforcer." "Self monitoring can increase a skill." "Recognizing and preparing for problematic tasks makes a difference." Yet each one of these statements represents tasty therapeutic spice.

The treatment described in this book would help some of the people, some of the time, with some of their problems. The change that would come out of this therapy would be meaningful and enduring.

Our understanding of how clients with ADHD get better has at times been characterised by cognitive errors. Getting better is not black (no change) or white (remission). For the vast majority of clients change is qualified. Getting better is not a race to the finish line, in which how fast you get better is more important than how long you maintain that improvement. This is a struggle, or a journey as the authors frame it, in which time, persistence, creativity, resilience, and insight empower the greatest change in longer term developmental gains. These authors have a developmental perspective on ADHD, but they also have a developmental perspective on how to optimise enduring functional change and quality of life.

DSM and ICD define the paradigm that allowed ADHD to obtain visibility. As a result of the research underlying the diagnostic systems for ADHD, we were able to move from a moral view of laziness into a neuropsychologically informed understanding of executive function and inhibition. However, DSM and ICD have been both a friend and a foe. The history of ADHD is defined by a chronic and essential tension between a narrow definition of the core symptoms and broader schemas of the associated symptoms carried by this population. Contemporary research in ADHD has benefited profoundly from use of a narrow definition of ADHD. On the other hand, clinicians such as Rosemary Tannock, Tom Brown, Paul Wender are often pulled out of this cozy research nest by the clinical demands of clients who have other complaints and complex neuropsychological deficits. This book exists in that tension. It targets a population diagnosed by the symptoms and addresses clinical deficits in a wide range of associated symptom areas.

Adults with ADHD may be anxious, even when their anxiety is either not specific enough or not severe enough to meet criteria for an anxiety disorder. Young and Bramham observe that ADHD symptoms lead to difficulty with anxiety and depression, while anxiety and depression divert power away from the working memory engine that mobilises attention and inhibition. You cannot divorce internalising and externalising symptoms and still engage and carry a client with ADHD through therapeutic change. When someone with ADHD has to do something they are not equipped to handle (homework, taxes, housework, taking a test, driving, being on time) they will sense their own danger and remember their own failures.

One of the more energetic controversies of recent academic and clinical forums is the differential between bipolar disorder and ADHD. One has to wonder why this particular problem continues to generate such interest. It was therefore with some delight that I observed these two psychologists wrestle with this demon. They describe clients with ADHD as "passionate" (a very un-DSM word), such that when they are low, they are "passionately low". They note that ADHD is often associated with dramatic mood swings within the hour rather than within the week. One might even say that they have impulsive mood swings. The clinical reality for people who work with ADHD is that these clients often suffer impairment from mood and anxiety symptoms. These symptoms overlap with but are not identical to the disorders described in DSM or ICD.

The focus of treatment for ADHD has been on symptoms rather than functioning. This truly puts the cart before the horse. Symptom-based assessment is only a conceptual gateway to knowing how to help someone get better at day-to-day living. The trick to helping clients is to target the areas where they have problems. This is the underlying structure which defines the modules of the Young and Bramham programme. Most clients do not need (or could not handle) the whole of this programme, however, any client would benefit from some of it.

The modules provided include many of the most common problems these clients complain of: time management, procrastination, anger management, interpersonal problems. The authors always start with symptoms and end with functioning. For example, the module on attention starts with a discussion of the varieties of attention deficits and how these manifest clinically. What follows is a description of how to support the development of executive function skills. The module on sleep starts by describing sleep itself, the sleep problems we see in clients with ADHD, and ends with a description of time tested, common sense sleep hygiene. This is all the more original given that while adults with ADHD commonly complain of sleep problems, there is almost no research on the sleep problems specific to ADHD in adulthood.

The modules deal with many different problems. The authors note that although circumstances will dictate the usefulness of one or another module, the skills that develop are cumulative. When clients address one problem, they obtain a framework for establishing change that permits them to rework the same skills in another arena of impairment. The core modules on assessment, treatment, attention, impulsivity, and termination are likely to be relevant to any client.

The section on impulsivity starts with a description of impulsive behaviour, affect, and cognitions and ends with practical strategies. If the client has consequence blindness, reinforce the immediacy and salience of rewards. If the client makes impulsive decisions, have them write down the pros and cons of decisions before acting. If the client jumps to conclusions, teach them to review the evidence. Clients with ADHD could not learn these skills when they were symptomatic, but nor do they necessarily reverse a lifetime of habit when the neuropsychiatric potential for change becomes available. For someone with ADHD to grow the symptoms have to be manageable, expectations need to match potential, and the client has to make up many lost years of potential skill development. The disabilities that accompany ADHD are varied enough to leave room for multiple treatment options.

The module I enjoyed the most was the discussion of social relationships. This is a description of ADHD symptoms seen through the distorting lens of the non-ADHD companion. If the client zones out, they are not interested. If the client is staring, they are aggressive. If the client is fidgeting, they are trying to bother you. If the client forgets to call, they do not love you. It is also a description of the profound social handicaps that ADHD symptoms engender such as hanging out with the wrong crowd, promiscuity, difficulty with pragmatic language, trouble listening. This is one of the first attempts to describe ways in which we might assist adults with ADHD with their interpersonal difficulties.

I appreciated the authors sensitivity to what is one of the greatest sources of psychological injury in ADHD: isolation. Clients with Asperger syndrome often come in as adults and discuss their wish to have a friend, but they are not actually lonely. They have grown into an awareness that there is an aspect of human gregariousness that they are not a part of, but they do necessarily feel what it is they are missing. By contrast, clients with ADHD are intensely social and what they see is denied to them. The authors have made an important beginning in making the client's experience of social rejection a focus of treatment.

There are many aspects of ADHD we do not understand. A good clinical book will by its nature defy categories. It will also be enriched by insights that make no theoretical sense. For example, the authors note that clients with ADHD may apologise for misdemeanors they have neither processed nor understood. I am reminded of the husband who does not remember what he said to his wife, or the child who tells the principal he "didn't do it" and is not lying in as much as he does not know at that moment that he actually did do it.

Of all the clinical wisdom in this book, by far the best is that the authors practice what they preach. Motivational interviewing and cognitive behavioural therapy are contingent upon helping the client see the cup as half full. And yet as clinicians how often we focus our interview on what is wrong rather than what is right? Young and Bramham capitalise on the greatest strength of ADHD clients: courage and resiliency. The authors note that these are clients who try, try again. Some clients with ADHD have great successes to attach to their name. Some have very few. All of them have tried and tried again and this is a powerful therapeutic niche. Young and Bramham use a metaphor o describe this. They say that clients with ADHD are "life's true entrepreneurs". This is true, and like all entrepreneurs they risk bankruptcy as well as wealth.

The authors note that adults with ADHD "often feel that they are 'survivors' of a syndrome that has left them with significant personal, social and occupational consequences. This is anecdotally known as the 'hangover' of ADHD." There is long term damage to self esteem that ensues from a childhood corrupted by inattention, hyperactivity and motoric, cognitive and behavioural impulsivity. The focus on strengths capitalises on the opportunity to rewrite a life history of injury and disability as a history of bouncing back. ADHD clients can be proud of their resiliency.

The constant refrain in lectures on ADHD has been to highlight the impairment, so as to make an invisible disability transparent and open the way to provision of both credibility, accommodation and service. This has been important and successful. However highlighting the functional impairment associated with ADHD has also had dangerous consequences. First, it has led to confusion between the consequences of ADHD and conduct disorder. Second, it has left clinicians with a feeling of therapeutic nihilism and thus indirectly increased the stigma associated with the disorder. Third, it has led to a reactive initiative where ADHD is perceived as a gift and "being" ADHD has become a culture in its own right.

People with ADHD have a disability, but they are human and human beings react to disability with plasticity. This is not a strength of ADHD, it is a strength of being human.The blind may be musical, but being musical does not make being blind a gift. Struggling with ADHD is long and lonely. The last module of the book helps the therapist recapitulate with the client where they are in the space and time of development, and the meaning of the relationship that has developed. Termination is a difficult and significant moment in every short term therapy, but it is all the more salient for clients caged by symptoms in a cell of social isolation. The authors know how to deal with the bittersweet aspects of a therapeutic success that foreshadows the difficulty of letting someone go it alone when life is never going to be easy.

There are many types of therapy in the food court of psychology manuals. This one borrows from psychoeducation, cognitive behaviour therapy, interpersonal therapy, behaviour therapy, social skills training, anger management, motivational interviewing, problem solving, cognitive remediation, relaxation therapy, sleep hygiene and coaching. It is perhaps a sign of our times that the only major psychological intervention which I did not see was dynamically oriented psychotherapy. ADHD does not grant immunity from conflict. While psychodynamic psychotherapy may not be an effective treatment for ADHD symptoms, ADHD does not preclude clients benefiting from psychotherapy for life problems.

Clients with ADHD will enter therapy thinking about medication, on medication, or having failed medication. Any psychological treatment has to help them integrate the experience of taking a pill to assist with focus and restraint. An effective treatment needs to capitalise on the strength and limitations of the context of attributions around medication. Clients may use medication and psychoeducation as a way of excusing them from the forced effort required for change. Good psychological treatment is an antidote. This book is grounded in the questions clients ask. "What is ADHD and what is me?" "Should I tell people or should I keep it a secret?" Medication treatment is a rapidly evolving area and no book can do justice to the latest innovations. If the client does not take the pill, has misguided expectations, or sees himself as in a contest with the pill, medication will not be as effective. The authors have tried to formulate a way of providing a pharmacotherapy alliance.

Research on psychological treatment of ADHD is very much in its infancy. Yet the very early, and methodologically limited studies of psychological treatment consistently showed improvement in symptoms, improvement in skills and deterioration in self esteem. Insight brought its rewards, but also carried side effects. The side effect of realistic assessment of oneself is diminished grandiosity. Shrinking narcissism is good for the soul if one endures, but if the client's only strength is the capacity to try, try again then it is not without its dangers. Young and Bramham learned this well. You cannot get better if you fail to bounce back. Throughout every module one hears the therapist negotiate between the twin dangers of unrealistic grandiosity that leads to repeated failure and despair that precludes continued effort.

Our ADHD programme started to see adults two years ago. We have a wait list of one year. Every day we are confronted with the impossibility of making up the difference between the hopes and dreams of our clients and what we can realistically provide. It is therefore with fear and trembling that we are now starting a psychotherapy programme. From this strategic point of view some therapy is better than no therapy. We have to find a way to provide education, skills, and coping strategies to many people, with many different problems and levels of functioning. This is a manual which lends itself to being delivered in a group or workshop modality. With limited manpower and explosive demand, this allows us to find a way to begin to deliver the essentials to our clients in a cost effective manner.

The group forum has potential to deal with the here and now of social interaction. Group treatment capitalises on peer support. It is easier to illustrate how symptoms put a stamp on life history when more than one example is under discussion. Most of all, if one of the trademarks of disability is isolation, then the brand equity of good treatment is companionship. The hardest part of ending a group for clients with ADHD is that for many of the clients there, this will have been their first experience with being understood. They fear it will be their last. This is the first published manual I am aware of dedicated to providing a guide to psychological treatment that can be accommodated in group and workshop formats.

The single most difficult task for a client with ADHD is to prioritise. Clients complaint that they procrastinate, lack motivation, become easily distracted, and cannot stay on task. There are many coping strategies that are useful to deal with these problems. However, when the rubber hits the road, the hardest thing to explain to a client is how to know what matters most. The early formulations of cognitive behaviour therapy described cognitive errors. They did not provide instruction in cognitive talents. Seeing the forest for the trees is a talent that underlies both the strength and the weakness of cognition in the face of an attention deficit. The problem solving, CBT and motivational sections of this manual attempt to draw out therapeutic maneuvers not just for getting it right, but getting what is most important.

This book is open to interpretation by each therapist and flexible enough to help most clients. The therapeutic approach is multi-faceted, appropriately reflecting the complexity of individuals who have ADHD. What the Young and Bramham programme contributes is perspective. They figured out what is most important and why it matters. In so doing they also helped us to begin to figure out how to help clients also develop this skill.

Margaret Weiss, MD, PhD
Director of Research, Division of Child Psychiatry

and

Candice Murray, PhD
Director Psychological Treatment, Provincial ADHD Program

Children and Women's Health Centre, Vanconves, Canada

PREFACE

We have frequently been asked for advice from clinicians working with adult ADHD clients in many different settings, including general adult mental health services, learning disability services, children's transition to adulthood services, forensic services, neuropsychiatry and neuropsychology services. From time to time we have also been approached for advice about how best to support and/or manage people with ADHD by people working in further educational and occupational settings, prison and probation services. In response, we wrote the Young–Bramham Programme to develop a conceptual framework and a unique approach for assessing and treating people with adulthood ADHD and associated problems. The Young–Bramham Programme is intended to help clinicians who have some knowledge of psychological approaches or cognitive behavioural therapy with clients with mental health difficulties, but who may not have worked with many adults with ADHD. It will also be useful for therapists who have some knowledge of childhood ADHD, who are interested in how the disorder progresses and in potential treatment strategies for ADHD 'graduates' or young adults. We also hope that the book will be useful for clients who are motivated to learn more about their condition and who wish to develop techniques for managing their own difficulties.

Since their childhood years, many of our clients have commonly had multiple presentations to educational and mental health services in their attempts to access help, support and treatment. They often report feeling that they have been misunderstood and not taken seriously. Even though ADHD is much better recognised these days, there seems to be far too many people who do not get the help they need. Furthermore, once diagnosed, many clinicians seem to feel apprehensive about providing treatment for this client group, whom they regard as requiring 'specialist' service provision. Both of us are clinical psychologists and clinical neuropsychologists, and we have spent several years working in a national referral service for adults with ADHD at the Maudsley Hospital in London. Between us, we have assessed and treated many hundreds of people with adult ADHD, have gained considerable insight into their problems and developed skills in working with this client group. In this book we have drawn on our knowledge and experience and provided case examples for illustration. All case examples provided throughout the book have been adapted so that clients remain anonymous. The book is accompanied by the Young–Bramham Programme Companion Website, www.wiley.com/go/adhdadults, which provides all the materials outlined in the chapters. These materials can be downloaded for use in sessions and by clients outside of the sessions.

The Young–Bramham Programme may be delivered either on an individual or group basis. We have been delivering a foundation programme to our clients in a group workshop format at the Maudsley Hospital. We are in the process of evaluating the effectiveness of the programme and outcome data suggest a marked improvement in the primary outcome measure of self-efficacy compared with individuals receiving medication alone. We have learnt a great deal from our clients and, in writing this book, we hope to convey many of our positive experiences of working with adults with ADHD. For us, their determination to access services, their motivation to change and receive psychological therapy has provided a consistent incentive to share our knowledge and experience.

Susan Young
Jessica Bramham

ACKNOWLEDGEMENTS

First and foremost, we wish to thank our clients who have shared with us their experiences, hopes and challenges. Second, we thank Charlotte Young for her patience and cups of tea. We are also very grateful to Professor Gisli Gudjonsson for reading and commenting on the book in draft, Philippa Bramham for proofreading the manuscript, Josip Lizatovic for providing some of our illustrations and Helen Fleck for helping with administration. Finally we would like to thank our friends and family, in particular Séamus O'Ceallaigh and Jane Adams, for their encouragement and support throughout the preparation of the book.

PART I

BACKGROUND, ASSESSMENT AND TREATMENT

1

INTRODUCTION

This book aims to provide clinicians with a comprehensive psychological guide to practice when working with adults with ADHD; from the assessment and diagnosis stage, through to treatment of both core symptoms and associated problems. As ADHD is a heterogeneous disorder, each individual is likely to present with a different constellation of symptoms covering a range of psychological strengths and weaknesses. For this reason, this book contains several stand-alone modules that have been devised and collated to form the Young–Bramham Programme. The Young–Bramham Programme provides an innovative and intensive practical approach to the presentation of adulthood ADHD using cognitive behavioural and motivational interviewing techniques, which are described in detail using case examples. Each module is presented in a separate chapter of this book and can be used independently or in conjunction with other modules.

Clinicians often report feeling under-equipped to treat this client group and that there is relatively limited literature regarding psychological treatment. This is despite ADHD adults seeking help for assessment and/or treatment of their presenting complaints in increasing numbers. Approximately one-third of children with ADHD continue to be fully symptomatic into adult life and the remainder often retain some residual problems that warrant treatment. In addition, although the diagnosis of the disorder of ADHD relies on a categorical perspective, many of the core attentional and impulsivity difficulties are continuously distributed within the normal population. Therefore, there are many individuals with attention, impulsivity and hyperactivity problems that fall below the threshold for formal diagnosis, but who nevertheless may also benefit from treatment of their functional impairments. Thus, the Young–Bramham Programme is appropriate for individuals who have a formal ADHD diagnosis; individuals who previously had a diagnosis and continue to have residual symptoms or problems; and individuals who present with an undiagnosed constellation of attention and/or hyperactive impulsive symptoms, and related problems.

Literature regarding pharmacological treatment of the disorder has been evolving in conjunction with increased recognition of its longstanding nature (e.g. Horrigan,

2001). However, stimulant medication is not effective for up to 20–50% of adults with ADHD as they may not experience symptom reduction or they are unable to tolerate the medication (Spencer et al., 1995; Wender, 1998; Wilens, Spencer & Biederman, 2002). Moreover adults who have benefited from pharmacological intervention may not experience a considerable reduction in their core symptoms (Weiss, Hechtman & Weiss, 1999) and they may continue to experience a number of symptoms and/or associated problems more suitable for treatment with psychological interventions. Cognitive remediation techniques that target problems associated with adult ADHD, such as attentional difficulties, poor motivation, poor organisational skills, impulsivity and anger management problems, have been shown to be effective in improving daily functioning skills (Stevenson, Whitmont, Bornholt, Livesey & Stevenson, 2002).

People with ADHD have often developed secondary conditions following lifelong ADHD-related frustration and failure (Murphy, 1995; Young, 2002). Indeed, a number of outcome studies have demonstrated a wide range of comorbid conditions associated with ADHD including anxiety disorder, depression, substance misuse and dysfunctional anger (for reviews, see Brassett-Grundy & Butler, 2004a; Murphy & Barkley, 1996; Shekim, Asarnow, Hess, Zaucha & Wheller 1990). Whilst these conditions are effectively treated by psychological interventions for individuals without ADHD, clinicians sometimes feel discouraged from intervening in the same way with clients with ADHD as they fear there may be complicating factors. We therefore decided to write this book to share our knowledge and provide guidance for clinicians who are working with adults with ADHD.

A second reason for writing the book was that we have talked to our clients and listened to their life histories. This led us to conduct an investigation into their thoughts and feelings about receiving a diagnosis of ADHD and their experience of treatment with medication (Young, Bramham, Gray & Rose, in submission). The results of the study formed the theoretical basis of the Young–Bramham Programme (see Chapter 3).

THE COMPANION WEBSITE

The Young–Bramham Programme book is supplemented by a Companion Website, which provides practical and pragmatic exercises that allow the client to identify personal specific problems and methods to address them. Strategies that involve writing ideas down or making lists of potential consequences target difficulties in organisational skills and memory problems which are inherent in adulthood ADHD. The therapist therefore needs to maximise the opportunity to create lists and structure plans during sessions. Examples, charts, diaries, figures, diagrams and illustrations are presented in both the book and on the Companion Website (the latter in a format suitable for use in sessions) to clarify information, and/or to improve accessibility and understanding of the concepts and issues presented. The Companion Website provides psychoeducational handouts and blank copies of relevant materials introduced in the programme. The materials can be downloaded, copied and used in treatment sessions to determine, evaluate and treat specific symptoms, problems and strategies. The materials will help the therapist and the client to collaboratively tailor the Young–Bramham Programme interventions according the client's specific needs.

ATTENTION DEFICIT HYPERACTIVITY DISORDER IN ADULTHOOD

Attention Deficit Hyperactivity Disorder was originally regarded as a childhood disorder in which the core symptoms of hyperactivity, impulsivity and attentional difficulties were thought to dissipate during adolescence. However, prospective studies examining the long-term outcome of childhood ADHD indicate that the condition can persist into adulthood (Brassett-Grundy & Butler, 2004a; Mannuzza, Klein, Bessler, Malloy & LaPadula, 1993; Taylor, Chadwick, Heptinstall & Danckaerts, 1996; Weiss, Hechtman, Milroy & Perlman, 1985). Estimates of prevalence vary widely and range between 3 and 9% of young people and 2% of adults are likely to meet DSM IV diagnostic criteria (Shaffer, 1994). A high proportion of young people may retain lesser residual symptoms as young adults. A Canadian longitudinal follow-up study suggested that up to two-thirds of young adults retain at least one disabling symptom of ADHD (Weiss, Hechtman, Milroy & Perlman, 1985). Symptom expression in adulthood seems to change as the disorder progresses (Bramham, Young, Morris, Asherson & Toone, 2005a, 2005b; Weiss & Hechtman, 1993). In our investigation of clinical referrals to the Maudsley Hospital, London, we have found that impulsivity and hyperactivity seem to diminish with age, but attentional problems persist into the middle adulthood years and beyond (Bramham et al., 2005a, 2005b).

It has been established that ADHD has a strong genetic component, with heritability estimates of 60–90%; that is, identical twins demonstrate greater concordance for symptoms of inattention and hyperactivity compared with non-identical twins (e.g. Thapar, Holmes, Poulton & Harrington, 1999). Family studies have also provided support for the heritability of ADHD; the risk of a parent with ADHD having a child with the disorder is 57% (Biederman et al., 1995) and the rate of ADHD among parents of ADHD probands falls about 20% (e.g. Faraone, Biederman & Monuteaux, 2000a). However, the challenge is now for researchers to determine how genetic susceptibility is translated into the disorder, through examining the relationship between genes and environmental risks (Asherson, Kuntsi & Taylor, 2005). Environmental risk factors include prenatal and perinatal events (e.g. prematurity, birth complications, mother's tobacco and alcohol use during pregnancy) as well as psychosocial factors (e.g. neglect, poor parental management, family discord, etc.). In addition, neurobiological risk factors may also contribute to the manifestation of ADHD, such as closed head trauma and lead exposure (Asherson et al., 2005).

Sex Differences and ADHD

Prevalence studies of childhood ADHD suggest wide variability between the extents to which males outnumber females, with ratios ranging from 1.5:1 to 12:1 (Heptinstall & Taylor, 2002). The sex differences may relate to underlying biological factors as males in general seem to be more susceptible to neurodevelopmental abnormalities (Gualtieri & Hicks, 1985). Further support comes from neuroimaging studies, such as that by Ernst et al. (1994) who found that global cerebral glucose metabolism in ADHD girls was 20% lower than in ADHD boys, although this study had very small sample sizes. Furthermore, Castellanos et al. (2001) found fewer structural abnormalities in the brains of girls with ADHD in comparison with those of boys.

Contrary to the hypothesis of biological predisposition is the finding that girls with ADHD have similar rates of affected relatives as boys with ADHD (Faraone et al., 2000b). Additionally, there has been no difference between the sexes in treatment response to methylphenidate and dexamphetamine (Sharp et al., 1999). It may be that females tend to be underdiagnosed due to referral biases from parents, teachers and health professionals (i.e. more boys are sent for clinical assessment of ADHD than girls) (Gaub & Carlson, 1997; Taylor, 1994). Boys may be overrepresented in clinics due to higher rates of comorbid conduct disorder and disruptive behaviour leading them to attract more notice from health and educational professionals, and resulting in more frequent referral for treatment (Biederman et al., 1999; Gaub & Carlson, 1997).

Whatever the difference, the sex ratio appears to rebalance with age. Cohen et al. (1993) found that the prevalence rate for boys declines by 20% during the ages of 10–20 years, whereas it remains relatively constant for girls. This is supported by data from the Maudsley Adult ADHD NHS service, where we found the ratio of female/male ADHD adults falls from 1:4.3 in teenage years to 1:1.5 by their thirties (Bramham et al., 2005a). A UK Cohort Study also reported a similar ratio of 1:1.7 for a 30-year longitudinal follow-up of children born in 1970 (Brassett-Grundy & Butler, 2004b).

Sex differences have been shown to exist in several key domains of functioning for individuals with ADHD. In non-ADHD groups, females have fewer attentional problems and less hyperactivity than males (Bauermeister, 1992). However, in the ADHD population, females are reported to be more inattentive and to have greater overall cognitive impairment and language dysfunction. By comparison, males exhibited increased motor activity, and aggressive and antisocial behaviour (Gaub & Carlson, 1997).

There also appear to be differences in comorbid psychological difficulties. Epidemiological studies suggest outcomes for adolescent girls relate to psychosocial problems especially disruption to peer relationships, whereas boys seem to have high psychiatric comorbidity and antisocial behaviour problems (Taylor et al., 1996; Young, Heptinstall,

Sonuga-Barke, Chadwick & Taylor, 2005a; Young, Chadwick, Heptinstall, Taylor & Sonuga-Barke, 2005b). These findings are supported by Carlson, Tamm and Gaub (1997) who reported that girls with ADHD received higher peer dislike scores than boys, and with increasing age, girls were more often rejected by peers. The peer relationships of boys, by contrast, did not change over time and appeared to be more stable. In adolescence, females with ADHD have been reported to be more impaired than males with ADHD in self-reported anxiety, distress, depression and locus of control (Rucklidge & Tannock, 2001), and to have a higher risk of substance misuse than boys (Disney, Elkins, McGue & Iacono, 1999). An epidemiological 8-year follow-up study of girls found that at 14–16 years, girls had greater state anxiety and ambivalence about their future (Young et al., 2005a, 2005b).

By adulthood, these problems appear to become more ingrained, with ADHD males reporting to be engaging in antisocial or criminal behaviour and females obtaining higher rates of psychiatric admission than males 10–30 years later (Dalsgaard, Mortensen, Frydenberg & Thomsen, 2002). There may be a particular risk for females with hyperactive subtype and comorbid conduct disorder as 60% of this group received inpatient admissions for their problems.

There is a growing body of evidence documenting sex differences in the expression of ADHD and its associated problems that argues strongly for gender specific treatments. Females seem to experience greater mood instability, anxiety and interpersonal problems whereas males seem to present with antisocial behavioural problems, including verbal and physical aggression. The modular approach of the Young–Bramham Programme is therefore helpful for therapists who may select interventions appropriate to females (e.g. social relationships, anxiety) and males (e.g. anger management and impulse control techniques). It is particularly striking that for people with ADHD, strengths and weaknesses in coping skills may be contrary to those typically reported (i.e. females usually being more prone to using emotional coping strategies and males tending to be more adept with problem-focused strategies). Indeed, female adolescents have been reported to adopt a variety of ineffectual coping strategies (Young et al., 2005a). Thus, psychological treatment needs to facilitate clients to select, develop and apply functional strategies to overcome their problems.

Learning Difficulties, Learning Disabilities and ADHD

ADHD is experienced by people throughout the intellectual spectrum. However, confusion may arise regarding the comorbidity of learning disabilities and ADHD due to differences in terminology used between North America and Europe. In Europe, the term 'learning disability' is used synonymously with the North American term 'mental retardation', whereas in North America, the term 'learning disability' is more consistent with the European understanding of specific 'learning difficulty'. Specific learning difficulties are characterised by a skill, such as reading, spelling, writing or arithmetic, being differentially affected in the context of otherwise adequate mental functioning, i.e. the individual's overall functioning is not globally low.

Some clinicians suggest that ADHD and learning disabilities are indistinguishable (e.g. Prior & Sanson, 1986) and that the core features of ADHD are expressed as a learning disabilities characteristic. Although it has been suggested that the disorder is more prevalent in individuals with a learning disability, even in those who have severe levels of intellectual impairment (Fox & Wade, 1998), DSM-IV criteria (American Psychiatric Association, 1994) may be more reliable for people with mild learning disabilities compared with individuals falling in the moderate to severe learning disability ranges (Seager & O'Brien, 2003). Others caution that ADHD is difficult to diagnose in children or adults with a learning disability because of the confounding factor of low IQ and the increased rates of challenging behaviour (Young & Newland, 2002).

Psychostimulant treatment of adults with learning disabilities and ADHD seems to be effective and well-tolerated (Jou, Handen & Hardan, 2004) but larger studies are required in order to fully determine their efficacy. Guidance regarding psychological intervention with clients with comorbid ADHD and learning disabilities is very limited in the current literature. Whilst the Young–Bramham Programme is primarily devised for use with non-learning disabled individuals, this does not preclude use with learning disabilities clients with ADHD, but several adaptations would be required.

First, attentional difficulties may be more pronounced for people with learning disabilities (Fox & Wade, 1998), which will further limit their ability to sustain attention in sessions. Thus, if possible, the sessions need to be on a 'little and often' basis; that is, frequent, brief time periods, such as half an hour, twice per week. Second, the primary therapeutic approach should be behavioural, as many individuals with learning disabilities have difficulty in accessing and applying cognitive strategies. Behavioural experiments in sessions, practical examples and simple explanations are particularly important for successful intervention with this client group. The therapist may also wish to recruit the assistance of a family member or carer who can reinforce what has been learned outside of the session, as well as support homework tasks.

Specific learning problems such as dyslexia and dyscalculia have also been reported as more prevalent in individuals with ADHD (e.g. Rabiner & Cole, 2000). As a result, some individuals may be assessed for their specific learning difficulties whilst their underlying ADHD symptoms remain unrecognised for some time. Whilst there is comorbidity between ADHD and specific learning difficulty, some individuals find their learning problems appear to be due to the latter but clinical assessment and formal testing indicates that an attention deficit is the primary problem.

There are three possible explanations for the association between ADHD and specific learning difficulty: (1) attention impairments impede learning; (2) working memory difficulties can affect the ability to unravel complex grammar; and/or (3) both conditions share similar neurobiological underpinnings, particularly those relating to executive dysfunction (e.g. Denkla, 1996). Indeed, frontal lobe systems involving cognitive control are likely to be affected and can result in attentional and information processing difficulties common to both disorders (Duncan et al., 1994).

Individuals with comorbid ADHD and dyslexia may be under-represented in clinical services because they have difficulty in completing screening questionnaires and this deters them from following through referrals. Such individuals may be helped by having written materials relating to the diagnostic and/or treatment process presented in an appropriate form for their needs, for example enlarged text using black and white simple characters. Some treatment exercises may be adapted from written form to verbal records using a Dictaphone and sessions may be recorded in a similar fashion.

A COGNITIVE-BEHAVIOURAL MODEL OF ADHD IN ADULTS

Based on our research and experience in working therapeutically with adults with ADHD, we have devised a cognitive-behavioural model to formulate their presentation (see Figure 1.1). This figure is included on the Companion Website. It may be helpful to work through the figure and 'personalise' the formulation with the client.

Due to their longstanding neuropsychological impairments such as poor concentration, forgetfulness, problem-solving difficulties and a need for immediate gratification, adults with ADHD are likely to have experienced numerous negative life events. Such experiences include academic underachievement, occupational difficulties, problems in making and maintaining both friendships and intimate relationships as well as experiences associated with novelty seeking and risk-taking behaviours.

When faced with certain situations or tasks, such as social encounters, dealing with conflict, or having an interview, people with ADHD may find that their neuropsychological impairments hamper their performance. Due to a history of failure, they can be prone to negatively appraise a situation with a pessimistic bias. Failure is likely to impact on their self-esteem; they may begin to doubt their own abilities, and in a self-fulfilling prophecy, expect failure in the future. Following negative appraisal, an individual may engage in negative behaviours such as verbal or physical aggression or they may withdraw or engage in maladaptive coping, such as misusing substances. They are likely to have negative thoughts and beliefs about their abilities and focus on weaknesses. The combination of negative behaviour and negative thoughts or beliefs is likely to induce or worsen a negative mood stage such as anxiety, frustration or anger. Being in a negative mood state means that an individual is more likely to appraise a subsequent situation in a negative way, and so the cycle continues.

However, there is both anecdotal and research evidence to suggest that adults with ADHD have an aptitude for the reappraisal or cognitive reframing of stressful

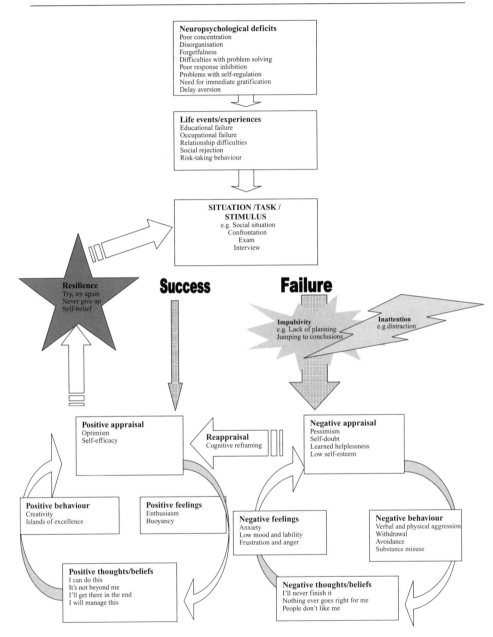

Figure 1.1   A cognitive behavioural model of ADHD in adults

situations (Young, 2005). It is possible that the negative cycle itself becomes a motivational force that compels change in a situation. A 'Drive Theory' was initially proposed by Hull in 1943. According to this theory, humans are driven to reduce arousal or tension so that they may maintain a sense of comfort and equilibrium (Hull, 1943). Whilst adults with ADHD may engage in a spontaneous process of reappraisal, this is likely to be negatively influenced by their cognitive impairments, resulting in the process being dysfunctional or unsuccessful. Nevertheless, a cycle is re-entered by the ADHD individual positively reframing the negative outcome, causing them to try again in the hope of achieving success. This explains the resilience commonly found in people with ADHD and suggests that this is underpinned by a belief in self-efficacy. Therefore, the way they interact is associated with their ability to continually compensate and adapt. This adaptive aspect of the syndrome may also be expressed as creative and entrepreneurial personality characteristics (Young, 2005).

STRUCTURE AND CONTENT OF THE YOUNG–BRAMHAM PROGRAMME

The Young–Bramham Programme is divided into four sections: (1) background, assessment and treatment; (2) core symptoms; (3) comorbid and associated problems; and (4) the future (see Table 1.1). The first section covers the background issues regarding ADHD in adulthood, an outline of the Young–Bramham Programme, as well as assessment and treatment methods. The second section focuses on the core ADHD-related symptoms of inattention, memory problems, time

Table 1.1   The Young–Bramham Programme structure

Part 1: Background, assessment and treatment	
Chapter 1	Introduction to the Young–Bramham Programme and adulthood ADHD
Chapter 2	Assessment
Chapter 3	Treatment
Part 2: Core symptoms	
Chapter 4	Inattention and memory problems
Chapter 5	Time management
Chapter 6	Problem solving
Chapter 7	Impulsivity
Part 3: Comorbid and associated problems	
Chapter 8	Social relationships
Chapter 9	Anxiety
Chapter 10	Frustration and anger
Chapter 11	Low mood and depression
Chapter 12	Sleep problems
Chapter 13	Substance misuse
Part 4: The future	
Chapter 14	Preparing for the future

management, problem solving and impulsivity. The third section presents common comorbid difficulties that can develop as a result of the core symptoms, including social relationship difficulties, anxiety, anger management problems, depression, sleep difficulties and substance misuse. Finally, issues around individuals' expectations and plans for the future are presented in the concluding chapter.

Assessment and Treatment of ADHD in Adults

The Young–Bramham Programme includes guidelines for how to apply the diagnostic classification of ADHD to an adult age group, as most diagnostic criteria were written with respect to childhood problems. However, given that many symptoms of ADHD are typical of normal behaviour and are present to a greater or lesser degree in the general population, it can be difficult to ascertain what constitutes a 'symptom'. ADHD can be viewed as representing one end of a continuum, e.g. a category of impairment or dysfunction. As such, the identification of ADHD involves an element of subjective judgement to determine whether someone falls into the area defined as 'abnormal'. From our experience of assessing adults with ADHD, we have elaborated how each symptom may present in adulthood. We also outline common hallmarks or symptomatic features of adulthood ADHD that may assist clinicians in making the diagnosis.

Since individuals with ADHD are prone to developing a range of comorbid conditions, differential diagnosis and comorbidity can make assessment particularly complex in adulthood, especially given that the symptoms of ADHD are also present in many other psychiatric disorders. Indeed, some psychiatric disorders can mimic the core symptoms of ADHD and, in Chapter 2 on assessment, we suggest how these may be excluded before a diagnosis can be made.

The diagnosis of adult ADHD is strengthened by gaining an accurate and comprehensive history of childhood functioning. Unfortunately clinicians often have to rely on the memory of the client and/or family members for this information and retrospective information is often affected by distortion. For example, some parents may minimise their child's difficulties or symptoms, whereas others may overestimate them as their memory has only retained the most serious and significant events. Thus, the reliability and validity of such data is uncertain. We therefore give practical recommendations regarding useful information sources for making the diagnosis in Chapter 2. In particular, we evaluate the use and limitations of psychometric rating scales and the contribution of neuropsychological tests to the assessment process, and provide guidance regarding the administration and interpretation of results.

The primary objective of the Young–Bramham Programme is to impart the psychological treatment outlined in Chapter 3, which can be combined with or used in preference to pharmacological therapy. The Programme has two primary aims:

1. *Change from the outside in* – to provide clinicians with ways of encouraging adults with ADHD to change their environment and optimise functioning.
2. *Change from the inside out* – to provide clinicians with ways of encouraging the individual to develop psychological strategies for adaptive functioning.

The clinician needs to instil hope and confidence in the individual in order that they can make progress with appropriate treatment, combined with hard work and support. This perspective needs to be offered in light of the information that there is no 'magic cure' for ADHD. However, it is possible to change how the individual copes with the disorder and to maximise individual strengths. We do this in the following chapters by drawing on various techniques, including: a psychoeducational process to inform the individual about the history, treatment and prognosis of the disorder; motivational interviewing to overcome ambivalence towards treatment; cognitive remediation to help control core symptoms; and cognitive behavioural therapy for comorbid and associated problems.

Psychoeducation is a specific therapeutic approach that can be used from the start of the diagnostic process (Jackson & Farrugia, 1997). The way that the diagnosis is communicated to the individual is paramount to their understanding of the disorder and their future adjustment to the diagnosis (Murphy & Levert, 1995; Young, Bramham, Gray & Rose, in submission). Throughout their lives, clients may have been told that they are stupid, lazy and unmotivated. It can therefore be extremely therapeutic and provide a sense of relief for the individual to understand that ADHD has a neurological basis and their problems are not due to a character defect.

We introduce how to adapt techniques applied in paradigms of cognitive remediation, cognitive behavioural therapy and motivational interviewing for people who are impulsive and inattentive, for example by introducing variety in treatment sessions to sustain focus and interest (e.g. shifting topics, visual aids, role play, etc.), by introducing frequent breaks in sessions and by including a reward system. Individuals with ADHD are motivated to satisfy a need for immediate gratification and it is important that treatment is structured to include regular immediate rewards in addition to delayed rewards. Specific tools such as worksheets, role-plays and exercises are employed to maintain motivation and attention. Shifts in topic and the incorporation of a variety of teaching techniques (including practical exercises) are attractive to individuals who have significant cognitive deficits, high intolerance and a low boredom threshold. A feature of the Young–Bramham Programme is the incorporation of practical exercises that will help individuals and clinicians identify and treat pertinent problems, either core symptoms or associated problems.

Core Symptoms

Inattention, impulsivity and hyperactivity are the hallmarks of ADHD. In adulthood, these symptoms are strongly associated with disorganisation, poor time-management and inadequate problem-solving skills, and the Young–Bramham Programme therefore includes modules on these topics.

Inattention and memory problems

Attentional problems tend to be the primary complaint of adults with ADHD, who describe experiencing difficulty focusing on a task and shifting the focus of their attention as necessary. Some individuals develop compensatory skills to deal with their inattentiveness, such as only obtaining employment where prolonged attention is not required (Wender, 2000). For others who have not developed such strategies, inattentiveness can impact on their ability to succeed in their adult life.

There are four facets of attention that are commonly affected in ADHD (selective; divided; shifting; sustained) and examples of these in everyday living are provided in Chapter 4. Attentional impairment can lead to many problems in day-to-day functioning, including difficulties listening, failure to finish and being easily distracted. In particular, two types of distraction can be observed in individuals with ADHD:

1. *External distraction*, e.g. noticing irrelevant details.
2. *Internal distraction*, e.g. having the urge to do something more stimulating.

For adults with ADHD, the difficulty with sustaining attention may be the most disabling problem as individuals struggle to engage in activities that are long, boring, repetitive or tedious. In contrast, when activities are particularly interesting or motivating and/or involve immediate gratification (such as computer games), individuals with ADHD are able to concentrate. Such inconsistencies can be difficult to understand for people around them and can be a source of tension and frustration.

In Chapter 4 we also discuss how clients need to be able to recognise tasks that are likely to be problematic and respond appropriately and adaptively. Methods of adapting the environment to minimise distraction are outlined, which often involves selecting the most appropriate surroundings suitable for success. Chapter 4 considers strategies for the individual to achieve their potential within the constraints of the environment, for example by maximising their ability to sustain attention by setting small achievable goals and introducing an 'immediate' reward system and regular breaks within a time-management structure. Given that memory problems are another common complaint in the context of poor attention, we also cover strategies for improving forgetfulness and poor recall.

Time management

Due to their attentional difficulties, poor time management and chaotic organisational skills can be particularly prominent for people with ADHD and these problems may become more marked in adult life. The ability to organise and prioritise is particularly challenging for people who tend to flit like butterflies from task to task, especially when an activity is mundane, or when beckoned by a seemingly more important task. Unfinished tasks are a source of frustration and leave the individual with a sense of failure. People with ADHD respond well to imposed structure, particularly in terms of scheduling time. Thus, Chapter 5 on time management presents ways of applying a methodical approach to make plans by reviewing goals for a set time period (short- and long-term), listing activities, devising a schedule, sequencing and prioritising activities, and planning breaks and rewards. We also include methods for avoiding pitfalls, such as ways of maintaining attention on a task, ways of adhering to a plan, advice regarding reviewing priorities and avoiding procrastination.

Problem solving

People with ADHD can have difficulty with solving problems for many reasons. They may respond impulsively, which leads to rash decision making without full evaluation of a situation. They may find it hard to generate multiple alternative options and focus on, or expect, negative outcomes. They may additionally worry unnecessarily about minor more immediate issues and lose sight of the whole picture. In addition, limitations with attentional control may prevent effective problem solving due to poor concentration and distractibility. We have therefore included Chapter 6 on problem solving to show how, by using a methodical approach, clients can be guided to achieve more optimal outcomes. The chapter provides methods to distinguish between 'problems' and 'worries', generate solutions, consider alternatives, perform accurate appraisal and avoid inaccurate and rapid decision-making processes. A methodology for choosing solutions is introduced through the rehearsal of solutions to evaluate consequences, role-playing appropriate scenarios and challenging cognitive distortions. In addition, practical advice regarding setting targets and goals, and evaluating success is provided.

Impulsivity and hyperactivity

Impulsivity in ADHD seems to be closely linked to a low tolerance of frustration. This feature appears to be a stable and enduring characteristic of ADHD as well as childhood ADHD. ADHD individuals seem to have a preference for short-term reward and an inability to delay gratification, which can lead to problems with wait-ing. This means that people with ADHD may seem demanding or self-centred. In addition, ADHD individuals find it difficult to consider the consequences of their behaviour before acting. There are obvious social ramifications when individuals present in this manner and they may appear to lack consideration for the feelings and needs of others. The consequences of their impulsivity appear to be more seri-ous in adulthood as poor impulse control, combined with a 'short fuse', may lead to antisocial behaviour, aggressive and/or violent behaviour, speeding tickets, road-rage, traffic accidents and criminal acts. In many respects, ADHD may be regarded as a potentially life-threatening disorder due to violent behaviour towards others, accidental injury, (e.g. road traffic accidents), and deliberate self-harm.

Chapter 7 introduces self-monitoring techniques to identify situations in which clients are vulnerable to responding in an impulsive way, and determine the appropriate self-restraint strategies they may apply in these circumstances. Stop-and-think techniques are introduced to maximise self-control, including self-instructional training, the use of self-statements, and role-plays involving consideration of personal and social consequences of behaviour.

Hyperactivity is the symptom most commonly reported to reduce over time as the ADHD disorder progresses through the lifespan. By adulthood, hyperactivity has usually considerably diminished and is objectively and subjectively perceived as an objective or subjective sense of restlessness. Clients seem to dislike sitting still and relaxing, and Weiss et al. (1999) have suggested that restlessness may be purposeful and adaptive for adults with ADHD as it has a motivating function, e.g. it might motivate the ability to achieve more physically taxing tasks. However, feelings of inner restlessness may also lead to relationship problems, as friends and family may feel exhausted by the client's inability to relax. In Chapter 7, we introduce methods for the individual to capitalise on excess energy and introduce a methodology for structuring and organising the day to anticipate and prepare for hyperactive difficulties.

Comorbid and Associated Problems

There are several additional features of ADHD in adults that often present in conjunction with the core symptoms, but are not necessary for the diagnosis (e.g. Nadeau, 1995; Ratey, Greenberg, Bemporad & Lindem, 1992; Weiss & Hechtman, 1993; Wender, 2000; Young, 2000). These may be viewed as consequences of the core symptoms of ADHD and have been described as the secondary characteristics or social and emotional sequelae of ADHD in adulthood (Young, 2000). These sequelae include: impairment of social skills and poor interpersonal relationships; anxiety; mood lability, especially frustration and poor anger control; a sense of failure and low self-esteem; sleep difficulties; and substance misuse. We have therefore devised treatment strategies that can be applied to address these areas of comorbid difficulty. However, the problem of low self-esteem is so common and debilitating for people with ADHD, we have included this as a common thread that is implicitly provided in each of the Young–Bramham Programme modules.

Social relationships

Disruption to interpersonal relationships is well-documented in the ADHD literature. Clients are likely to have experienced a lifetime of adverse interactions with other people and a lack of opportunity to develop effective social skills. Core symptoms of ADHD may be misinterpreted by others, for example a difficulty maintaining a conversation may be perceived by others as a lack of interest or fickle behaviour. Impulsivity may feature as a difficulty in turn-taking and social reciprocity. Some clients report a long-standing awareness that they are 'different' from others in some way, leading to feelings of rejection and social isolation (Young et al., in submission).

It is important for clients to understand the relationship between symptoms and interpersonal relationship problems. In Chapter 8, we emphasise a need to develop positive attributions and attitudes in order to improve social skills. We introduce techniques to improve macro-skills, for example to increase self-awareness, develop the ability to take another's perspective and accurately perceive others' emotions. This is achieved by developing micro-skills, for example evaluation of facial expressions, posture, voice quality, gestures, non-verbal communication, verbal communication, conversational skills and listening skills. A crucial social dilemma for people with ADHD is whether to disclose to others that they have the disorder and coping with perceived or actual rejection, so we discuss this issue in detail.

Anxiety

Due to their history of academic problems, school failure and interpersonal relationship problems, generalised anxiety problems often present in ADHD adults. Social anxiety may also develop, as one of the most commonly experienced sources of anxiety reported by our clients is when they are in group situations (either in unfamiliar or intimate settings). Due to their uncertainty in such settings, they have difficulty adhering to social norms and/or inhibiting inappropriate behaviour. Some clients have such little confidence in such situations that they avoid them altogether. This seems paradoxical given their often gregarious presentation, but this can be used to mask underlying anxiety and a lack of confidence.

In Chapter 9, we outline how conventional Cognitive Behavioural Therapy (CBT) techniques may be applied and adapted for patients with ADHD to maximise successful outcomes. In order to address social anxiety and avoidance, we discuss how to modify behaviour in varying social situations, including controlling the impulse to over-compensate for feelings of inadequacy by 'playing the fool' and attention seeking behaviour. We also introduce methods to re-interpret common reactions/responses to anxiety by evaluating thoughts, feelings, behaviours and bodily reactions. A version of the Clark (1986) cognitive behavioural model of panic is presented with appropriate coping strategies for intervention. Relaxation and breathing exercises are reviewed and tailored for use in different settings. We suggest ways to overcome avoidance and increase confidence by applying techniques of graded exposure, systematic desensitisation and behavioural experiments, and outline methods to evaluate success.

Frustration and anger

People with ADHD are likely to experience both trait and state anger. Trait anger may be expressed by feelings of general dissatisfaction and irritability towards friends, family, employers and clinicians, especially if they believe that they are misunderstood or negatively evaluated. Symptomatic individuals may be particularly predisposed to have an explosive temperament and express their feelings in emotional outbursts. Clients may have developed maladaptive ways of coping with their feelings of frustration and irritation. Indeed, anger is more likely to be expressed outwardly than inwardly suppressed, possibly due to poor impulse control, emotional lability and a low boredom threshold. This behaviour may lead to negative outcomes including relationship breakdown, termination of employment and involvement with the police. It is likely to be perceived by others as a negative character trait and clients may be assumed to be unpredictable or in some cases even dangerous.

In order to effect change, the client needs to understand the function of anger. Reasons for becoming angry are often an unmet desire for immediate gratification and this may escalate due to feelings of frustration and inner restlessness, which are then inappropriately and impulsively expressed. Chapter 10 examines the stages of anger from a cognitive behavioural perspective and focuses in particular on teaching the individual to recognise physical indications of anger and learn when and how to interrupt the anger process. In addition, ways of dealing with insults and criticisms are presented to clients, including sessions to help the client recognise the difference between insults and criticisms, appreciate constructive criticism and learn to accept criticism appropriately.

Low mood and depression

Some people with ADHD may be predisposed to experience depressive symptoms due to their history of negative life events and low self-esteem, such as academic failure, relationship difficulties and financial problems. Their cognitive problems may escalate the development of depression. As many ADHD individuals lack the ability to plan, they are poorly motivated to start projects and have difficulty finishing tasks. This means that they may lack the opportunity to experience a sense of achievement and mastery, and when things go wrong, the individual may rapidly spiral into depression. Depression in people with ADHD needs to be taken very seriously because of their lack of behavioural control, which may cause them to act on an idea or impulse to self-harm. Once medicated, they may develop better insight into past problems but ruminate more, e.g. with reduced distractibility, over past failures and maladaptive interpersonal relationships with important people in their lives. Their risk of becoming depressed may increase shortly post diagnosis and treatment (Young, Bramham et al., in submission) and clinicians need to be aware of the serious risk of self-harm and suicide in this population due to poor impulse control. Chapter 11 stresses the necessity of risk assessment in addition to the need for regular monitoring of low mood and the impact of medication on impulse control.

In Chapter 11, we have adapted the Beck (1976) cognitive-behavioural model of depression to incorporate the negative thinking and thinking errors common to people with ADHD. We provide suggestions of how to break the negative cycle and introduce techniques to challenge their negative automatic thoughts, reduce the self-talk that perpetuates low mood and develop positive self-statements according to ADHD strengths.

Sleep problems

People with ADHD often complain of sleep problems when they present to services. Some sleep problems may be explained by core symptoms of ADHD as an incessant feeling of inner restlessness may prevent people from getting to sleep. Other sleep problems may be more similar to disturbance associated with affective disorders, such as early wakening in depression. Sleep problems may also relate to medication for treating ADHD, particularly following withdrawal of stimulant medication, or drug holidays or changes in dose.

In Chapter 12, we review the function of sleep, describe the different stages of sleep, and consider how the core symptoms of ADHD may exacerbate sleep problems such as hypersomnia and insomnia. We detail the management of sleep problems, outlining sleep hygiene programmes and relaxation techniques adapted for individuals with ADHD.

Substance misuse

People with ADHD may become involved with substances via two mechanisms. Poor impulse control may lead to increased risk-taking behaviour, experimentation with drugs and subsequent addiction. A second route is when individuals with undiagnosed and/or untreated ADHD use illicit substances to self-medicate. In these circumstances, for pharmacological reasons, the drug of choice is likely to be amphetamine-based but alcohol and cannabis are also often taken by adults with ADHD who claim they induce a sense of calm and relaxation. Chapter 13 describes the different categories of substance misuse and their relationship with ADHD. Psychological dependency is addressed by suggesting motivational interviewing techniques to motivate the client to engage in a process of change. We present the vicious cycle of substance misuse and discuss dysfunctional beliefs that may have developed for adults with ADHD around substance misuse. The chapter also outlines techniques to build self-confidence and cope with physical cravings and urges by applying distraction techniques, activity scheduling and motivating support.

Preparing for the Future

Many people with ADHD have negative assumptions about themselves and an expectation of failure, and it is therefore useful to explore how expectations of the self influence future outcomes. Thus, in the course of the Young–Bramham Programme, and particularly in our conclusions in Chapter 14, we discuss the influence of self-fulfilling prophecies on self-esteem. We emphasise the creative, resilient and flexible aspects of the ADHD personality and discuss how the client may have previously applied these characteristics successfully to achieve personal goals. Through the reappraisal of personal capabilities and the application of techniques and skills developed throughout the Young–Bramham Programme, people with ADHD can be encouraged to develop a sense of self-efficacy and purpose.

It is important to impart how people with ADHD may apply characteristics adaptively to achieve success in everyday challenges, as well as working towards medium and longer term plans. Unless this perspective is included in sessions, the therapist is likely to have difficulty fostering engagement and developing a therapeutic alliance. We suggest, therefore, that the final module is always included to summarise the techniques introduced in previous modules, and determine and/or reiterate those which have been beneficial for the client. The module follows a relapse-prevention approach whereby a plan to identify and manage 'risk' situations is developed to support the individual and refer to when they feel vulnerable and are most likely to slip back into old habits. The identification of periods of vulnerability and a management plan will prepare the client for their eventuality and increase the likelihood that the client will respond by applying useful coping strategies and avoid impulsive or dysfunctional responding patterns. It is important that these relapse-prevention plans include a variety of options that can be applied as appropriate in a range of situations, for example cognitive techniques, avoidance of troublesome situations/persons, seeking family/friends' support, seeking professional advice.

CONCLUSIONS

The primary intervention for ADHD is treatment with medication and this has been reliably shown to provide a reduction in symptoms for many individuals with the disorder. However, symptom reduction is but one treatment objective of adults with ADHD, who have accumulated a host of concurrent difficulties. Our clients at the UK National Adult ADHD service are positive regarding pharmacological treatment, which, they say, gives a sense of 'normality' and helps them to achieve their potential (Young, Bramham et al., in submission). However, the level of satisfaction is variable and clients have stated that medication does not resolve all of their difficulties. Furthermore, as the effects of medication wear off, the rapid emergence of symptoms makes clients realise that this is not a 'miracle cure' for their problems. Treatment with medication appears to help clients distinguish between problems that are strongly associated with their symptoms and those that are less influenced by the presence of symptoms. This means that clients become personally motivated to engage in a process of change, especially with respect to symptoms and/or problems they perceive to be resistant to treatment with medication.

There is clearly a role for psychological intervention for people who are diagnosed with ADHD in adulthood in order to facilitate their adjustment and acceptance of the disorder. These individuals, as well as those who were fortunate to be diagnosed and treated in childhood, also require psychological interventions to help them cope with the psychological, social and occupational demands they will meet as adults. The Young–Bramham Programme provides treatment strategies to address these needs by applying techniques drawing from psychoeducation, to engage the client in a learning process; motivational interviewing to encourage change; cognitive remediation and cognitive behavioural treatments to teach coping strategies and develop skills.

2

ASSESSMENT OF ADHD IN ADULTS

Although ADHD is now recognised as a condition that is present in adulthood, many clinicians lack the confidence to make the diagnosis. The central tenet in performing an assessment is that adults with ADHD will have had their symptoms through their childhood. Thus, when conducting an assessment of ADHD in adulthood, there are two fundamental questions to be answered:

1. Did the client have ADHD as a child?
2. If so, to what extent is the client still symptomatic?

This chapter provides a guide for clinicians to gather sufficient information to answer these questions and conduct a comprehensive assessment. The diagnostic classification systems and the manifestation of symptoms in adults are presented, along with consideration of typical additional features. The comorbid conditions commonly associated with the disorder are discussed in addition to differential diagnoses. We review the strengths and limitations regarding sources of information, including the structured clinical interview, neuropsychological assessment, rating scales and corroborative documentation.

DIAGNOSTIC CLASSIFICATION OF ADHD

There are three recognised symptoms of ADHD – inattention, hyperactivity and impulsivity – and two formal diagnostic classifications to draw on, the US Diagnostic and Statistical Manual (DSM-IV) (American Psychiatric Association, 1994) and the World Health Organization's International Classification of Disease (ICD-10) (World Health Organization, 1992). Different prevalence rates are likely to be at least partly influenced by the adoption of these differing classification systems. There are 18 items that are required to make a diagnosis of ADHD. These items are the same in ICD-10 and DSM-IV. Both classification systems require that symptoms are maladaptive, inconsistent with developmental level and present for the past six months. Overall there must be clear evidence of clinically significant impairment in social, academic or occupational functioning; that is, pervasive across different environments. However, ICD-10 adopts a more restricted definition of 'hyperkinetic syndrome' than DSM-IV and requires that all three symptoms are present independently.

Longitudinal follow-up studies have established that approximately one-quarter of children followed up into young adulthood will continue to meet criteria for ADHD (Mannuzza et al., 1993; Taylor et al., 1996). However, the heterogeneous nature and trajectory of the ADHD syndrome means that for each individual the experience of the disorder, and their response to treatment, is different. Symptoms do not conveniently and uniformly remit, some clients will retain predominantly poor impulse control, and others will retain predominantly poor attentional control. Whilst motor overactivity is likely to be found unusually in adults, this may take a different form and present as a feeling of internal restlessness. Children with ADHD struggle in compulsory environments where they have to conform and sit still, either defined by the educational setting (e.g. attending class in school), or by a social setting (e.g. watching a film at the cinema). However, it would be unusual to assess an adult for ADHD, for example, who gets off the chair, rolls around the floor, picks the desk lock, plays with the light switches, and puts all the papers on a desk into complete disarray. What is more likely, is that adults will talk about feelings of internal restlessness, and/or ceaseless mental activity.

Thus whilst the ICD-10 classification may be helpful for the diagnosis of childhood ADHD, it is less so for adult symptoms. Longitudinal follow-up of both normal and hyperactive children suggests that concentration is likely to improve with age and activity levels are likely to decrease (Biggs, 1995; Fischer, Barkley, Fletcher & Smallish, 1993; Taylor et al., 1996). Marsh and Williams (2004) found that hyperactivity-impulsivity problems declined more rapidly with age than attention difficulties.

For these reasons, the DSM-IV criteria are more flexible and better able to accommodate residual symptoms as they remit. Using these criteria ADHD may be diagnosed as three distinct typologies shown in Table 2.1.

Table 2.1   Classification of DSM-IV symptoms for ADHD diagnosis

Predominantly inattentive type	Six out of nine inattentive symptoms rated as 'often'
Predominantly hyperactive-impulsive type	Six out of nine hyperactive/impulsive symptoms rated as 'often'
Combined type	Six out of nine inattentive symptoms rated as 'often' *and* six out of nine hyperactive/impulsive symptoms rated as 'often'

ADHD combined type represents the more severe form and predominantly inattentive type or predominantly hyperactive impulsive type may account for heterogeneity or remitting symptoms. Additionally, there is a category for disorders with prominent symptoms of inattention or hyperactivity-impulsivity that do not meet the above stringent criteria, known as 'ADHD Not Otherwise Specified'.

Thus, when applying DSM-IV criteria, an assessment of ADHD needs to ascertain the presence of six out of nine inattentive symptoms as being present 'often'; and/or six out of nine hyperactive/impulsive symptoms as being present 'often'. These may be assessed by a checklist of symptoms in a semi-structured interview format (see Table 2.2, which shows how this may be completed for a client with predominantly inattentive symptoms). It is recommended that each positive self-rating is endorsed by the assessor on the basis of supplementary questioning or other information (e.g. independent documentation or information from a different source). The Companion Website includes two versions of Table 2.2, one for completion by the client (Table 2.2a) and the other, indicating scoring and guidelines for diagnosis to be used by the therapist (Table 2.2b).

However, there remain a number of difficulties with the DSM-IV criteria. When looking at the above criteria, it can be seen that there is an immediate problem

Table 2.2   DSM-IV checklist of symptoms for clinician

In the past six months, do you think you:	*Never* 0	*Sometimes* 1	*Often* 2
Failed to give close attention to details or made careless mistakes in studying, work or other activities?			✓
Had difficulty sustaining attention in tasks or leisure activities?			✓
Have not seemed to listen when spoken to directly?		✓	
Did not follow through on instructions and failed to finish studies, chores or duties in the workplace (not due to oppositional behaviour or failure to understand instructions)?			✓
Had difficulty organising tasks and activities?			✓
Avoided, disliked or were reluctant to engage in tasks that require sustained mental effort (e.g. studying, homework, leisure activities)?		✓	
Lost things necessary for tasks or activities (e.g. pens, books, tools, study papers)?		✓	
Were easily distracted by outside events and stimuli?			✓
Were forgetful in daily activities?			✓

(continued)

Table 2.2   *(continued)*

	In the past *six **months***, do you think you:	Never 0	Sometimes 1	Often 2
1	*Inattention criteria met? (i.e. six or more items rated 'often')*			(Yes)/No
	Fidgeted with hands or feet or squirmed in seat?			✓
	Left seat in situations where remaining seated is expected (e.g. in classes, church, movies)?			✓
	Experienced feelings of restlessness, especially in situations where it is inappropriate?			✓
	Had difficulty engaging in leisure tasks quietly?		✓	
	Felt 'on the go' or as if driven by a motor?	✓		
	Talked excessively?			✓
	Blurted out answers before questions have been completed?	✓		
	Had difficulty waiting turn?		✓	
	Interrupted or intruded on others (e.g. butting into conversations)?		✓	
2	*Hyperactivity/impulsivity criteria met? (i.e. six or more items rated 'often')*			Yes/(No)
A	Either 1 and 2 (or both rated yes)			✓
B	Were some hyperactive-impulsive or inattentive symptoms present before age 7?			✓
C	Some impairment from the symptoms is present in two or more settings (e.g. in educational setting, work setting, at home)?			✓
D	Is there clear evidence of clinically significant impairment in social, academic or occupational functioning?			✓
E	The symptoms do not occur exclusively during the course of a severe psychiatric illness (e.g. schizophrenia) and are not better accounted for by another mental disorder (e.g. mood disorder, anxiety disorder, dissociative disorder or a personality disorder).			✓
3	*Combined (A-E **and** items 1 **and** 2 rated yes)*			Yes/(No)
4	*Predominantly inattentive type (A-E **and** item 1 rated yes)*			(Yes)/No
5	*Predominantly hyperactive-impulsive type (A-E **and** item 2 rated yes)*			Yes/(No)
6	*Total score obtained for symptoms by applying ratings of 0 = never, 1 = sometimes, 2 = often*			26
7	*In partial remission of symptoms? If (3), (4) and (5) above are scored 'no' **and** if score obtained for (6) above is 17 or greater*			Yes/No (N/A)

when diagnosing the disorder in adults as there is unequal weighting between the impulsive and hyperactive symptoms. If impulsive symptoms are more likely to be retained than hyperactive symptoms in young adulthood, then clearly individuals may fall short of these stringent criteria. Bear in mind also that clients may not have these problems 'often' or all the time. Adults, unlike children, are likely to have more control over their impulses not least by being able to exercise choices over their environment. They can select their work environment, for example, long distance lorry driving may be a more attractive employment than a 9–5 office job. Others may prefer to be self-employed. Professions in information technology appear to be favoured – most likely because this satisfies a thirst for immediate gratification as computer work provides individuals the opportunity to multi-task using lots of different windows, etc. Hence, although such adults may well be symptomatic, their symptoms may not impair their functioning.

Although not formally part of the diagnostic criteria, there are other difficulties that present in adult ADHD such as procrastination, low tolerance of frustration, mood lability, low self-esteem, disorganisation, attitudinal problems, disinhibition and ceaseless mental activity. The ways these problems commonly present in adult ADHD are presented in Table 2.3.

Table 2.3   Symptomatic features of ADHD in adulthood

Procrastination	Individuals with ADHD do not put things off for hours or days, they put things off for weeks or months. They have loads of projects half started but they do not see things through. They may get into debt because they don't pay bills on time or miss deadlines. If they do meet deadlines, it is only because they have crammed in last-minute information or stayed up all night to do so. They are always late and have loads of excuses as to why they have been unable to do a task on time.
Low tolerance of frustration	This is often presented as being irritable or 'tetchy'. Individuals are often impatient and quick to become cross especially when others do not appear to understand them or follow what they are saying.
Mood lability	Mood states can change rapidly and possibly without apparent triggers. These symptoms may be misdiagnosed as bipolar disorder, but the difference is that, for ADHD, lability occurs over a matter of hours whereas in cases of bipolar disorder it will occur over a period of weeks.
Low self-esteem	Individuals have a history of failing (which they may perceive as the incompletion of projects). They commonly feel that they are underachieving according to their potential and constantly seek reassurance or approval. They are sensitive to criticism and motivated to seek social recognition and approval. At the same time they often have a sense of self-efficacy and resilience, which drives them to constantly seek new opportunities and successes. Their entrepreneurial nature may appear incompatible with a lack of self-esteem.

(continued)

Table 2.3 (*continued*)

Disorganisation	This is often presented as poor planning and sequencing. They may have difficulty organising and prioritising information in addition to imposing order and structure in their world. This may be for particular tasks, e.g. household chores resulting in mess and chaos in their living environment, or more functionally, e.g. being late for work, taking a long time to prepare a meal. This problem may present as a lack of co-ordination and a tendency to adopt a haphazard, chaotic approach to tasks.
Attitudinal problems	Individuals may present as irritable and oppositional, and argue for the sake of the argument. They may seek arousal and stimulus in this way, thus presenting as 'difficult individuals' who do not take criticism well. They may be bad employees, who do not accept line management. Attitudinal problems may result in the falling out with friends and colleagues. They may have a high turnover of jobs.
Disinhibition	This may be expressed as both verbal and physical disinhibitive behaviours. Individuals may not be able to inhibit the impulse to speak out and say the first thing that comes into their head, resulting in them being hurtful and insensitive towards others. Their impropriety may get them into trouble in their interpersonal relationships with friends, colleagues and the law. They may be unable to inhibit the impulse to express anger physically by either lashing out at others and/or destroying property. Antisocial behaviour is likely to be opportunistic and unplanned. If feeling depressed, poor impulse control may be a risk for acting out suicidal ideation.
Sensation-seeking behaviour	A need for high stimulation and immediate gratification will often lead to individuals engaging in risk-taking behaviours. This may be expressed as an obsessive eagerness to explore new ideas and gain new experiences. Leisure pursuits may contain a sense of danger and recklessness, e.g. mountaineering, bungee jumping. Individuals may deliberately heighten the excitement by increasing the odds or risk. They tend to live life to the excess and push limits to extremes. This symptom may be expressed in illicit drug taking behaviour, they may present as accident prone, and/or engage in unsafe sex.
Ceaseless mental activity	Individuals will talk about their brain working too fast and a speeding up of thoughts that rapidly change. They are unable to keep track of these thoughts or write them down and they may feel completely overwhelmed and exhausted by this experience. Other people present as being able to relax and appear calm, but still report having racing thoughts. If a client presents with speeded up thoughts/ideas as opposed to a flooding of thoughts/ideas then one might consider hypermania to be the primary problem.

The Canadian longitudinal follow-up study conducted by Weiss et al. (1985) found that two-thirds of hyperactive children retained at least one disabling ADHD symptom in young adulthood. What does that mean for the individual? Does it mean that they no longer have ADHD and thus cannot access treatment in spite of retaining a symptom that may cause them to have significant adjustment problems? The prevalence of ADHD declines with age. Nevertheless, impulsivity, disorganisation, impaired concentration and poor planning can remain as disruptive symptoms and, for individuals who currently have symptoms that no longer meet full criteria, 'in partial remission' should be specified. However, there are no formal diagnostic guidelines to help identify this important group, who may as a result be prevented from accessing appropriate services. Genetic studies support the notion that ADHD represents a dimensional trait rather than a pathological category (Levy, Hay, McStephen, Wood & Waldman, 1997) and the DSM-IV criteria may be applied in this way by allocating the following scores to responses:

0 = never
1 = sometimes
2 = often

A score of 17 on the DSM-IV checklist of symptoms represents one standard deviation above the mean average score obtained in a normal control group (Young, 1999); that is, falling at the 84th percentile. Thus, individuals who do not meet the categorical diagnosis usually applied, and who are in partial remission of their symptoms may be identified using this method (see section 7 in Table 2.2).

DIFFERENTIAL DIAGNOSIS AND COMORBIDITY

Clinical assessment of adult ADHD should only be made by a professional trained in differential diagnosis of adult psychiatric disorders, for example psychiatrists, neurologists or clinical psychologists. Multidisciplinary assessment is recommended. It is important for professionals to remember that adults with other psychiatric problems may appear to have symptoms of ADHD. A difficulty with attentional control is common to many psychiatric disorders, but this is usually excluded from an alternative diagnosis when it involves a very serious psychopathology. Poor impulse control is commonly associated with conduct disorders and antisocial behaviours. Adolescent-onset socialised conduct disorders or hypomania might appear superficially similar. The age criterion is crucial to distinguish ADHD from later onset conditions, thus care must be taken when diagnosing subtypes (either predominantly inattention, or predominantly hyperactive-impulsive) or, unless such care is taken to rule out the existence of the other conditions, there may be a higher rate of false positive diagnoses (Weiss et al., 1999).

There is considerable comorbidity with childhood ADHD including conduct disorder, oppositional defiant disorder, anxiety disorder, depressive disorder, pervasive developmental disorder, Tourette's syndrome and substance misuse. Language, learning and motor developmental delays are also commonly reported. In adulthood, comorbid problems include personality disorder (particularly antisocial), bipolar disorder, obsessive-compulsive disorder and, to a lesser extent, psychotic disorders. Adults with severe mental illness, such as schizophrenia, or severe learning disability often have problems with attention and activity levels yet these disorders do not occur any more frequently in people with ADHD than in the normal population (Mannuzza, Klein, Bessler, Malloy & LaPadula, 1998).

A competent adult ADHD assessment requires a thorough history taking involving a much more detailed developmental history than is undertaken as part of a conventional general adult psychiatric interview. When considering whether a diagnosis is differential or comorbid, it is helpful to bear in mind the age of onset. Children with ADHD often have comorbid problems whether they are anxiety, depression, emotional lability or substance misuse. However, most of these difficulties are likely to have had a later onset than ADHD.

Thus, to summarise, when assessing adult ADHD one needs to have the following checklist in mind:

1. Obtain a comprehensive childhood history particularly with respect to presence of ADHD symptoms.
2. Evaluate the presence of current ADHD symptoms.
3. Evidence that these symptoms are causing the individual significant impairment in their everyday life (e.g. relationships, job, emotional adjustment).
4. Assess for differential diagnoses – assess for the existence of comorbid conditions. It may well be that the comorbid condition(s) is impacting more on the individual's life than the ADHD and, as such, this may be the primary target for treatment.

The persistence of the ADHD syndrome beyond childhood and the complexity of its assessment as an adult disorder give rise to the need for the development of reliable and valid assessment procedures in adolescence and adulthood. This is hampered by diagnostic criteria that do not account for the heterogeneity and/or remission of symptoms in adulthood. It is also important to screen for comorbid problems and rule out differential diagnoses. In the case of severe comorbid symptoms, such as substance misuse, it will be important to treat these prior to formal re-assessment.

SOURCES OF REPORTING

Studies have suggested that children with ADHD are not reliable informants of symptoms of ADHD (Danckaerts, Heptinstall, Chadwick & Taylor, 1999; Smith, Pelham, Gnagy, Molina & Evans, 2000) and parents have been shown to be more reliable informants than their adult children in predicting treatment response

(Wender, Reimherr & Wood, 1981). However, adulthood studies have also reported that ADHD adults are able to give reliable and valid accounts of ADHD symptoms (Murphy & Schachar, 2000; Young & Gudjonsson, 2005). Thus, the reliability and validity of the reporting of ADHD symptoms by adult clients and their parents may depend on the context of what is being reported and whether it refers to a prospective or retrospective evaluation. For example, a parent may know less about the severity and frequency of ADHD symptoms experienced by an adult child who may be employed and living independently. Parental information may be particularly unreliable for antisocial behaviour (Young, 2004; Young & Gudjonsson, 2005; Young & Gudjonsson, in press).

It can be helpful to encourage the client to think about their past experiences in a structured way and to identify important gaps in their knowledge about their history. In such cases, the therapist could provide Exercise 2.1 (outlined on the Companion Website), which aims to facilitate taking a developmental history.

Clinicians need to be cautious when faced with 'self-diagnosed' ADHD symptomatology (particularly since clients could self-refer in anticipation of being prescribed a drug of potential misuse). Although the 'first question' identified earlier regarding whether the client had ADHD as a child requires an assessment of a history of hyperactivity in childhood, this may not be easy to elicit in retrospect and/or reliability may be questionable. Client's recollections have been found to show poor agreement with parental recall, whilst the latter seems to be a better predictor of treatment response (Wender et al., 1981). In order to make a diagnosis with confidence, whenever possible an assessment should include information from various sources, including psychometric measures.

There are few validated measures appropriate for adults that distinguish adult ADHD from other disorders. This is in marked contrast to childhood ADHD, where several well validated measures of attention and impulsivity can be implemented, as well as access to informants other than the client who can provide reliable historical information and behavioural observations. Parents and teachers may be useful sources of information for adolescents, but clinicians may need to turn to other sources such as partners (Young, 2004) or put more weight on other sources, such as observational, cognitive or neuropsychological measures. Cognitive impairments can be assessed by neuropsychological measures and moderate-to-severe impairments will have a negative influence on the individual's academic and social functioning.

NEUROPSYCHOLOGICAL ASSESSMENT

Several domains of neuropsychological dysfunction have been documented as being associated with ADHD in childhood (e.g. Barkley, 1998). However, there is a relative paucity of literature regarding a neuropsychological profile of the disorder in adulthood. Studies that have endeavoured to investigate different cognitive functions have generally involved only small sample sizes with limited power to detect even moderate effect sizes and provided little information regarding how clients with this disorder may differ from clinically similar but non-ADHD clients, such as those with anxiety disorders. Also, researchers tend to have focused on employing laboratory-based experimental tasks rather than standardised tests, which are readily available.

Nevertheless, when assessing an individual for ADHD in adulthood, it is important to conduct a neuropsychological assessment for three reasons. First, it may contribute to the diagnostic evaluation of adults with ADHD as they commonly exhibit impairment in domains of cognitive function. However, a neuropsychological assessment should never be solely used to determine a diagnosis, as it is generally accepted that no single individual test or battery of tests has sufficient specificity to reliably diagnose ADHD (Barkley, 1998). A neuropsychological assessment can, however, be used to support a diagnosis, in conjunction with information gained from childhood, current sources regarding behaviour and a comprehensive clinical interview.

The second reason for performing a neuropsychological assessment is that it can be used to exclude other diagnoses such as learning disabilities or diffuse brain injury leading to a global impairment, rather than specific attentional and/or impulse control difficulties. Third, it can be used to provide a functional expectation or hypothesis regarding the client's ability to perform in areas of daily living, for example educational attainment, occupational and domestic activities, from which discrepancies may be identified.

When conducting a neuropsychological assessment of adult ADHD, the following areas of cognitive functioning need to be assessed: intelligence; attention; other executive functions, such as response inhibition; planning ability; working memory; and processing speed. Behavioural observation is an extremely important aspect of the assessment and one which may be overlooked. Common behavioural features of an adult ADHD assessment include inattention (e.g. repetition of instructions, distraction, daydreaming), hyperactivity (e.g. fidgeting, restlessness, foot tapping, leg shaking, fiddling with papers) and impulsivity (e.g. turning pages of tests prematurely, blurting out irrelevant questions or answers, rapid shifts in topic of conversation). Deterioration in performance may be accounted for by the client's inability to sustain attention as evidenced by complaints about the duration of the assessment, requests to leave the room for breaks (for cigarettes, coffee, toilet) and an overall reluctance to perform tasks.

Intelligence

Tests of intellectual functioning can be used either as a baseline measure from which to predict a client's estimated level of functioning in other domains or as discriminatory tools; that is, to indicate clients who may have ADHD.

Baseline intellectual predictions may be made from tasks that do not load heavily on the cognitive functions commonly impaired in ADHD. For example, Digit Span and Arithmetic subtests from the Wechsler Adult Intelligence Scales (WAIS-III) (Wechsler, 1997a) draw heavily on attentional and executive functions whereas verbal comprehension tasks, such as Vocabulary and Information may be better indicators of intellectual potential. Non-verbal tasks, including the Kaufman Brief Intelligence Scale (Kaufman & Kaufman, 1990) and the Matrix Reasoning subtest of the WAIS-III (Wechsler, 1997a), are not timed and have the advantage of being less culturally specific than most neuropsychological tasks. They are also less sensitive to the effects of educational attainment and problems such as truancy. Hence, if an ADHD child missed out on education due to attentional difficulties or behavioural problems, performance intellectual tasks are less likely to underestimate their IQ due to lack of exposure to similar materials. However, behavioural observations during these tasks can sometimes indicate underperformance due to impulsive response styles, or adopting a 'stab in the dark' or guessing approach when the client has lost concentration.

Certain verbal tasks may also be used to estimate a baseline of intellectual functioning. Reading tasks are commonly used in clinical neuropsychology for predicting premorbid intellectual functioning, for example, the National Adult Reading Test (Nelson, 1992; Nelson & Willison, 1991) and the Wechsler Test of Adult Reading (WTAR) (Wechsler, 2001). These tests are often used to evaluate intellectual decline, as reading abilities are relatively resistant to many forms of brain damage, disease or mental disorder and hence may be employed to estimate a previous overall level of ability (otherwise referred to as a premorbid or 'former' functioning level). However, for adults with ADHD, the investigation of premorbid intellectual functioning is not particularly relevant as the clinician is not aiming to identify intellectual deterioration. The purpose of an intellectual assessment is to determine discrepancies between domains of cognitive functioning, for example specific impairments in attention, in comparison with average levels of intelligence. Reading tests can be employed to do this but they do have two major limitations. First, reading is a skill that is commonly acquired in primary school and early secondary school, and these are the ages at which a child with ADHD may be exhibiting particular difficulty in sitting still and learning due to hyperactivity and poor attention. Hence, they may be deprived of the opportunity to sit quietly with adults in order to be taught reading skills appropriately. The second limitation is that there is a high comorbidity of ADHD with dyslexia (e.g. Semrud-Clikeman et al., 1992) and therefore an adult's reading ability may be compromised for reasons due to a specific learning difficulty rather than reduced general intellectual functioning.

An alternative method of estimating verbal intellectual functioning in order to provide a baseline intellectual assessment is through the use of the Vocabulary subtest of the WAIS-III or the Wechsler Abbreviated Scale of Intelligence (WASI) (Wechsler, 1999). This reduces the previously described problems associated with reading tests and dyslexia as the individual is required to provide word meanings as opposed to reading the word. However, educational disruption and lack of exposure to written material may also limit a client's knowledge of word meanings, although this task is somewhat less dependent on educational attainment than reading ability as clients may be exposed to words aurally in contexts where they have been able to abstract a meaning.

Intellectual measures which have been shown to discriminate ADHD in adults from normal controls include subtests of the Wechsler Scales: Digit-Symbol Coding, Arithmetic, Block Design; Digit Span (Hervey, Epstein & Curry, 2004; Quinlan, 2001). This may be due to these tasks loading heavily on working memory and processing speed abilities. As yet, no research has been published regarding the Working Memory (WMI) and Processing Speed (PSI) indices of the WAIS-III (Wechsler, 1997a) but it is likely that these are more sensitive to ADHD symptoms in comparison with other indices.

Aside from examining formal intellectual performance and comparison of subtest scores, it is important to bear in mind that ADHD individuals are less likely to have achieved their intellectual potential. Thus, it is helpful to compare occupational and academic attainment to that of family expectations and sibling achievement. For example, it is not uncommon to find a young man of average intellect employed in unskilled factory work or manual labour, but whose siblings are at college or in skilled or professional employment.

Attention

Attention inevitably affects all aspects of testing as the ability to focus on any task requires attentional functions. Hence, it could be argued that poor attention may contaminate all test results, even for tests which are not specifically designed to assess attentional functioning (e.g. IQ scores may be depressed). It is therefore advisable to assess attention independently using appropriate measures.

Attentional functions can be fractionated into several domains. Four commonly acknowledged areas are selective attention; divided attention; shifting attention; sustained attention.

1. Selective attention is the ability to focus attention on one stimulus source and screen out distracting irrelevant stimuli.
2. Divided attention is the ability to attend to two or more stimuli simultaneously.
3. Shifting attention is the ability to switch attention between two or more sources of information.
4. Sustained attention is the ability to maintain attention over a long period of time, with only a limited frequency of reinforcement.

Tests assessing selective attention include the Letter Cancellation Test (e.g. Lezak, Howieson & Loring, 2004) (see Figure 2.1), the Trail Making Test (Reitan, 1958;

Instructions

On this page you will see lines of letters. I want you to go through these letters and put a slash through all the letter 'e's. Work as quickly as you can but without missing any letter 'e's.

Example

1   plmkoijuhubgyvftgbhfdcdscczvatwabfhsyxmjewqpoiuytredfrtgvcxzswqaszxcfrtgvbjrmc

2   plokmjiikmchtsgbxvzfatagsfxcsdweqwqsaczdsewfcvctdhnvjlkomjhdngtsgbcvpoiuytlmikm

Figure 2.1   Letter cancellation test

Spreen & Strauss, 1998) and the Stroop Task (Stroop, 1935; Trenerry, Crosson, DeBoe & Leber 1989). Attentional control has been shown to load on certain subtests of the Test of Everyday Attention (Robertson, Ward, Ridgeway & Nimmo-Smith, 1994), including the Map Search and the Telephone Search tasks. A client with ADHD will typically race through tests of selective attention, completing the tasks rapidly but making errors by missing target items. However, as individuals mature, they seem to learn from past experience and recognise that by speeding through tasks they are liable to make errors and hence apply a strategy of performing the task extremely slowly in order to ensure they achieve accuracy.

Divided attention can be assessed by the TEA: Telephone Search Whilst Counting task (Robertson et al., 1994). On this occasion the client is required to listen and count a series of tones in series played on a tape recorder. The dual task decrement, (i.e. deterioration in performance when required to do two tasks simultaneously) is a measure of divided attention.

There are several neuropsychological measures of attention shifting. The most widely available is Part B of the Trail Making Test (Reitan, 1958; Spreen & Strauss, 1998), which requires shifting attention between numerical and alphabetical sequences. Other tests of attention shifting include the Visual Elevator subtest from the Test of Everyday Attention battery (Robertson et al., 1994), which provides measures of both speed and accuracy. Laboratory-style tests of attention shifting, can be found in the CANTAB battery such as the Intra-dimensional-Extra-dimensional shift (ID-ED shift), although this task is also a test of rule learning and mental flexibility (MacLean et al., 2004). Clients with ADHD are likely to have increased error rates on such tasks, although this has not been found reliably (Hervey et al., 2004).

Sustained attention can be assessed using various versions of the Continuous Performance Test (e.g. Lezak et al., 2004). It involves attending to computerised stimuli that are presented at a slow rate with a low target frequency. A client with ADHD may typically lose concentration early in the task and hence miss several targets. An ecologically valid sustained attentional task is the Lottery subtest of the Test of

Everyday Attention (Robertson et al., 1994), which involves listening out for target lottery numbers over a 10-minute period. However, this has relatively few target items and thus may be less sensitive to deficits.

Response Inhibition and Executive Functioning

Response inhibition is an executive function or higher order cognitive process, which is engaged when situations require voluntary control over responses, often when there is a change of context. Tasks assessing response inhibition for children include Go-No-Go and Stop tasks, but these have been shown to be less sensitive in adulthood ADHD (Lovejoy et al., 1999). One task which has been documented to discriminate well between ADHD individuals and patient controls is the Matching Familiar Figures test (Cairnes & Cammock, 1978; Young & Gudjonsson, 2005; Young, Channon & Toone, 2000). This task requires identification of a target amongst five distractor items. A typical ADHD response involves a speeded time to respond score, but an increased number of errors in comparison with control subjects. Other response inhibition tasks include the Stroop test (Trenerry et al., 1989) where the Colour-Word version requires inhibition of the prepotent response of reading the colour name rather than identifying the colour of the ink. A study by Young, Morris, Bramham and Tyson (in press) showed that a deficit in response inhibition existed even when controlling for colour naming speed; that is, subtracting the time taken to perform the basic word reading task which loads on selective attention.

Attention and response inhibition are two aspects of a more overarching constellation of symptoms manifested by patients with ADHD forming a dysexecutive syndrome. This is perhaps unsurprising given the wealth of literature implicating the prefrontal cortex in neuroimaging studies to be significantly smaller and less active for individuals with ADHD than matched controls (e.g. Rubia et al., 1999; Rubia et al., 2000).

Executive dysfunction beyond the core cognitive deficits in ADHD has been identified with tasks assessing spontaneous verbal production (FAS/COWAT tests, e.g. Lovejoy et al., 1999) and cognitive flexibility (e.g. Wisconsin Card Sorting Test; Milner, 1963). In a study by Young, Morris, Toone and Tyson (2006), a computerised version of the Tower of London test was used to investigate both planning and problem solving in a group of adults with ADHD. It was found that the control subjects increased their planning time as a function of task difficulty, whereas the ADHD group used the same amount of planning time regardless of difficulty. In contrast, the ADHD group increased their time to complete the solution in proportion to difficulty whereas controls did not follow the same pattern. It was concluded that normal adults plan and think through the solution for the task before beginning, whereas ADHD patients do their thinking during the task. This performance style obviously has major implications for a group of patients who are liable to be distracted during their everyday 'on-line' planning.

We have found that the Behavioural Assessment of Dysexecutive Syndrome is less sensitive to adulthood ADHD than more traditional neuropsychological tests of executive functioning, although it may provide more valuable qualitative detail. For example, some patients may have difficulty in developing a search strategy in the Key Search subtest. Others may be unable to plan the route in the Zoo Map subtest or sequence and organise their time for the Modified Six Elements subtest. Again, behavioural observations are particularly crucial throughout assessment of executive functioning.

Memory

Several studies have investigated memory functioning in adults with ADHD, possibly because forgetfulness or 'losing track' of thoughts is one of the most commonly reported difficulties experienced in everyday living for this patient group. However, measured memory deficits appear to vary as a function of the tests that measure them. There have been consistent findings of difficulties with working memory as measured by tasks such as the Digit Span and Spatial Span subtests of the Wechsler Memory Scale – 3rd edition (WMS-III) (Wechsler, 1997b). Short-term memory deficits have been reported, for example, using Figure Recall and Logical Memory subtests. However, the nature of the impairment is unclear as it is possible that retention is affected by poor attention in registration of information rather than dysfunctional storage per se. In addition, studies (e.g. Dowson et al., 2004; Young, Morris, Toone & Tyson, 2006) have shown that deficits in short-term working memory are also exhibited by adults with ADHD.

Verbal learning tests have also been shown to be performed poorly by adults with ADHD (Hervey et al., 2004). Again, this may in part be due to poor attention and therefore faulty initial encoding. In addition, adults with ADHD have been shown to have a reduced ability to use the optimal strategy of organising their learning according to semantic clusters and instead attempt to learn lists according to serial clustering instead; that is, they did not group the list in categories such as fruit, vegetables, etc., but learnt the list just in the order it was read to them.

Processing Speed

Studies of differences in processing and motor speed scores between adults with ADHD and healthy controls report smaller effect sizes than those seen in the other cognitive domains. However, there seems to be a strong relationship between response time and cognitive processing demands, whereby if cognitive processing co-occurs with motor activity, there is a relative increase in response time. Tests which can be used to assess processing speed include the Information Processing subtests from the Adult Memory and Information Processing Battery (AMIPB) (Coughlan & Hollows, 1985) and subtests of the WAIS-III (Wechsler, 1997a) that load on the Processing Speed Index (e.g. Digit-Symbol Coding; Symbol Search).

Differences in motor speed may be non-significant for some studies, although when this has been controlled for then impairment in other domains is still apparent (e.g. Young Morris et al., in press; Young, Morris, Toone, & Tyson, 2006).

Limitations of Neuropsychological Assessment

Clinical research has shown that, whilst abnormal scores are good predictors of ADHD, normal scores are poor predictors of the absence of ADHD; that is, there is an increase of false negative errors. This suggests that it is possible that a client may receive a diagnosis of ADHD in the absence of impaired test results.

A major limitation of using a neuropsychological assessment for diagnostic purposes or to evaluate functional ability, is the unnatural setting of a typical testing session. Assessments are usually conducted on a one-to-one basis in a quiet setting with only limited distractions. However, the situations in which ADHD symptoms may pose the most difficulties for the client are those where there are multiple competing demands on their time which require prioritisation and planning in the context of many distractions. In the clinical environment, the examiner is effectively acting as the client's frontal lobes by organising the sequence of tests, thereby minimising distraction. The importance of an assessment somehow enforces the client to stay seated and motivated to perform optimally. This latter aspect has been shown to be important in childhood ADHD where cognitive dysfunction is mediated by motivation; that is, children with ADHD were able to perform a task within normal limits when motivated by rewards but unable to do so in the absence of reinforcement. It is therefore likely that the presence of the examiner will provide some form of reinforcer, thus inducing motivation. It is likely that more ecologically valid neuropsychological tests will provide a more realistic assessment of true level of attentional and executive functioning, and this may also give the individual the opportunity to demonstrate adaptive strategies they may employ to overcome difficulties.

Conversely, patients who do not have ADHD may also exhibit impairment on tests of attention, working memory and executive function. For example, the Stroop test has been shown to be sensitive to depression (Katz, Wood, Goldstein, Auchenbach & Geckle, 1998). Mood disorders, such as anxiety and depression, have been shown to be associated with poor attentional functioning, which may contaminate results on other tests such as memory assessments (e.g. Elliott, 2002). Unfortunately, these disorders may masquerade as adult ADHD due to their similar attentional symptoms or they may co-exist with the disorder. It is therefore crucial to obtain as detailed a history as possible regarding the chronicity and longevity of all cognitive symptoms.

RATING SCALES

Assessment of behavioural symptoms can be performed using various standardised rating scales in order to determine the extent to which they differ from accepted behaviour. The advantages of using rating scales are that they offer a method for a consistent approach to assessment across a service and that they can be used to quantitatively monitor progression of the disorder and treatment response. Rating scales can also be used as a screening measure since, if retrospective ratings of childhood ADHD symptoms are low, it is unlikely that an individual has ADHD in adulthood. Nevertheless, it is important to stress that scoring above a threshold score on a rating scale does not constitute a diagnosis but may provide support to clinical information regarding symptoms.

It is advisable to use rating scales in order to attain information regarding both childhood and current behaviour from clients and someone who knew them as a child. Several childhood and adulthood ADHD measures are available for this purpose and may be selected according to speed and comprehensiveness. The most straightforward scale is the DSM-IV checklist of symptoms (see Table 2.2) where clients are required to rate each symptom according to frequency from 0 = never to 1 = sometimes and 2 = often. A score of 17 or above is an indication of moderate ADHD symptoms (Young, 1999). This can be done by both clients and their informant (e.g. a parent) for current and childhood symptoms in order to determine presence and magnitude of difficulties. However, this scale does not allow assessment of behaviours commonly associated with, but not forming part of, the ADHD diagnostic criteria, such as emotional lability.

Childhood ADHD Rating Scales

Comprehensive and well-established childhood measures include the Conners' Rating Scales – Revised available in long and short forms for parents and teachers (Conners, 2000). The long form includes assessment of DSM-IV symptom subscales and comorbid disorders. The short form can be scored according to a symptom count or in comparison to norms. The Conners Global Index additionally provides information regarding restless-impulsive factors and emotional lability in childhood.

The Wender Utah Rating scale (Ward, Wender & Reimherr, 1993) is a retrospective rating scale with a subset of 25 items rated with a 0–4 severity scale. It has been shown to be valid in differentiating adults with ADHD from those without and with more ambiguous psychopathology (Ward et al., 1993). However, this has not been standardised on a UK population, and its wording may have a North American bias.

Adulthood ADHD Rating Scales

A Conner's Adult ADHD Rating Scale (CAARS) (Conners, Erhardt & Sparrow, 1998) can be rated through self-report and by an observer in a parallel form. The long versions have 66 items, which form nine subscales of problem behaviours. The short versions have 26 items with abbreviated subscales and hence can be used for screening purposes.

Although the Brown Attention Deficit Disorder Scales (BADDS) (Brown, 1996) do not thoroughly assess impulse control and hyperactivity, they are particularly useful in assessing executive functioning deficits that are associated with ADHD in child and adulthood versions. Ratings of six domains of functions can be identified: (1) organising, procrastinating and activating to work; (2) focusing, sustaining and shifting attention to tasks; (3) regulating alertness, sustaining effort and processing speed; (4) managing frustration and modulating emotions; (5) utilising working memory and access recall; and (6) monitoring and self-regulating action.

Limitations of Rating Scales

There are disadvantages in using rating scales, the most obvious being that the questions are answered subjectively. Given that many clients who present at an assessment for ADHD are motivated to receive a diagnosis (Van der Linden, Young, Ryan & Toone, 2000), it is possible that biases towards overrating symptoms may be in operation. Conversely, clients who have been encouraged to attend the clinic by parents or other influential people may have only limited insight into their difficulties. It is therefore advisable to obtain corroborative ratings wherever possible. This is particularly so for retrospective ratings regarding childhood behaviour as reporting may not be reliable (e.g. Mannuzza, Klein, Klein, Bessler & Shrout, 2002) although other studies have shown greater reliability (e.g. Murphy & Schachar, 2000).

CONCLUSIONS

Assessment of adulthood ADHD requires the consideration of a wide range of sources of information in order for a diagnosis to be made. The existence of the disorder in childhood is necessary for an adult to be diagnosed with ADHD, therefore presence of symptoms that meet diagnostic criteria within the inattentive and/or hyperactive/impulsive domains needs to be established both within childhood and currently. Given that attentional and impulse control difficulties are common in other psychiatric disorders, careful consideration must be applied to differential and comorbid diagnoses. The information required can be obtained from several subjective and objective sources, which vary regarding sensitivity and reliability. The subjective sources include interview and rating scales with the client and informants, such as parents, for childhood history or a partner for current difficulties. More objective sources for consideration include school reports and current documentation regarding functioning, in addition to formal neuropsychological evaluations. Table 2.4 on the Companion Website provides an Assessment Checklist, which summarises the information to be gathered in order to conduct a comprehensive assessment of adulthood ADHD.

3

TREATMENT OF ADHD

There is a range of clinical approaches to working with adults with ADHD. This chapter will briefly review the different therapies recommended to be helpful in treating ADHD and outline the principles of the Young–Bramham Programme, which draws on cognitive behavioural, psychoeducational and motivational interviewing therapeutic paradigms.

As in the management of ADHD in childhood, pharmacotherapy has a major role in treating ADHD, and when taking appropriate medication an individual is better placed to access psychological treatment as they may be better focused, less distracted and/or restless. For childhood ADHD, the combination of pharmacological and behavioural treatments has not been shown to be more efficacious than medication alone (MTA Cooperative Group, 1999) but this is less likely to be the case in the treatment of ADHD adolescents and adults (Wilens et al., 1999). Although medication helps alleviate core symptoms of ADHD, the additional comorbid psychiatric problems, psychosocial problems and skills deficits which have developed over a lifetime of having ADHD may be usefully addressed by the psychological interventions presented in the Young–Bramham Programme.

MEDICATION

Stimulant medication (usually methylphenidate or dexamphetamine) forms the mainstay of treatment across the ADHD lifespan (Spencer et al., 1996). However, efficacy is heterogeneous, ranging from a 25% success rate to as much as 78% (Spencer et al., 1995). Thus, some individuals benefit less from medication than others.

Medication can be prepared in immediate release (e.g. Ritalin) and slow release forms (e.g. Concerta). Immediate release forms act within 20–30 minutes, peak after approximately 1–2 hours and wear off after 3–4 hours. Some patients report a 'rebound' effect, when they become more irritable and experience more

Table 3.1   Medication tips

1.	Slow release preparations reduce the need for remembering to take medication as frequently as immediate release preparations
2.	Work out the best time for taking tablets in order to optimise sleep – for some people, medication helps them sleep; for others, it can keep them awake and therefore the last dose can be taken mid-afternoon
3.	Reminders for taking medication can be programmed into mobile phones or watches. Otherwise, cues can be made at other times of day, e.g. when television programmes or mealtimes begin. It is important to take medication at regular times
4	Repeat prescriptions should be organised well in advance of medication running out. This could be done by planning several appointments ahead with the client
5.	Planned 'drug holidays' are sensible from time to time, to establish the extent to which symptoms are still problematic. However, these should be planned carefully and not be taken just when medication runs out
6.	Clients should be encouraged not to view medication as a 'magic pill' but as one of several strategies for improving their functioning
7.	Some clients who respond well to medication initially may become depressed after a period of treatment. This may be because their improved cognitive function allows them to ruminate, and hence may increase low mood as they reflect on regrets about their past and present lives. This possibility should be mentioned when patients begin treatment

pronounced symptoms as their medication wears off. Slow release preparations can be advantageous as they reduce the need to remember to take medication and have been reported to have a smoother action, although some patients still experience a rebound. Medication tips are presented in Table 3.1, which is also on the Companion Website in a format suitable for use as a handout.

Other non-cerebral stimulant drugs can also be effective although few studies directly compare their effects with stimulant medication. Anti-depressants, such as desipramine and venlafaxine, can be effective and, more recently, atomoxetine has been marketed as an alternative to stimulants. Such preparations may be preferable for patients with comorbid depression and those who have adverse reactions to stimulants.

Commonly reported side effects include insomnia, nausea, headaches, weight loss and anxiety. Less common side effects are psychosis and tics. In a very few cases, hair loss has been reported. Some of the techniques introduced in the Young–Bramham Programme will help clients in the management of medication side effects (see Table 3.2). However, any side effect should be discussed with a medical professional before attempting any of the described techniques.

Table 3.2 Methods to counteract the side effects of medication

Side effect	Recommendations
Insomnia	See Chapter 12 on sleep hygiene
Nausea	Tends to remit, take medication with meals
Headaches	Relaxation techniques (see Chapter 9) and medication for pain relief
Weight loss	Take medication with food or just after meals
Anxiety/edginess	Psychoeducation. See Chapter 9 on anxiety
Psychotic symptoms, e.g. paranoia, hallucinations	Stop medication immediately and seek medical advice
Tics	Stop medication and seek medical advice

THE YOUNG–BRAMHAM PROGRAMME

We have conducted in-depth interviews with our clients to ascertain their beliefs and feelings about receiving a diagnosis and being treated with medication (Young, Bramham et al., in submission). From these interviews, three themes have emerged:

1. *Review of the past – feeling different from others.* Clients reported that they had always felt different from their peers and family. They had been compared unfavourably with siblings and often told they were stupid, lazy or disruptive. For some individuals, this led them to internalise the negative feedback, which in turn had a detrimental impact on their self-esteem. However, other individuals described being relatively resistant to the criticisms of others. This may in part have been due to the protective role of their inattention and impulsivity, which prevented them from ruminating about their difficulties. They described not having the ability to dwell on an issue for long enough for it to become distressing or problematic. In addition, some individuals described reviewing their own childhood through observing their children with ADHD and reflecting on how the disorder affected them in their youth.

2. *Emotional impact of the diagnosis.* On being diagnosed with ADHD, clients often felt a sense of relief and elation that there was an explanation for their difficulties. This was quickly succeeded by turmoil and confusion as they tried to make sense of past experience in light of the diagnosis. They began to consider what might have been, how their lives may have been more successful if they had been diagnosed with the disorder and received treatment earlier. For example, they may have been able to achieve academically rather than experiencing concentration problems in the classroom, which meant they were unable to gain appropriate qualifications commensurate with their potential. There was also anger that they had not been given appropriate support and advice during their childhood and adolescence. Clients then felt particularly sad and regretful that they had come to expect themselves to fail and underachieve. There was a

period of adjustment during which they came to realise that they may have a lifelong chronic disorder and this elicited some anxiety. However, in the final stages of adjustment, individuals came to accept the diagnosis and the need to take medication.

3. *Consideration of the future.* Clients were able to acknowledge how medication had improved their motivation and ability to function in their everyday lives, particularly regarding interpersonal relationships. It also allowed them to recognise the difference between their symptoms when they had taken medication and when it had worn off. However, they were aware that all their difficulties did not disappear with pharmacological treatment and that certain problems required them to makes changes in their behaviour. This distinction was important for clients in understanding the features of their own presentation. Some individuals were worried that others would believe they were using ADHD as an excuse for all their difficulties and hence it was useful for them to understand what was and was not attributable to the disorder. There were also concerns about the stigma attached to ADHD and this influenced their disclosure of the diagnosis.

These findings identify a role for psychological treatment in three areas. First, it is necessary to help clients through the process of adjustment and make sense of the past. Second, in order to reduce anxiety about the future therapists should emphasise the clients' strengths and positive characteristics that will allow them to make changes in the future. Finally, there is a need for skills development, particularly in domains that do not improve directly with medication, in order to allow individuals to function more successfully.

AIMS AND OBJECTIVES OF THE YOUNG–BRAMHAM PROGRAMME

This Young–Bramham Programme promotes two primary aims of psychological treatment:

1. *Change from the outside in:* whereby it is aimed to provide clinicians with ways to encourage and help the individual to change the environment in order to optimise their personal, occupational and social functioning.
2. *Change from the inside out:* whereby it is aimed to provide clinicians with ways of encouraging the individual to develop psychological strategies for adaptive functioning within different environments. This is achieved by amalgamating aspects of independent evidence-based psychological treatments, drawing on a cognitive behavioural, motivational and psychoeducational paradigm and applying techniques to meet the needs of adults with ADHD.

However, the neuropsychological presentation of patients with ADHD is not unique to this disorder. Indeed deficits of attentional control underlie many psychological conditions and certain modules of the Young–Bramham Programme may be helpful more generally for individuals with cognitive deficits of this type (e.g. those suffering with traumatic brain injury, schizophrenia, mild learning disabilities, etc.).

The objectives of the Young–Bramham Programme are:

1. To provide information about ADHD.
2. To provide psychological strategies for coping with symptoms and associated problems.

If the delivery of the programme is in a group format, then a third objective is:

3. For ADHD adults to meet others with similar difficulties and experiences.

The Young–Bramham Programme draws on three core psychological techniques, Cognitive Behavioural Therapy, Psychoeducation and Motivational Interviewing. It is intended to enable the individual to develop self-efficacy and the confidence that change can be achieved, to develop strategies to effect positive lifestyle change and cope with challenges. This involves education about the disorder, adopting psychoeducational techniques, overcoming ambivalence drawing on motivational interviewing decisional balance, cognitive-restructuring and reframing the past by challenging negative automatic thoughts, self-monitoring performance, recognising errors in thinking and evaluating cognitive distortions and misattributions. Whenever possible, it will also be important to elicit core beliefs that the individual holds about themselves, other people and the world. Behavioural techniques such as graded task assignments, modelling and role-play are employed to develop and rehearse new skills.

We introduce how to adapt these core techniques for people who have cognitive deficits of impulsivity and inattention, for example by applying a variety of techniques in sessions (shifting topics, visual aids, role-play, etc.) and introducing frequent breaks. In particular, individuals with ADHD are motivated to satisfy a need for immediate gratification, and treatment needs to be structured to include regular immediate and delayed reward systems. Specific tools such as worksheets, role-plays and exercises are presented as ways of maintaining attention and motivation, and reducing impulsivity. A fast-paced structure incorporating a variety of cognitive behavioural techniques (including practical exercises) will be attractive to individuals who have significant cognitive deficits, high intolerance and a low boredom threshold.

THERAPEUTIC ALLIANCE AND ENGAGEMENT IN TREATMENT

A central tenet of the therapeutic programme is collaboration. It is vital to engage and motivate an individual by setting agendas and goals of therapy together. This approach is likely to have face validity for individuals who may feel ambiguity over engaging with a clinician. It is important that the client has confidence in the therapist and perceives that the therapist understands their problems and the prognosis of ADHD in adulthood.

By adulthood, individuals with ADHD have frequently had many encounters with various education and mental health services (Young, Toone & Tyson, 2003). However, the diagnosis of ADHD has often not been made or the individual may have been given contradictory information. Individuals diagnosed for the first time in adulthood may lack trust in services and feel they have been unfairly treated by a system that has failed to identify their problems. Also, clients with ADHD may have more difficulty in coping with waiting for an appointment and become frustrated by any delay before assessment. Once diagnosed, they may feel angry and bitter that their condition had not been recognised sooner. It is important that they develop confidence in what they may perceive as yet another clinician before them. A collaborative and supportive relationship is crucial for the success of therapy for those adults who may have had difficulties in forming long-term healthy relationships and have experienced rejection. Previous relationships may have been intense but only lasted for a short period.

Nadeau (1995) identifies several roles that the therapist should adopt when treating an individual with ADHD:

1. *Supporter:* this involves supporting the client to convert from being a victim to being empowered.
2. *Interpreter:* here the therapist should facilitate interpretation of the constellation of difficulties making up the individual's ADHD. This information can be communicated to others who are in contact with the client to help them to understand the disorder.
3. *Structurer:* in order to provide a foundation for someone who has difficulty in planning and organising, the clinician should become more active and structured.
4. *Educator:* education may be provided through reading, writing session notes collaboratively, or ongoing (verbally) as part of the therapeutic process.

We propose a fifth additional role, and perhaps a more primary role:

5. *Trainer:* the predominant function of the therapist is, through guided discovery, to help the individual build a bridge between their internal and external world. The individual needs to identify and develop appropriate coping strategies to overcome difficult situations and obstacles to progress.

Developing a successful therapeutic relationship is crucial regardless of the mode of treatment. This is essential in the early stages of therapy, particularly if this is at a time when the client adjusts to their diagnosis.

THE IMPACT OF THE DIAGNOSIS

Treatment for adults begins at the time they are diagnosed. Following diagnosis, we found that an adult passes through six stages: (1) initial relief and elation; (2) confusion and emotional turmoil; (3) anger; (4) sadness and grief; (5) anxiety; and finally (6) accommodation and acceptance (Young, Bramham, Gray & Rose, in submission). Thus the way that the diagnosis is communicated to the client is crucial in their understanding of the disorder and their future adjustment to the diagnosis. Our research has supported this proposal as we found that many individuals do not absorb much information when being given positive results regarding the diagnosis. It is not until a second appointment that clients are able to process the experience of having a diagnosis of ADHD, take in relevant information and ask questions. Thus factual information regarding diagnosis and treatment should be presented in written format and reinforced at a subsequent appointment.

Many people feel relieved after they have received a diagnosis of ADHD. They say they always knew there was something wrong and it is reassuring to know that it is not their fault. Although people have often thought about ADHD for some time before receiving the diagnosis, hearing the words 'you have ADHD' can still be a shock requiring emotional adjustment. Many people report that, following diagnosis, they experience an emotional reaction, such as feelings of regret, guilt and sadness, which are natural and part of an acceptance process. They then attempt to reframe past events – what can be attributed to ADHD and what cannot? How could things have been different? Following treatment with medication they report a sense of change in identity saying they see themselves as becoming more serious and less 'zany'.

It is therefore important to encourage clients to talk to those who know them well and to reassure themselves that they are still the same person as before. Furthermore, helping clients to become more informed about their condition will allow them to understand themselves better and optimise their abilities. Reviewing helpful coping strategies will reassure them. Undoubtedly they will have already developed numerous ways of helping themselves without therapeutic input and this should be explored as it will give clues to what will be helpful to adopt in treatment and what will not.

PSYCHOEDUCATION

Psychoeducation should be applied from the start of the diagnostic process (Jackson & Farrugia, 1997). The aim is to promote knowledge about the disorder, the meaning of the diagnosis, and the impact it has had on the individual (Weiss et al., 1999). The first part of the education process is to provide fundamental information about ADHD, as there is still a surprising amount of erroneous 'lay' information that is misleading and confusing to the client. Murphy (1998) suggests that the therapist should explain the reason why the individual fulfils the criteria for a diagnosis of ADHD to enhance their understanding of the disorder. Education about treatment methods is important at this stage as many individuals may have preconceptions about the impact of stimulant treatment and the utility of psychological approaches. A written handout is helpful.

Following sessions promoting psychoeducation, we have found that there is a greater shift to a biological definition and understanding of the disorder. For example, a client who previously thought ADHD was a 'personality disorder that affects your attention span and thought processes', after psychoeducation described it as a 'condition which affects brain chemistry, and contact mechanisms in the brain'. Additionally, following psychoeducation sessions, individuals recognised how emotional and self-esteem problems are also related to the primary disorder, whereas previously they thought that the disorder was restricted to the core symptoms of inattention, hyperactivity and impulsivity.

We have examined how individuals tend to view treatment for ADHD and found that individuals strongly focus on medication as being the sole treatment available. For example, when asked how ADHD can be overcome, responses included: 'drugs', 'medication' and 'death'. However, after psychoeducation sessions, individuals tended to encompass a greater range of possibilities and recognise a biosocial model, for example 'medication, psychological strategies, environmental changes to your home/work so it no longer affects your life'.

Through a psychoeducation treatment model, the therapist should inform the individual about the aetiology of ADHD, its prognosis, comorbid problems, cognitive deficits and their expression in daily living. Associated factors of the ADHD syndrome should also be explained, such as skills deficits and the likelihood of maladaptive coping strategies. However, this should be put constructively with emphasis on targets for treatment.

Understanding that their problems stem from an underlying neurodevelopmental basis will be an important step in repairing the self-esteem of people who have long believed themselves to be stupid and/or who have been labelled as stupid or lazy by others. Furthermore, by acknowledging and understanding their limitations, individuals can develop realistic expectations for performance. This will be especially important when applied to psychological therapy, for example, the rehearsal of new skills requires repetition and patience. These are unlikely characteristics of adults who tend to seek novelty and stimulation. Acknowledging that sometimes the Young–Bramham Programme will be challenging and providing information about the disorder can help individuals appreciate that learning new strategies requires ongoing practice until a new skill becomes automatic and routine. Working collaboratively, individuals must be motivated to complete the Young–Bramham Programme and not give up half way through.

MOTIVATIONAL INTERVIEWING

Motivational interviewing techniques, based on Prochaska and DiClemente's (1982) model, are helpful as they draw on a theoretical background where change is regarded as a cycle of stages (see Figure 3.1). The transactional model of change is a paradigm that views change as a dynamic process with the early stages requiring a greater supportive role by others (e.g. therapist, family) and in later stages the individual becomes self-reinforcing and autonomous. Individuals with ADHD may lack confidence in the ability to effect change. So ambivalence and resistance to change can be overcome by introducing motivational interviewing techniques into treatment.

Motivational interviewing is client-centred and therefore focuses on the client's current concerns and perspectives. It is directive, aiming to resolve ambivalence through reinforcement of talk which involves changes and thus diminishing resistance. Rather than imparting a set of techniques, motivational interviewing is a means of communication that facilitates change. Miller and Rollnick (2002) state there are four general principles of motivational interviewing:

1. *Expressing empathy*; that is, using reflective listening techniques to understand the patient's feelings and accepting them, whilst acknowledging that ambivalence is normal. This will be particularly important when treating adults with ADHD, as they may have found themselves rebuffed or ridiculed by others when expressing any interest in trying to make changes in their lives.
2. *Developing discrepancy*; that is, motivating change by highlighting a discrepancy between their current behaviour and important goals or values. For example, helping a client recognise that their disorganisation means they have occupational problems, e.g. they may be unable to gain or sustain a job, which in turn affects their perception of self-worth.
3. *Rolling with resistance*; that is, not arguing with the client for change and using resistance as a signal to respond differently, but inviting new perspectives without

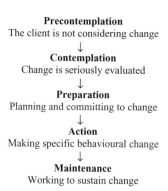

Precontemplation
The client is not considering change
↓
Contemplation
Change is seriously evaluated
↓
Preparation
Planning and committing to change
↓
Action
Making specific behavioural change
↓
Maintenance
Working to sustain change

Figure 3.1   Stages of change

imposing them. This is particularly appropriate when working with clients who become defensive and confrontational, as it is less challenging for them to take the perspective of an 'onlooker'.

4. *Supporting self-efficacy*; that is, by imparting the idea that the therapist can facilitate change but cannot change the client. The aim is to promote a client's belief in the possibility for change and enhancing the client's confidence in their capability of coping with obstacles and succeeding.

COGNITIVE BEHAVIOURAL THERAPY (CBT)

Adults with ADHD present with multiple problems and complex histories. Their strengths may be buried under a mountain of negative thoughts and experiences. Thus it is important to identify goals of treatment. These may be:

- *general:* e.g. motivation to engage in treatment
- *modular:* e.g. to reduce social anxiety
- *specific:* e.g. to complete homework tasks.

Individuals with ADHD require structure in terms of personal organisation, social boundaries and practical help to cope with everyday problems. They achieve best in an environment where there are clear rules and expectations of behaviour. Therefore, a cognitive-behavioural approach is effective for adults with ADHD, whether applied on an individual or group basis, because it is structured and has a strong evidence base for mood-related disorders. Cognitive behaviour therapy has been successfully applied to this client group even with minimal contact (Stevenson et al., 2002; Wilens et al., 1999). CBT emphasises action as a means of addressing change, thus individuals who adopt a role of a 'passive recipient' are unlikely to be successful and require more intensive motivational interviewing treatment as outlined above.

There are a number of challenges in the adaptation of CBT for this client group. These vary from pragmatic difficulties, for example resistance to completing 'homework' tasks, to generic problems, such as core symptoms. In the following chapters, specific modules of the Young–Bramham Programme are presented, outlining CBT techniques, which are helpful for treating adults with ADHD. More generally, the cognitive behavioural treatment aims to provide cognitive remediation, cognitive reframing of the past, cognitive restructuring and cognitive reasoning strategies, rationalisation, development of internal/external compensatory strategies as well as drawing on behavioural techniques.

Cognitive Remediation Strategies

Cognitive remediation strategies are an important method for the treatment of core symptoms of adult ADHD as they may be used to enhance memory, attention and organisation in everyday life. Weinstein (1994) suggests that they are an important active adjunct to other psychological treatment interventions. Learning to apply strategies that directly address and/or compensate for the core symptoms may help individuals to feel they have greater self-control and to reduce feelings of learned helplessness.

The neuropsychological assessment of clients is useful for establishing a profile of cognitive strengths and weaknesses. For example, individuals who have deficits in selective attention will benefit from learning attentional and memory enhancing strategies. Learning to ignore external distractors and develop techniques to stay on task will be important for individuals who have difficulty sustaining attention. Others may have difficulty with impulse control and require input in this area.

Cognitive Reframing of the Past

Adults with ADHD will have experienced a history of failure in many aspects of their life. Often they will have been given the message that they are stupid, lazy and unmotivated. The cumulative effect of this is often low self-esteem and a belief that the situation can never be changed (Murphy, 1998). Helping the individual to understand that ADHD has a neurological basis and is 'not a character defect or moral weakness' should begin to provide the person with some hope for the future (Murphy, 1995).

Once individuals are diagnosed with ADHD for the first time in adulthood they may go through an adjustment period coming to terms with the diagnosis and the impact of the disorder on their lives. They may reflect on past experiences and ruminate on these from a different perspective. Some individuals may feel relief that there is an explanation for the ways events have unfolded but others may feel resentment and/or regret that their situation could have been different. There is a risk that individuals may become depressed if they ruminate over past underachievements and lost opportunities. The therapist should acknowledge feelings of distress and confusion and normalise these thoughts and feelings. The therapist should then seek to elicit examples of positive aspects of having the disorder and direct the individual to learn from the past and focus on the future in a constructive manner.

Cognitive Restructuring and Reasoning Strategies

Some people with ADHD are creative and have no difficulty applying helpful CBT strategies, such as thought monitoring, challenging negative thoughts and assumptions, and generating alternative cognitions. Others have specific difficulties in abstract reasoning. In the latter case, clients will require greater support and practice to master techniques. In particular, impulsivity may impede the development of reasoning strategies as clients do not think through a course of action or sequentially develop an idea, for example causing them difficulty applying social perspective-taking techniques and/or interpersonal problem solving. These issues are addressed in Chapter 8.

Rationalisation

Adults with ADHD may become over-focused on current thoughts, and hence their preoccupation may mean they have difficulty distancing themselves from distorted cognitions in order to challenge and replace them. This may be the case especially soon after treatment with stimulant medication, when individuals (who are less likely to be distracted) may become preoccupied with negative beliefs whilst re-framing the past. It is important that clients are coached using a 'guided discovery' framework to encourage them to reason critically, engage in consequential thinking and rationalise beliefs.

Development of Internal/External Compensatory Strategies

Given that adults with ADHD will have experienced ADHD symptoms throughout their life, it is likely that they will have already developed an extensive repertoire of compensatory strategies, both adaptive and maladaptive. Compensatory strategies can be divided into those which:

- Require change from within (i.e. internal strategies such as 'stop and think' techniques).
- Involve the adaptation of the environment to suit the individual (i.e. external strategies such as removing potential distractions).

Many problems can be alleviated with a combination of both compensatory approaches. Presenting strategies in this two-pronged format will empower the individual to address future problems by looking for ways of changing themselves and ways of changing aspects of their environment. It is important to emphasise these two methods throughout the Young–Bramham Programme as adopting a dual approach will optimise its success.

Behavioural Techniques

When treating clients with learning disabilities and ADHD, the clinician will need to draw more heavily on behavioural techniques. Whilst much of the Young–Bramham Programme draws on cognitive techniques, changing behaviour requires the re-hearsal of new actions that are modified, applying positive and negative reinforcement and punishment techniques. The individual will be required to observe and record identified behaviours, and monitor change in homework tasks. However, some adults with ADHD may have difficulty organising themselves to follow a Behavioural Programme and make observations about themselves. Similarly, some adults with ADHD may find difficulty applying a reward system appropriately. Impulsivity could mean that they reach for the reward even if they are not entitled to it or may become easily frustrated if they feel that they are being deprived of something. It will be im-portant for the therapist to be aware that difficulties may arise in the maintenance of a Behavioural Programme and to watch out for intermittent reinforcement of maladaptive behaviours. Weiss et al. (1999) suggest that all of these difficulties need to be taken into consideration when designing a programme and discussed fully with the individual concerned. Methods regarding organisation of time and the introduction of a reward system into a timetable or week schedule are produced in Chapter 5.

STRUCTURE OF THE YOUNG–BRAMHAM PROGRAMME

The role of the therapist in the early stages is to explain and clarify the therapeutic rules and boundaries. This means asserting that treatment is a collaborative process and displacing potential power struggles. Many individuals with ADHD have personality problems, for example, they may be pedantic, challenging and confrontational in presentation. A tendency to procrastinate will particularly hamper progress. Whilst most clients with ADHD will be motivated, interesting and creative, it is important to recognise that others will be therapeutically more demanding.

Concentration problems may mean that individuals have difficulty following a train of thought or developing a theme using cognitive techniques. They may have difficulty keeping to time limits and/or struggle to cope with the duration of a 50-minute session. Adaptations to the therapeutic process will need to take account of these problems by introducing shorter sessions, scheduled breaks, structured changes in topic and/or variety in treatment methods (e.g. switching between visual aids, written exercises and role-plays within sessions).

Cognitive-behavioural therapy is usually time limited, ranging between 8 and 12 sessions, sometimes more. However, individuals with ADHD may require longer term treatment in order to address their multiple problems. It is advisable that sessions are held at a specified time and day each week as making different appointment times can increase the likelihood of non-attendance. Nevertheless the therapist should expect clients to be late for appointments but try not to accommodate this by extending the session. Instead, techniques should be identified that can prevent this occurring and set homework tasks to address the problem. Telephoning the client the day before their session may improve attendance and time keeping, or asking the client to identify a person or method (e.g. telephone alarm) to remind them. Prompting by the therapist should be faded out during the course of treatment.

As discussed in Chapter 1, the Young–Bramham Programme is modular, so specific topics can be selected as appropriate. Alternatively the therapist can work through each module until the Programme is complete (see Chapters 4–14 in Table 1.1).

If modules are to be selected, we recommend these are chosen collaboratively so that the client is empowered by the process. Due to attentional and working memory deficits, it is recommended that sessions allow additional time for consolidation of information and rehearsal of new material. It is recommended that 3–4 sessions are spent on each module, but this may be shortened or lengthened according to need. However, due to the underlying desire for immediate gratification, we suggest that no more than six sessions are spent on one module at any time. If the material is not fully covered or needs to be repeated, we suggest that this is re-introduced at a later stage and following alternative modules in order to avoid boredom and disengagement. Due to the Young–Bramham Programme's modular design, skills acquisition is cumulative. Thus, if client has difficulty with a module presented early in the programme, this can be revised at a later stage when new skills have been acquired and this may make it seem easier to understand.

Group Therapy

The Young–Bramham Programme may be applied in individual sessions or in a group format. Group work provides normalisation, mutual understanding and peer support; these are considered important factors since adults with ADHD may feel socially isolated and misunderstood by others. A group forum provides the opportunity to meet people with similar problems and to share strategies for coping with difficulties. Individuals can validate their own experiences by sharing their thoughts with other adults with ADHD (Hallowell, 1995). In addition it provides opportunities for acquiring and rehearsing key skills within a supportive non-critical environment.

We have successfully delivered the core aspects of the Young–Bramham Programme in a one-day 'group foundation workshop' format. In traditional group therapy, clients meet weekly for 1–2 hours over a set period, but we have found that a workshop paradigm also works with ADHD individuals as they respond positively to the 'immediacy' of workshops, for example by presenting one topic in the morning and a different topic in the afternoon. It also means that it is possible to provide treatment to individuals who are unable to commit to weekly meetings. However, by delivering the Young–Bramham Programme in an intensive workshop format, it is essential that techniques and teaching aids are introduced in order to shift attention and maintain interest and motivation, for example inclusion of group role-plays, working in pairs and/or small groups, group discussions. We recommend that frequent breaks are introduced in Programme Workshops (e.g. 10 minutes every 1½ hours) and participants are provided with detailed handouts that contain exercises to complete within the workshop and/or later at home to reinforce the techniques presented.

Agendas

Agendas are a method of providing structure within each session and should be drawn up collaboratively. The therapist needs to adhere closely to the agenda and not be distracted by 'crises', which may be presented by the client week by week. This will provide a model for the clients on how to deal with difficult situations in a rational and non-catastrophic manner. For example, an issue arising one week may be put on the agenda for the subsequent session, by which point it may no longer be construed as such a difficult area.

Goal Setting

The therapist must introduce the concept of the modular approach by clarifying with the client that treatment cannot address everything at once. Much as the client may wish to address multiple problems in one disorganised session, this is unhelpful and will leave both the therapist and the client feeling dissatisfied. Clear specific goals need to be established collaboratively at the onset of therapy, which are carefully broken down into stages. The client is likely to require assistance in this latter task, as it may be difficult for the client to see beyond one overarching goal, such as 'I want people to like me', or 'I want to succeed'. Goals should be reviewed regularly in order to maintain focus and prevent the temptation to become distracted, for example, by lurching from crisis to crisis. The modular structure of the Young–Bramham Programme will be helpful in this respect.

Rewards

Rewards are important for individuals with ADHD as they find it difficult to delay gratification and tend to opt for a short-term smaller reward rather than wait for longer term larger reinforcement. This feature of ADHD needs to be incorporated into treatment so that individuals are rewarded regularly for achievement, otherwise they are likely to lose interest in therapy and become distracted.

Homework

Homework tasks are set at the end of each session. It is important that clients learn to take responsibility for rehearsing and endorsing techniques learned in sessions in an applied setting. Resistance to homework tasks needs to be addressed, obstacles identified, anticipated and overcome by planning alternative strategies.

Treatment Termination

Given that ADHD is a chronic disorder, it can be difficult to identify a point at which to end therapy. It is therefore important to clearly specify tangible goals at the beginning of therapy and to regularly review progress. Nevertheless, it may be necessary to offer more sessions than other clients require, as it may take a client longer to acquire skills. This may result in dependence on the therapist and the concept of termination must be introduced early in treatment to avoid a situation in which the client feels isolated, abandoned and without the confidence to apply the structure and techniques learned in the Programme. The transition from treatment to autonomy needs to be planned carefully with collaboration, for example reducing the frequency of sessions and/or conducting brief planned follow-ups in person or by telephone.

Relapse Prevention

Adults with ADHD have the potential to catastrophise when they encounter future difficulties. Motivational interviewing techniques are therefore useful for reframing problems as slips and lapses. Pre-planned booster sessions are a sensible way of supporting a client through termination of therapy and prevent relapse. Treatment needs to incorporate a plan for 'risk' situations and/or times when the client may feel vulnerable. By identifying such times/situations, the client can consider appropriate coping mechanisms and avoid responding impulsively. By forward planning and thinking through the consequences of proposed behaviour, clients may learn to avoid challenging situations and/or cope better when faced with them. Relapse plans need to be multi-faceted, for example including seeking social support and/or advice, applying cognitive techniques and avoidance of troublesome situations/persons.

CONCLUSIONS

ADHD is a disorder that presents with core symptomatology, comorbid problems and skills deficits. Treatment for adults with ADHD typically follows a pharmacological route, which is helpful to alleviate core symptoms in ADHD adults and results in clients being better placed to succeed in psychological interventions. The Young–Bramham Programme with its modular cumulative skills acquisition provides treatment according to the needs of the clients.

The Young–Bramham Programme provides an integrated framework for understanding ADHD, adjusting to the diagnosis and developing techniques to cope with symptomatology and associated problems through: the provision of psychoeducational information; drawing on motivational interviewing techniques; and the use of cognitive behavioural therapy. The following chapters introduce the Young–Bramham Programme modules and describe the treatment techniques in detail.

PART II

CORE SYMPTOMS

4

INATTENTION AND MEMORY PROBLEMS

This chapter is the first of four chapters in the section outlining treatments for the core symptoms of ADHD, beginning with the hallmark of ADHD – attentional problems. The following chapters in this section include methods to assess and treat time management, problem solving and impulsivity in adults with ADHD.

People with ADHD have attentional impairments that can disadvantage them in a busy society with its high demand for multi-tasking. Attentional impairment can lead to many problems in day-to-day functioning, including difficulty listening, failure to finish tasks and being easily distracted. This means that completing tasks simultaneously and to an acceptable and satisfactory standard is difficult for people with ADHD. The ability to attend and concentrate comprises a number of stages of mental skill required for personal, social and occupational adaptive functioning. The human brain has several attentional systems serving different functions in everyday behaviour, and impairment in the central executive component of working memory may lead to inefficiency in the allocation of attentional resources (Baddeley, 1986; Baddeley & Wilson, 1988).

This chapter will discuss the domains of attention most likely to be affected by ADHD, the relationship between motivation and attention, the impact of anxiety and stress on attention, methods to teach individuals to recognise tasks that are likely to be problematic and strategies to help clients cope more appropriately and adaptively. The latter includes ways in which the client may adapt their environment to minimise distraction and thus maximise their ability to concentrate; that is, external strategies that involve the selection of the most appropriate surroundings in which the client is most likely to succeed. Internal strategies to sustain attention and motivation are also suggested and these can be rehearsed in sessions with the therapist. The chapter also discusses how ADHD impacts on an individual's memory processing and introduces strategies that the individual can adapt to achieve their potential within the constraints of an environment. Specific techniques to improve memory are outlined, again by applying both external and internal strategies.

ATTENTION AND ATTENTIONAL CONTROL

Attention is the process that allows us to focus on particular features of our environment such that we are aware of them at a particular moment in time. Attentional control processes determine at any given moment where to prioritise effort and to which stimuli to attend. These control processes are complex 'higher order' cognitive functions that allow attention to be selective to one stimulus, divided between several stimuli and shifted between stimuli. In some ways, difficulties in attentional control could be regarded as being at the centre of the cognitive deficits underpinning all aspects of attentional impairment in ADHD. If an individual is unable to govern what they will listen to, look at and focus on, then they have lost attentional control, and they are likely to exhibit the problems presented by people with ADHD. Norman and Shallice (1986) and Shallice and Burgess (1996) theorise that attentional control is achieved through the organisation of a 'supervisory attentional system', which is similar to Baddeley's (1986) concept of the 'central executive' (discussed later in this chapter). These models propose that the supervisory attentional system/ central executive is a 'higher order' cognitive function that determines which stimuli in the environment are prioritised with regard to attentional focus, particularly in novel situations. Certain activities make greater demands on the supervisory attentional system than others, for example, forward planning, responding to feedback and self-monitoring. Conversely, problems within the supervisory attentional/central executive system can lead to various attentional deficits and ultimately can affect memory functioning. For people with ADHD, these types of attentional deficit can be subdivided into four domains.

Domains of Attention Affected by ADHD

There are several domains or types of attention, but the main four are: selective attention, divided attention, attention shifting and sustained attention. Examples of attentional impairments in each of these domains of attentional functioning are given in Table 4.1. We also have provided this description of the different types of attention which can be affected by the disorder in a handout format on the Companion Website, as, in our experience, people with ADHD want to develop their knowledge and understanding about attentional processes and this will help them to identify, apply and/or adapt strategies to overcome their problems.

Selective attention involves the ability to focus on a specific task in hand. For example, being able to read whilst traveling on public transport and ignoring all other distractions. However, in some situations it is necessary to be able to attend to two or more sources of information, or 'divide attention'. This is a common demand of everyday life, for example, making conversation whilst driving. A similar ability is that of 'attention shifting' where there are competing demands on cognitive functions, and attention needs to be shifted from one source to another, for example using a recipe to cook a meal.

Table 4.1   Examples of attentional impairments

Domain of attention	Associated problems
Selective	Being unable to see detail
	Being 'slapdash'
	Making mistakes in reading or filling in forms
	Skipping lines in questionnaires
Divided	Not being able to focus on a conversation or task when there is background noise
	Not being able to do two things at once to an acceptable standard
Shifting	Getting stuck on one topic and not being able to change track
	Always starting tasks but never finishing because it is difficult to resume an original task
Sustained	Losing track of a conversation, film, book, etc.
	Being distracted by own thoughts (internal) or anything else going on around (external)

An example of the types of attentional problems experienced by clients with ADHD can be seen by their performance on the Test of Everyday Attention (Robertson et al., 1994). As a measure of selective and divided attention, the participant is required to perform a task involving identification of stimuli from an array, in other words, they are presented a page from the *Yellow Pages* and asked to identify plumbers which are marked with a double cross, star, circle or square. They are then required to perform the same task, but this time it is done simultaneously with an equally important task of counting tones played on a tape recorder. For people without ADHD, their speed and accuracy at performing the original task is reduced by performing a second task. However, adults with ADHD become increasingly error prone and they become unable to do both tasks simultaneously. This means they often stop one task in order to concentrate on the other. This strategy leads to a suboptimal speed. To put this into the context of everyday life, this means that people with ADHD have great difficulty multi-tasking. In order to complete a task well, and without making errors, they have to apply all their resources to focusing on that task. This is difficult for three reasons:

1. They find it difficult to maintain the degree of attentional control.
2. They are easily distracted from the task.
3. They give up on the task because they are not reaching their goal (i.e. a lack of positive reinforcement).

For adults with ADHD, difficulty with sustaining attention is probably the most pronounced and disabling attentional problem as individuals often struggle to engage in activities that are long, irrespective of whether they are repetitive or tedious. If a task is lengthy and also tedious, the client with ADHD is likely to completely give up on the task. The chores that we have to do in our daily lives are by definition routine and many are boring and repetitious. It is not possible to have a daily routine that is consistently full of excitement and high stimulation. When people with ADHD are faced with mundane tasks they respond with irritation, which is a source of frustration for the individual with ADHD as well as those who live or work with them. These feelings, coupled with a lot of unfinished tasks, are likely to leave the individual with a sense of failure and low self-esteem. In contrast, when activities are particularly interesting or motivating and/or involve immediate gratification (such as the rapid feedback and reinforcement introduced in many popular computer games), people with ADHD are generally able to concentrate. Such inconsistency can be difficult for people around them to understand. We have heard many complaints from partners about half-finished household do-it-yourself jobs. One of our clients had a half-painted lounge, a half-plumbed washing machine, the shell of a wardrobe built in the bedroom, and tiles for the bathroom had been purchased six months earlier but remained stacked up on the bathroom floor. It can be confusing to observe the individual with ADHD being competent in one domain (e.g. surfing the internet), yet unable to achieve in another one which is perceived as more important (e.g. writing a CV). The primary difference between the tasks is fluctuating levels of motivation, which is not always under control of the person with ADHD.

Motivation and Attention

There are two forms of motivation: extrinsic motivation and intrinsic motivation (Deci, Koestner & Ryan, 1999). Both can be affected by ADHD and can fluctuate considerably throughout any given time period:

1. *Extrinsic motivation* refers to rewards or incentives for people for performing well, or avoiding negative consequences.
2. *Intrinsic motivation* is determined by interest in an activity.

With regard to extrinsic motivation, the person must have some expectation that they can achieve the desired goals, otherwise they will feel demotivated regardless of the reward or incentive. However, people with ADHD often feel demotivated as they have experienced years of underachievement. When motivation drops, attention and effort also drop. A status of learned helplessness may develop. A person can change the way they view a task and their ability to achieve it by setting clear goals and rewarding their attention to the task with incentives. External reward systems need to be realistic, appropriate and achievable. Goal setting is a motivational strategy that has been shown to enhance attentional performance when difficult but achievable goals are set (Deci et al., 1999). If goals are not achieved then failure will reinforce learned helplessness and the ADHD client will 'switch off'. We describe techniques that will help with goal setting and their achievement in Chapter 5 (Time Management) and Chapter 6 (Problem Solving).

Feedback is a crucial component of intrinsic motivation as it helps the person determine the discrepancy between desired and actual performance. If a person has a sense of self-efficacy and believes they can do something, they will feel they have control. A sense of control will improve their motivation and optimise their attention for the task. However, if a task is perceived to be out of a person's control, the person may lose interest and stop attending. This means the task will be unfinished, which will reinforce a sense of failure. A negative feedback loop may develop from repeated failures and learned helplessness. Conversely, a sense of self-efficacy will be associated with successful and persistent performance.

Identifying Attentional Deficits and Their Functions

The attentional impairments associated with ADHD affect different people in different ways. Some examples of reported attentional difficulties are described below:

1. They lose their train of thought. This is especially irritating if they forget what they want to say in the middle of speaking.
2. When there are a lot of people around or a lot of noise in the background they find it difficult to sustain a conversation.
3. They find it difficult to sustain an in-depth conversation about a single topic. Other thoughts or ideas come flooding into their mind which they cannot suppress. At parties, people get annoyed with them as they see them as fickle as they flit about, talking to different people and/or changing topics of conversation.
4. Their mind wanders and they 'drift off' or start to daydream when they watch television, read a book or study in class.
5. They start lots of tasks but never finish them. They get distracted into doing something different.
6. They find it difficult to do more than one task at a time, such as driving a car whilst having a conversation with a passenger.

There are, of course, individual differences in everything we do, and this is no different in terms of strengths and weaknesses of attentional control. For example, some people have greater difficulty with sustaining attention whereas others have greater difficulty with dividing attention. Different tasks present different challenges. Some people find that they are more productive with several activities on the go; that is, providing themselves with 'constructive' distraction to reduce the likelihood of becoming bored with a primary task. Others find this impedes their performance. Mood and motivational processes may also affect performance. The goal of the therapist is to identify specific areas of weakness and help the individual develop compensatory strategies to facilitate achievement. The client should be taught to recognise tasks that are likely to be problematic and respond appropriately and adaptively. This goal will be influenced if there is a dominant symptom of ADHD (e.g. predominantly inattentive type or predominantly hyperactive/impulsive type), what the person wants to achieve and what support they have. In many ways, 'forewarned is forearmed', so recognising and preparing for tasks that are likely to be problematic is the first major step towards improving attentional difficulties. Once specific tasks have been identified for which the individual has difficulty with attentional control, then these should be targeted for improvement by applying both external strategies and internal strategies. External strategies involve adaptation of the environment and internal strategies involve a process of self-monitoring.

Applying External Strategies to Cope with Attentional Problems

External distraction refers to all outside sensory information (i.e. both auditory and visual) that is being processed at the expense of the required task. Cutting down on irrelevant distraction can help the individual focus on the subject of interest. The application of external strategies requires the individual to make adaptations to their environment in order to maximise the likelihood that they may optimally achieve success. We describe this to clients as making 'change from the outside in' and describe some techniques in Table 4.2, which can be discussed in sessions with the client. The client must be encouraged to set up 'mini experiments' between sessions in order to test out which techniques are most suitable for them and work best.

There are many possibilities and the client themselves may have ideas to try out or already established strategies that are helpful. When following up the efficacy of a strategy, it is important to determine whether the client applied the strategy correctly and/or appropriately. Sometimes distractions are welcome, especially if the client is engaged in a tedious task.

Applying Internal Strategies to Cope with Attentional Problems

The application of internal strategies to optimise performance or 'change from the inside out' requires the individual to learn persistence of effort and the suppression of internal urges. It is important to encourage the client to maximise their ability to sustain attention by increasing interest and motivation. This can be achieved by setting small achievable goals and introducing an 'immediate' reward system and/or regular breaks. Indeed, a primary difference between treating people with ADHD and other clients is the introduction of systematic reward systems in the treatment as individuals with ADHD are unable to delay gratification and are averse to delay. This means they favour small regular rewards as opposed to having greater rewards that are spread out over a longer period. However, the client needs to be encouraged to focus on *completion* of a task over a long period, so introducing lots of small 'immediate' or regular rewards *and* a larger reward is recommended for completion of the overall goal or task. Aside from the set reward for finishing a task, completing a task is a reward in itself as it gives the client a sense of achievement. Achievement is a very strong reinforcer.

Table 4.3 outlines various suggestions that can be explored in sessions that may help the client improve attentional control. These include the introduction of a reward system, competition with others or themselves, maximisation of novelty, physiological arousal, cognitive challenges, repetition, goal setting, and allocating breaks. Of course, not every strategy will suit every client, and some clients will benefit more

Table 4.2 External strategies to improve attentional control

Source of distraction	Proposed techniques
Auditory	Listening to low level music without lyrics can be useful to mask out other more intermittent noises. Music with words should generally be avoided as this can interfere with thoughts and lead to further distraction
	Although it can be awkward to request that others around them try to reduce their noise, this strategy can be rehearsed in sessions. The client may then work out a way of making this request that is least likely to offend. Often people feel relieved when the environment is quieter, so their efforts may be supported and appreciated
	The simple strategy of using earplugs can be effective in blocking out all but the loudest of sounds without the individual needing to do their own filtration
	Telephone calls can interrupt concentration and output. Whilst it is acknowledged that some calls may be essential, this is rarely the case for all calls. Telephones can be switched to silent mode, and checked for messages at a convenient time, regular intervals, or when a task has been completed
	If a task is portable, it may be helpful for the client to move away from a noisy environment, for example, at home where the television and radio are blaring. If they cannot find a quieter room in their house, then they could negotiate with a friend to use a quiet room somewhere else or work in a library
Visual	Distracting visual material such as noticeboards, pictures, etc., should be positioned out of the line of vision where or when an individual is working
	Facing a window can be distracting even when nothing is happening outside as it is tempting for people with ADHD to gaze outside and daydream. However, facing a wall can lead to feelings of restlessness. Often facing into a room can provide the best compromise for limiting distractibility and reducing restlessness
	Using bright colours to attract attention to the task can be helpful. For example using post-it notes, and highlighter pens
	It can be useful to place a cue card (e.g. a photograph, a cut out from a magazine, a note) in 'risk' places to remind the person to pay attention. For example, 'Stop dreaming! Focus!' can be written on notes stuck onto the top of a computer monitor.

Table 4.3   Internal strategies to improve attentional control

Reward	The development of an incentive and reward programme is a priority. This should be introduced when targeting small goals as well as larger ones as it capitalises on the need of ADHD people for immediate gratification. Rewards can be simple activities like having a tea break or walking around the block
Competition	People with ADHD can be encouraged to increase their interest and stimulation in an activity by introducing a competitive element (e.g. let's see if this can be finished in one hour) or by incorporating a pre-existing interest (e.g. if a client enjoys using computers, encourage them to pay bills via the internet)
Novelty	People with ADHD may be more motivated in new situations, so they should be encouraged to capitalise on the 'novelty factor' by accepting new tasks in exchange for old, less interesting ones (e.g. taking on new roles with enthusiasm)
Snap!	Encourage clients to wear an elastic band around the wrist. This can be snapped in order to reorient attention at times when it has drifted and increases the overall level of alertness
Cognitive challenges	Develop strategies to cope with times when a client loses their train of thought, e.g. they should not be embarrassed to say to someone 'I'm sorry but I have forgotten what I was saying'. This can be rehearsed in role-play. Dysfunctional thoughts regarding what it means to lose attention and how this may be perceived by others can be cognitively challenged in sessions
Repetition	In cases when the client has difficulty following and retaining information (e.g. when being given instructions), they should be encouraged to ask for these to be repeated. Again this can be rehearsed in role-play so the client may overcome feelings of embarrassment and/or humiliation
Goal setting	Help the client to set achievable goals and avoid overarching intangible goals that may be difficult to operationalise. They should be encouraged to reflect on what it feels like to finish a task and gain a sense of achievement. Principles of pleasure and mastery may be incorporated (see Chapter 11 on low mood)
Breaks	It is important to break up activities. The client should train themselves to allocate enforced breaks in tasks, especially when these are mundane or tedious. The client should additionally allocate breaks immediately prior to a 'risk period' when they may lose concentration or interest, e.g. if they can concentrate for 30 minutes, they should break after 25 minutes

from some than others, so it is a matter of discussing potential techniques of benefit in the session, setting homework to establish what works by investigating 'mini-experiments' and evaluating outcome. The client will often have developed their own ideas and strategies, and these will be a helpful indicator of what will be most useful to them.

Distractibility and Restlessness

A particular problem for people with ADHD is that they are distracted from the task in hand. They find it difficult to stay on task for two reasons:

1. *External distraction:* i.e. noticing irrelevant details (e.g. someone walking past the window).
2. *Internal distraction:* i.e. having the urge to do something more stimulating (e.g. chatting when they are supposed to be working quietly).

Motoric overactivity is frequently a disabling symptom in childhood, but less so in adulthood. We have not met many ADHD adults running around the therapy room, jumping out of windows, climbing trees, or skateboarding down the hospital corridor. Whilst adults with ADHD may have developed better control over their hyperactive behaviour, they often report a feeling of 'internal' restlessness. Some people find it almost impossible to stay sitting down or have a feeling of being 'driven by a motor'. However, in adulthood, restlessness is most commonly expressed by pacing, tapping fingers, jigging feet, changing posture, fiddling with things, swaying from foot-to-foot, humming, and/or excessive talking. Such difficulties are commonly mistaken or misdiagnosed as generalised anxiety or manic depression.

Clients should be encouraged to capitalise on this energy by performing tasks that involve exertion. If appropriate, this may be introduced as part of the reward system with the day being organised to include regular periods when they are able to move around and dispel pent up restlessness and energy. At the same time, it is helpful to identify situations that the client finds more relaxing and restful, and structuring these into their day as part of an activity schedule (see Chapter 5 on Time Management). Such times can be helpfully timetabled following the completion of cognitively challenging and emotionally demanding tasks.

Anxiety, Stress and Attention

Attentional control decreases when a person is fatigued, stressed and/or worried. If the person is self-monitoring and thinking 'I can't do this, I'll fail' then their attentional ability is likely to be more impaired due to the competing demands of worrying about how well they will do it and their actual performance on the task in hand. The impairment then becomes exacerbated and becomes a function of stress and anxiety. The vicious cycle and self-fulfilling prophecy of stress and anxiety is

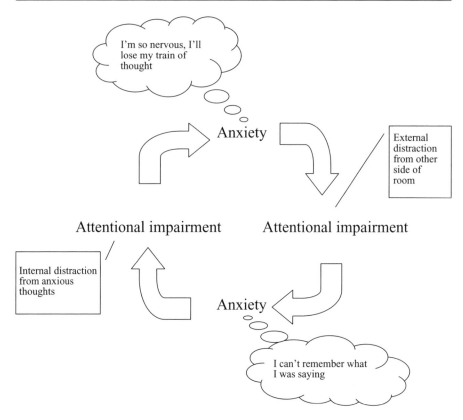

Figure 4.1   The spiral of anxiety and attentional control

presented in Figure 4.1 with an example of someone becoming anxious in a social situation (also on the Companion Website in handout form). When this occurs, clients become highly distractible. It is hard enough at the best of times for them to be motivated to remain on task, but if they feel acutely anxious about their perform-ance and/or lose their confidence to do well, they will become even less motivated, have many unfinished tasks (both important and less important) and feel even more stressed and distressed. Chapter 9 outlines specific characteristics of people with ADHD who have comorbid anxiety and techniques to help them.

MEMORY PROBLEMS

Memory problems are present in many psychiatric disorders, both with or without an organic basis. In people with ADHD, memory problems are often associated with their attentional problems. Memory problems are also the most obvious problem to the person themselves and to those around them as a poor memory is often more exposing than poor attention.

Common Memory Problems in ADHD

The types of memory problem reported by individuals with ADHD include:

1. Misplacing things, e.g. forgetting where they have put their glasses, keys.
2. Forgetting appointments, deadlines and activities that need to be done in the future, such as forgetting to pay the rent.
3. 'Losing time', i.e. not attending to time passing, or having a distorted sense of time resulting in them being late and not knowing where time has gone.
4. Forgetting instructions, if someone tries to explain how to do a task they have to slow down and repeat it a number of times.
5. Mental processing, e.g. mental arithmetic.

These problems arise due to disruptions in memory processes within the three major memory systems that are presented in Figure 4.2: immediate memory (i.e. very brief storage for all sensations); short-term/working memory (i.e. temporary storage where information can be manipulated); and long-term memory (i.e. storage over longer periods).

Both shorter and longer term memory deficits may be present in clients with ADHD, although 'working memory' or short-term memory deficits are more often identified (MacLean et al., 2004a; Young et al., 2006). A figural representation of memory processes is presented on the Companion Website, which can be used in sessions to

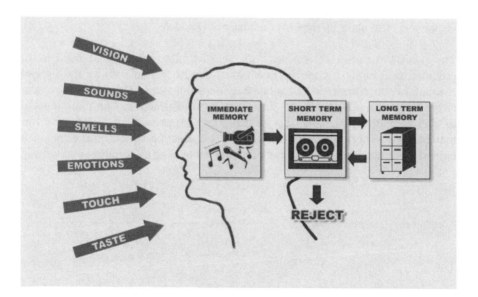

Figure 4.2 Memory systems
Adapted from *Head Injury* © Trevor Powell, 2004, Speechmark Publishing Ltd, Bicester.

explain the problems commonly experienced by people with ADHD in order to help clients understand their difficulties.

Immediate Memory

Immediate memory is often regarded as a 'sense' memory as it provides brief storage for all the senses including vision, sounds, smells, emotion, touch and taste. It is like a scratchpad or snapshot of information, which is quickly overwritten by new sensations coming online. For some people with ADHD, they may have particular difficulty if their immediate memory becomes overloaded with too much stimulation from too many different sources and this leads them to become extremely distractible. Attentional processes are also likely to determine the quality of information that enters the immediate memory. When information in immediate memory needs to be used it is then transferred into the 'short-term' memory or 'working memory' where it can be rehearsed or manipulated.

Short-term Memory/Working Memory

After the information has been received in the immediate memory system, it is then held for a very brief period in a 'short-term' or 'working memory' system. This is a temporary storage for information, like a rewritable cassette or video recording, before it enters long-term memory or is 'rejected' and thus becomes unrecoverable. Working memory has been shown to be disrupted in people with ADHD, possibly through poor attention or interference from distraction. Figure 4.3 shows the three components that make up the working memory (Baddeley, 1986).

The *central executive* determines what sensory information is attended to, or provides an attentional control system as discussed earlier, both for the subsystems of working memory and other cognitive functions. This can be particularly affected in ADHD due to susceptibility to distraction. The *phonological loop* is an auditory memory system that stores a few seconds' worth of information, like a short circular cassette tape. Information stored on the tape can either be rehearsed after it is recorded or erased by new information overwriting

Figure 4.3 Working memory model
From Baddeley (1986) *Working Memory*. Clarendon/Oxford University Press.

it. The *visuospatial sketch-pad* is a visual analogue, and can be likened to an 'etchasketch' toy where images can be stored then wiped out by further information. In ADHD it is possible that information does not enter working memory adequately and that the same length of material cannot be stored as for people without ADHD. Furthermore, problems with the 'central executive' can lead to difficulties attending to the appropriate material in order for it to be processed by the working memory.

Long-term Memory

Information is transferred from the working memory to long-term memory, which rather confusingly refers to all information from only a few minutes ago to years since the event. There are three stages of this memory system: encoding; storage; and retrieval. *Encoding* involves registering and processing information, and is highly dependent on attentional processes and hence can be affected in people with ADHD. *Storage* of learned information is affected by a large range of factors that interfere with brain functioning and is evidenced by forgetting. *Retrieval* of stored information involves explicit recall or implicit knowledge revealed in later performance.

Retrieval can depend on strategies for accessing information, such as trying to retrace one's steps in order to find a lost possession. In ADHD, this process may be more haphazard without a strategy. Retrieval can also be affected by the way information has been encoded. For example, ADHD clients have been shown to exhibit difficulties in organising information at the encoding stage, such as organising material into categories, and hence have resulting difficulties in optimal retrieval.

Applying External Strategies to Improving Memory

There are several strategies that the client may adapt to try to help them improve their memory. These commonly include the introduction of external aids; that is, using support systems to minimise problems arising from poor memory, such as the use of diaries, planners, etc., and specific strategies are listed in Table 4.4. Electronic organisers are invaluable. However, as we increasingly move towards advanced information technology, it is important for clients to ensure that electronic organisers are the servant of the individual and do not become the master and provide an opportunity for distraction and time wasting. Moreover, there are also internal strategies that can be applied and, for optimal results, the client should be encouraged to develop both internal and external methods to enhance memory. As discussed previously for developing attentional control, the therapist should investigate what the client has successfully applied in the past, identify new possibilities, set homework tasks to evaluate their efficacy and review with the client the best and most appropriate techniques.

Table 4.4   External strategies to improve memory

Diary	A diary is helpful for short-term planning. A 'page-a-day' diary is most useful as appointments can be recorded as well as additional notes, e.g. tasks to complete, items needed, etc. Having this information presented in a day format serves as a cue and reminder of tasks (or steps) that need to be completed to achieve longer-term goals
Weekly calendar	A weekly calendar allows family members to write reminders and instructions that may be helpful for the individual. For example, for a family birthday party, another family member may devise an action plan dividing up the responsibilities by noting 'book a taxi', 'buy a cake', 'book the restaurant', etc. It is additionally helpful for the person with ADHD to see how their activities integrate with those of their family
Annual wall planner	This can be used for longer-term plans and forward planning, e.g. by marking up school holidays, family vacations, birthdays and anniversaries
Portable dictaphone/ recorder	These can be used to make verbal lists and reminders for information that may quickly go out of mind. Some people find it helpful to carry a dictaphone around with them so they can quickly record ideas and reminders. The list of tasks or reminders can then be worked through systematically at a later point in time
Answerphone messages	Some telephone systems, including mobile phones, give the opportunity for individuals to leave themselves answerphone messages. This can help to reduce the need to remember information in the future
Lists	It will be helpful to get the person with ADHD into the habit of making lists. These will include daily lists of 'things to do', shopping lists, housework chores. Organising ideas into lists and categories can also help someone with ADHD to develop a sense of control. Ticking off completed items serves as feedback and can be a motivator through positive reinforcement
Help cards	Summarised forms of information such as 'help cards' can be useful for activities that are not performed regularly such as setting the video, or filling in tax return forms
Watches and clocks	Clocks can be positioned in obvious places, even in every room in the house, in order to remind the person with ADHD of the passage of time. Clocks with chimes or watches that beep can be useful for orienting someone to time when they have become distracted
Alarms and/or computerised reminders	These can serve as reminders over varying time periods ranging from a three hourly alarm to take medication to setting an annual reminder to prompt an individual about a friend's birthday
Personal organisers and mobile phones	Personal organisers and mobile phones can perform many of the above tasks. However, if their organisational functions are new to the client then these should be introduced and developed gradually into a routine, with goal setting agreed with the therapist to make sure that this is not yet another strategy that has been started and quickly abandoned. The aim is that these items are functional and not distractors. The organiser should only be kept in certain places and backed-up, as it may be even more disabling for a person with ADHD to lose the organiser and/or memory system in the organiser

Applying Internal Strategies to Improve Memory

Aside from the plethora of external strategies, internal memory strategies may also be used in conjunction with external memory strategies in order to enhance encoding and retrieval memory processes. Specific strategies are outlined in Table 4.5. If the client develops internal strategies for improving their memory then this will improve their confidence and self-efficacy, rather than relying entirely on external aids.

Table 4.5 Internal strategies to improve memory

Repetition and rehearsal	Repeating and practicing recall of information, e.g. through self-talk, can improve the likelihood of information being successfully processed by working memory and then encoded for longer-term recall
Create a visual cue	Pairing a verbal task with a visual image can improve verbal retention as it allows information to be encoded in both a visual and verbal form. This enhances the memory trace and increases the likelihood of later retrieval. The more bizarre and exaggerated the image, the easier it will be to remember. For example, if remembering to pay a water bill, think of white-water rafting to the bank!
Mnemonics	Learning cues or mnemonics can be a useful method of condensing information for later recall and can appear less overwhelming for someone with ADHD. For example, S.T.O.P. = sausages, tomatoes, oranges, potatoes
Spaced retrieval	Memory research has shown that gradually increasing the time span between retrieval times increases the likelihood of it being retrieved in the future, and thus improves storage through reinforcement of a memory trace (Ebbinghaus, 1885). Information should be rehearsed with increasingly longer gaps, e.g. 5 minutes, 30 minutes, an hour, next day, etc. Performing this exercise throughout a session and beyond can allow someone with ADHD to improve their self-efficacy
Problem solving	A good method for finding lost or mislaid possessions is to mentally retrace steps in a systematic way. This can be done by asking the client a sequence of questions such as 'when did I last have my keys?' 'where did I go when I got in?' or 'where would I put that key now?'
Keeping calm	High emotional arousal and feelings of stress can interfere with both attention and memory functioning. Therefore it is important to encourage the client to reduce anxiety and anger before attempting any recall. See Chapters 9 and 10 for specific strategies, including relaxation techniques

CONCLUSIONS

Attentional and memory difficulties are common cognitive deficits for adults with ADHD. However, there is much variation in the difficulties that arise due to individual variation in the disorder, motivational factors and state arousal. In addition, environmental factors also play a large part in attentional control. This chapter has explained the ways in which attention is affected in ADHD. It is important for individuals to develop an awareness of situations in which their attention becomes impaired. Once these have been recognised and established, the person can then develop strategies to improve attentional control and reduce both external and internal distractors. Attentional deficits also impact on memory functioning and internal/external strategies may be adopted to improve memory. In treatment, the clinician therefore adopts a two-pronged approach to overcome attentional and memory problems, by introducing the notion of 'change from the outside in', and 'change from the inside out'.

5

TIME MANAGEMENT

'Time management' is the Achilles heel of adults with ADHD. People with ADHD find it more difficult than others to manage their time due to their attentional problems inducing them to lack focus on the task in hand. They become easily distracted by other seemingly more important or interesting activities. Prioritisation is particularly difficult as people with ADHD tend to flit from task to task, irrespective of its importance. They often have many projects on the go, all at various stages of completion. People with ADHD are very spontaneous and they initiate lots of projects with good intentions, but their disorganised chaotic personal style means that they do not see these through. There are often difficulties in meeting deadlines and maintaining interest in order to complete a project. This can be a particular problem for more mundane tasks, which are necessary but boring. Due to their inability to organise time effectively and the tendency to fall into 'time-wasting traps' they are often regarded as 'unsuccessful entrepreneurs'. An analogy is that people with ADHD try to keep too many balls in the air at once but end up dropping most of them.

People with ADHD achieve more when a time structure is organised for them. Their difficulty is setting and managing this for themselves. Thus, the goal of time management sessions is to train an individual to structure their time appropriately, prioritise tasks and reward themselves for success. 'Success' becomes a positive reinforcer of achievement. The best way of doing this is to use a methodical approach and ensure that the client adheres to it. This chapter outlines methods to teach clients to structure their own time and help them feel that they are taking control of their life. This reinforces a sense of purpose and desire for achievement. The chapter also provides methods to reconceptualise time and set a time plan. Potential hurdles to success, such as 'time-wasting traps', are also discussed.

RECONCEPTUALISING TIME

To people with ADHD, time can seem like it is always against them. It is either going too slowly when they feel bored and frustrated, or can disappear quickly when they become engrossed in something interesting or immediately gratifying. Time passes quickly when their attention slips – this means they become easily distracted and may start to daydream. The end result is that they are often late, do not achieve or complete tasks and miss opportunities. It is therefore important for the therapist to establish a shared understanding with the client about how they perceive time. Time should be seen as a 'resource', which is applied to achieve set goals. Time is a tool. If clients are satisfied or happy with how they spend their time, and what they achieve in that time, then this will reinforce the need for structure. Thus, it is important to encourage clients to find something they enjoy in whatever they do. This may involve 'freeing up time' to integrate pleasurable activities and mundane tasks.

Table 5.1 outlines a measure, the Time Management Evaluation, which provides an example of a client's perception of their time management by measuring the frequency at which they experience time-management problems. This individual was particularly concerned about their memory problems. This measure can be repeated at various stages during treatment to evaluate change in the client's time management skills and demonstrate improvement. In the table, the scores range from '0' representing the absence of a problem to '4' representing experiencing the problem with high frequency. However, the numerical scores shown in Table 5.1 are not presented in the questionnaire given to the client and the Companion Website provides this table in an appropriate format for therapeutic use. Nevertheless, the scoring system illustrated in Table 5.1 can be applied to measure baseline difficulty as well

Table 5.1   Time management evaluation

How often...	Never	Rarely	Sometimes	Often	Always
1 Do you make plans for your time?	4	3	2	(1)	0
2 Do you write down your plans?	4	3	(2)	1	0
3 Do you complete everything you had planned to do for a day?	(4)	3	2	1	0
4 Is your time interrupted by seemingly urgent tasks?	0	1	2	(3)	4
5 Do you leave things unfinished?	0	1	2	3	(4)
6 Do you forget what you were supposed to be doing?	0	1	2	3	(4)
7 Do you arrive on time and prepared for appointments?	4	(3)	2	1	0
8 Do you know roughly what time it is?	4	(3)	2	1	0
9 Do you feel that you have wasted your time?	0	1	2	3	(4)

Total Score = 26

as progress in treatment. (Note that scores on items 4, 5, 6 and 9 are reversed). Thus a reducing total score indicates improvement. (A blank copy is provided on the Companion Website.)

In addition to the time management evaluation outlined in Table 5.1, it will be helpful to determine *how* the person actually spends their time before they begin learning time management strategies. This is achieved by keeping a log of activities using a weekly diary record (see Table 5.2, a blank version of which can be found on the Companion Website). This should be introduced by asking the client to map in the session what they have done in the recent past, for example, in the past two days. The client is then asked to complete the rest of the week prior to the next session and bring this to the next appointment. This will help determine how much time is usefully and constructively spent on tasks and highlight problem times when the client is vulnerable to time-wasting traps, for example reading junk mail, chatting at length on the phone, looking for items that have been lost, missing the train, surfing the internet. The time that the client usually takes their medication should also be recorded as it is important to establish the relationship between taking the medication and its effect on concentration; that is the ability to focus and periods of 'lost' or wasted time. Table 5.2 shows the completed diary activity log of David, a painter decorator, who was taking slow-release stimulant medication in the morning.

The diary activity log will guide the therapist about how the client actually spends their time and this should be used as a basis for discussion. The client may be surprised to see how much time they spend off-task. It is easy to forget how much time is spent reading junk mail, looking for items that have been lost, missing the train, etc. From examining his diary activity log, David could see that he was rather chaotic in his organisation of time. He had not been prompt or reliable in his attendance at work, and when he was criticised for this, he had reacted impulsively by walking out and losing the money for the job. He noticed he was distracted for large amounts of time and not using time efficiently. He was spending large amounts of time in the pub, getting home late and not having sufficient sleep. His meal organisation was haphazard and he frequently went for long periods without food. With regard to timing of medication, David realised that he was rather irregular as to when he took his medication. This meant that the optimal hours for him to concentrate varied from day to day. The day he walked out of his job in anger, he had forgotten to take his medication.

TIME PLANS

In order to manage time more effectively, the client should be helped to plan their time in advance by making up a time plan. This entails following the six steps outlined in Table 5.3.

Table 5.2 Diary activity log

Time	Monday	Tuesday	Wednesday	Thursday	Friday	Saturday	Sunday
7–8am	Asleep	Asleep	Asleep	Asleep	Asleep	Asleep	Asleep
8–9am	Asleep	Got up	Got up	Asleep	Asleep	Asleep	Asleep
9–10am	Felt too tired to go to work. Had breakfast	**TOOK MEDICATION** No food in house, bought breakfast on way to work	Breakfast and set off early for work	Overslept	Hungover so went to local café for big breakfast	Lie-in bed	Lie-in bed
10–11am	**TOOK MEDICATION** Watched daytime tv	Arrived late at job	**TOOK MEDICATION** Went to cafe for coffee and read papers	Went to warehouse for more paint	Arrived at work but no-one there to open up	Lie-in bed	Lie-in bed
11–12am	Watched daytime tv	Started preparing walls	Painting	**TOOK MEDICATION** Intensive painting as need to get it finished by end of day	Waited for owners to come	Lie-in bed	Lie-in bed
12–1pm	Rang mum	Have bought wrong paint	Painting	Painting	Owners arrived and say they will dock pay – tell them to stuff it and resign from job	Lie-in bed	Lie-in bed
1–2pm	Started looking for car tax form	Went to warehouse for more paint	Arrived late for meeting for new piece of work	Painting	Went to pub	Got up. Watched tv	Got up. Panic because supposed to be at parents for lunch
2–3pm	Found magazine had been looking for	Bumped into old workmate and go for coffee	Supposed to have another meeting but missed it to have lunch	Painting	Went to bookmakers for a flutter	Watched tv	Arrived late at parents – they have finished meal
3–4pm	Surfed internet for things in magazine	Went back to work	Caught up with a few tasks	Lunch	Lost £50 on horses	Watched tv	Sat around chatting

Time							
4–5pm	Felt hungry – no food in house so go to shops	Stripped walls	Run out of paint	Tried to finish by cutting corners	Went to pub	Watched tv	Sat around chatting
5–6pm	Noticed new cd has been released – look around shops	Got Distracted and stripped too much off	Went home early	Realised it is impossible to finish so gave up and left work early to go to gym	Friends arrived	Made a meal	Missed the bus home so dad drove me
6–7pm	Bumped into friend and go for drink	Just got to supermarket before it closed	Watched soap operas	Arrived at gym but had forgotten kit	Out with friends	Late to meet friend	No food in house so got a takeaway
7–8pm	Stayed out drinking	Microwave meal then watched tv	Started cooking food but forgot it is in oven because watching a film	Went out with friend from gym	Out with friends	Cinema	Watched tv
8–9pm	Stayed out drinking	Watched tv	Had to start cooking again	Out at pub	Out with friends	Cinema	Watched tv
9–10pm	Stayed out drinking	Watched tv	Watched dvd	Went to restaurant for food	Out with friends	Cinema bar	Watched tv
10–11pm	Stayed out drinking	Phone call from sister	Watched dvd	Restaurant	Out with friends	Got something to eat then go home	Watched tv
11–12pm	Stayed out drinking	Still on the phone	Bed	Missed last train home so had to get taxi	Out with friends	Watched tv	Watched tv
1–2am	Went home and watched tv	Go to bed	Asleep	Watch tv	Out with friends	Watched tv	Fell asleep on sofa
2–3am	Asleep	Lie awake	Asleep	Asleep	Fell asleep at friends	Bed	Asleep
3–4am	Asleep	Asleep	Asleep	Asleep	Asleep	Asleep	Asleep
4–5am	Asleep	Asleep	Asleep	Asleep	Woke up and walked home	Asleep	Asleep
5–6am	Asleep	Asleep	Asleep	Asleep	Asleep	Asleep	Asleep
6–7am	Asleep	Asleep	Asleep	Asleep	Asleep	Asleep	Asleep

Table 5.3   Six steps to making a time plan

1	Set goals
2	Make lists
3	Prioritise activities
4	Estimate time to complete tasks
5	Schedule tasks
6	Incorporate a reward system

The client must be encouraged to determine *set goals* within a time period. In the session, they should *list activities* that they are required to do for the week as well as activities that they would like to do. The next step is to prioritise the tasks. *Prioritising activities* is likely to require assistance from a therapist initially, until the client develops or improves these skills. This can be achieved by asking the client to allocate an importance rating, for example how vital is it to get a bill paid this week from 0 – 'not at all' through to 4 – 'essential'. Then the client must *estimate the amount of time* each task will take. This may take some practice as the client and therapist will need to determine together whether the client has a tendency to consistently overestimate or underestimate time. At this stage, the client should be ready to create a *schedule of tasks* to complete within a determined time period. When making a time plan, it will be important to explore 'contingency plans' as some important tasks may overrun. A final step is to incorporate a *reward system* for successful completion of chunks of time. This may be taking a break from a challenging task or switching to a more enjoyable, lower priority task, for a set period. Thus there are six stages to designing and achieving an effective time plan and these techniques are described in more detail in the following sections.

Step 1: Set Goals

The therapist must encourage the client to set and review goals routinely, as this will help the client to achieve where they want to go in life. Clients should consider their large-scale and longer-term goals. These include career, educational, family, financial, physical and pleasure-related goals. However, the client must learn to break these general goals down into smaller achievable 'mini-goals' that represent stepping stones to reaching the overall aim (see Figure 5.1). This will provide short-term focus and motivation in addition to encouraging the client to retain an eye on the longer-term outlook. It is important to focus on *specific* tasks as this will help the client to organise their resources. For example, Figure 5.1 describes David, the painter and decorator, who wanted to replace his van.

A blank version of this figure is available on the Companion Website, where the client can complete their own goals and then break them down. Once goals and steps have been established, the client should be encouraged to make a time plan for the

Figure 5.1   Example of breaking down goals into steps

week to organise achievement of the first steps. At this time, the focus is on the steps, working from the bottom upwards.

David wanted to replace his van, which he used for work. Previously he would have gone to a garage and bought one the next day on credit. However, he was aware that this impulsive behaviour had led to him spending far more in the longer term. He therefore needed to work out a financial strategy that would allow him to save. He also needed to determine how much money he would be able to make by selling his old van. Finally, rather than buying the first van he saw, he needed to spend some time researching his options and finding a good deal.

It is important that tasks are defined *precisely* so that it is clear when they have been achieved. For example, 'save £1000' can be measured, but 'spend less' is less obvious as to when it has been completed. Wherever possible, tasks should be performance-related rather than outcome-related, particularly for activities for which the client may not have absolute control. For example, 'find five possible vans to choose between' is a preferable (and more achievable) goal than 'buy a van'. Tasks that seem very large or overwhelming need to be broken down into several stages. If they still seem large, then break them down further. Achievement of realistic expectations is the key. It is easier and quicker to achieve a small step than a great step.

Step 2: Make Lists

Next the client and therapist must make a comprehensive list of what needs to be achieved, for example, in the coming week. This must include all the components outlined in Table 5.4.

The Companion Website includes this table in a format that can be used in sessions with the client. However, although clients may think that they will be able to remember the list, they probably will not. Lists should be written down whenever possible

Table 5.4   List components

1. Things that the client needs to do to achieve the step(s) they are focusing on
2. Things that the client really wants to do
3. Things that they have to do
4. Things that they might do if they have time
5. Things that they hate doing but are necessary at some point soon

to avoid expending valuable mental energy in rehearsing and reminding themselves of tasks. This in itself can be a distraction. Second, it is much more powerful to produce a written document to which the client is 'signed-up'. This is much more motivating as it can be used both within the sessions and applied on their own outside the sessions.

It is really important to include in the list activities that the client enjoys. Lists need not be chores! Listing mundane or uninteresting tasks that *have* to be completed will be boring and unappealing. The client will be unmotivated and not achieve their overall objective.

Making a 'to-do list' serves the additional purpose of inducing a sense of control and satisfaction as activities are co-ordinated in one place. This avoids a sense of feeling overwhelmed or that there are endless demands on the client's time. It is also particularly useful for looking at several commitments together. By imposing structure and order, the client can logically associate tasks, see how they contribute to an overarching goal, and integrate these with desired activities. This will reduce feelings of panic and anxiety.

For example, if the aim is to apply for a job, the steps may include:

1. Monday – go to the Job Centre
2. Tuesday – obtain relevant application forms by telephone or by writing
3. Wednesday – fill in personal details on application forms
4. Thursday – fill in previous employment history on application forms
5. Friday – fill in reasons why you want the respective job on application forms
6. Saturday – ask a friend or family member to look through the application forms and give feedback. Find an envelope and stamp
7. Sunday – make changes to application forms, re-read them and post them.

Step 3: Prioritise Activities

It is unlikely that *everything* on a comprehensive 'wish-list' of activities will be achieved in the allocated time. Therefore, it is important to *prioritise* as it is very easy to spend a long time doing a little job that does not actually progress the client

How important is it to go to the Job Centre the next day?

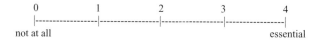

How important is it to play football on Sunday?

Figure 5.2   Prioritisation methods

towards a goal or affect the quality of their life. Prioritising involves the client asking the following four questions:

1. What *must* be done this week?
2. What can wait, and for how long?
3. What do I *want* done this week?
4. What will happen if I don't do it?

Use of a Likert scale will help the client determine the importance of tasks (see below). For each task the client should evaluate how vital it is to achieve this task within the set period (i.e. day, week, month). For example, if the client's goal is to get a job as quickly as possible because they are unemployed, they should ask the questions shown in Figure 5.2.

For clients who find that a Likert scale lacks sensitivity to help identify subtle prioritisations, it may be more helpful for them to allocate a percentage rating (ranging from 0% – 'not at all', to 100% – 'essential'). We have included both methods of measurement on the Companion Website.

The characteristics identified and learned from the diary activity log in Table 5.2 obtained at the beginning of these sessions and prior to intervention should be borne in mind. This will give helpful clues to how the clients naturally apply themselves; that is, the best time of the day to conduct work requiring concentration, physical activity and rest periods. It will also give clues to likely distractors and obstacles to achieving tasks. Forewarned is forearmed, so the sessions should be spent preparing for distractors and obstacles and working out a plan to avoid temptations. Once items have been prioritised, they should be ranked in order of importance. These activities can then be scheduled for times when the individual is able to perform at their optimal level. For example, David took his medication in the middle of the morning, which meant that he was best able to concentrate in the middle of the day.

Learning to prioritise is a skill that the client needs to develop. It should be modelled and rehearsed in sessions, for example, by using an agenda and prioritising work in progress. Clients may be reluctant to prioritise tasks and consider this activity to be a waste of time as they prefer to deal with issues as they present themselves. This reticence or lack of impulse control needs to be acknowledged and discussed in the sessions. It is not until the client engages in the process that they learn that engaging in a process of prioritisation takes time, but is a good use of time. It serves a valuable function and leads to positive results. Like all new skills, the process needs to be practiced until it becomes habitual.

For example, take the case of David. In the immediate term, David needed to find new employment. Additionally, he thought that if he learned plastering skills, this would improve his potential for gaining regular employment as a painter and decorator. He also enjoyed playing football and going to the pub with his friends. David was running out of ADHD medication. Before walking out of his job, David had intended to sell his old van and purchase a new van, but, as he was no longer employed, his priorities changed. Before engaging in the process of prioritisation, David was keen to go ahead and take a loan to buy a van that he saw one day when driving past a garage. However, in the session a list of goals and priorities was generated using the techniques described and it became clear that this was now a relatively low priority. Bearing in mind his new goals of getting a job and to learn plastering, David rated the importance of the tasks to be achieved and determined his priority task list as shown in Table 5.5.

Priorities are dynamic factors, thus it is important to allow clients to review them in a regular and planned way. If a priority task list is not regularly revisited, then the client may waste time on tasks that have been superceded by more important activities. They also become distracted and lose sight of their main priorities.

Table 5.5   Priority task list

0	1	2	3	4
least important				most important

Request a repeat prescription from his GP	4
Determine and organise financial situation	4
Go to job centre	4
Complete application forms	4
Find lists of courses from local college	3
Enroll on a course	3
Play football on Saturday	3
Go to pub after football	2
Buy a new van	1
Play football on Sunday	0

Step 4: Estimate Time to Complete Tasks

Next the client must estimate how long they think it will take to perform each task. In David's case, his most urgent priority involved incorporating several steps to schedule him to organise a repeat prescription from the GP, as follows:

1. Telephone the GP receptionist and place the request   5 minutes
2. Drive to the GP surgery and park   20 minutes
3. Wait in reception   10 minutes
4. Drive home   15 minutes

When making his time plan, David also needed to schedule time for 'unpredictable' circumstances, such as heavy traffic, difficulty finding a parking space, being late and the surgery being closed. It is better to overestimate and succeed than underestimate and fail.

Perception of time can be distorted for adults with ADHD (Young et al., 2000). Usually time passes quickly for a person with ADHD, for example 10 minutes can feel like two, so it is difficult to schedule a time plan that accurately reflects all that has to be done within a limited amount of time. Almost certainly this will guarantee failure, leaving a distressed client feeling disinterested, disenchanted and despondent about unfinished tasks and without the motivation to recommence them another day. In order to avoid this negative reinforcement, it is very important to accurately estimate how long it will take to complete a task. First, the client's general time perception can be determined by asking them to complete a set of exercises, such as those outlined in Table 5.6. These are illustrated as completed by David, but are presented on the Companion Website in a format for use in treatment. Of course, these exercises may be modified as appropriate as it is important that they are relevant to each client's way of life. First, David estimated how long it would take him to complete a task, and then he timed himself to see how accurately he had estimated the time (as his homework assignment). This behavioural experiment can be further extended by the client timing others performing certain tasks.

Table 5.6 Time estimation exercise

Activity: How long does it take...	David's estimated time	David's actual time
To have a shower and dry off	2 mins	8 mins
To get dressed in the morning	3 mins	5 mins
To make a cup of tea	1 min	3 mins
To go to the hairdressers/barbers	20 mins	30 mins
To buy a week's shopping	30 mins	1 hour
To change the bed linen	5 mins	15 mins
To clean the kitchen floor	5 mins	15 mins
To read a newspaper	20 mins	40 mins

This exercise will help the client realise the extent to which they consistently distort periods of time and find out how long regular activities really take, such as shopping, ironing, etc. It is important to identify is the client's general trait in time-estimation (i.e. whether they tend to overestimate or underestimate – it is most likely to be the latter) so appropriate adjustments to the time plan can be made.

When constructing a time plan, however, some tasks will obviously be new, in which case clients should always be encouraged to allocate additional time to complete them. Unscheduled gaps in time, i.e. 'free time', are viewed as additional rewards for successful completion of tasks.

Step 5: Schedule Tasks

By this stage, steps or tasks have been identified to achieve goals, a list has been determined to integrate these with tasks for the week, they have been prioritised and the time to complete them has been estimated. The next stage is to sequence the tasks or activities by setting out and organising the time plan. Ironically, it is crucial to schedule time to create a plan and organise time. Depending on individual preference, priority tasks may be organised according to particular inclinations. Some people prefer to do the worst task first to get it out of the way, others would rather ease themselves in gently. The time of day may also be a factor. Most people have a post-lunch dip in their energy levels, therefore it is advisable to avoid scheduling an activity that requires particular mental exertion during this period. The pre-treatment diary activity log will be helpful in this respect. Medication regimes of the individual should be noted, as a good time to schedule tasks that require concentration may be within the hours following taking medication. Additionally, when scheduling the time plan, it is important to balance the day evenly with pleasant and unpleasant activities.

Some activities will be difficult to accurately schedule (particularly novel activities for which completion times are difficult to estimate). 'Contingency time' needs to be scheduled in to account for tasks which overrun and/or for unexpected tasks that arise in the course of the day. However when these occur, it is important to distinguish between a genuine 'unexpected item' that is a priority and an idea that springs to mind which functions as a distractor from a mundane task. Irrelevant distractors must be discussed in sessions, so that the client can recognise them when they arise and can reject them as time-wasting traps representing obstacles to the client reaching their weekly goal(s). Ideas and initiatives, however, should not be discarded but temporarily put on ice by noting them for scheduling into a future set of activities and/or time plan. Creativity is not a resource to be stifled.

Table 5.7 shows the time plan devised in a session with David. David's specific goals for the week were to organise his finances, get a job, obtain a repeat prescription and enrol on a plastering course. In the week, David also wanted to play football on Saturday, visit his parents and look into the cost of replacing his van.

Table 5.7 Time plan

Set goals	Organise finances	
	Get a job	
	Repeat prescription from GP	
	Enrol on plastering course	
Make lists	Work out budget for next 3 months	
	Pay outstanding bills	
	Visit bank manager	
	Find out value of old van	
	Visit garages to look at vans	
	Go to job centre	
	Look in newspapers at job adverts	
	Ring old friend who may have work	
	Complete application forms	
	Ask sister to check application forms	
	Go to post office to buy stamps	
	Book GP appointment	
	Go to GP practice to collect prescription	
	Go to pharmacy	
	Find out about plastering courses	
	Enrol on plastering course	
	Visit mum and dad	
	Play football	
	Out with friends	
Prioritise activities	Work out budget for next 3 months	4
	Pay outstanding bills	4
	Go to job centre	4
	Book GP appointment	4
	Look in newspapers at job adverts	4
	Ring old friend who may have work	3
	Complete application forms	3
	Ask sister to check application forms	3
	Go to post office to buy stamps	3
	Go to GP practice to collect prescription	3
	Go to pharmacy	3
	Visit bank manager	3
	Find out about plastering courses	3
	Enrol on plastering course	3
	Visit mum and dad	2
	Play football	2
	Find out value of old van	1
	Out with friends	1
	Visit garages to look at vans	1
Estimate time to complete tasks	Work out budget for next 3 months	3 hr
	Pay outstanding bills	3 hr
	Visit bank manager	1 hr
	Find out value of old van	5–6 hrs

(*continued*)

Table 5.7   (*continued*)

Visit garages to look at vans	4 hrs
Go to job centre	4 hrs
Look in newspapers at job adverts	6 hrs
Ring old friend who may have work	30 mins
Complete application forms	5 hrs
Ask sister to check application forms	2 hrs
Go to post office to buy stamps	30 mins
Book GP appointment	5 mins
Go to GP practice to collect prescription	45 mins
Go to pharmacy	5 mins
Find out about plastering courses	1 hr
Enrol on plastering course	1 hr
Visit mum and dad	3 hrs
Play football	3 hrs
Out with friends	5 hrs

David then generated a weekly diary activity plan (see Table 5.8) in order for him to schedule his time so that he would complete all of his essential priority tasks as well as the lower priority activities that he wanted to achieve. Thus David scheduled his week to meet his target goals and his desired goals, for example playing football and exploring the possibility of buying a new van. Desired goals may be incorporated into a reward system to positively reward achievement.

Step 6: Incorporate a System and Reward

Planned breaks and rewards are a vital part of time management for people with ADHD and these are most likely to be omitted from a scheduled time plan. It is crucial to plan breaks and rewards as carefully as planning time on tasks as they provide time to relax and refresh in order to refocus attention. An additional function is that they provide the client with positive reinforcement by engagement in a pleasurable activity. A common problem for people with ADHD is that they do not take sufficient scheduled breaks, especially when tasks are interesting, resulting in them becoming fatigued. Attention dwindles when people become tired, and novel, frivolous tasks may seem more attractive and rewarding. In such circumstances, people with ADHD often become engrossed in the distractor task resulting in it becoming impossible to return to the original (now boring) task.

The length of time for which the client can concentrate needs to be evaluated and will vary accordingly to individual differences. As a rule of thumb, breaks should be scheduled *at least* every hour but this needs to be tested out, evaluated and adjusted accordingly. It is better for clients to break off at a 'cliff-hanging' moment in the middle of a task, as this raises interest and motivation and makes it easier to return to the task later.

A 'reward' may simply involve a break chatting to a colleague or wandering around the office (local shops, or going for a walk) for five minutes. The point is the individual must be 'off task'. More tangible rewards may be making a cup of tea/coffee, chocolate biscuits, watching TV, telephoning a friend, going on shopping trips, etc. The reward must be *desired* and enjoyed or it becomes an aversive stimulus and one to be avoided, thus having a contra-indicative effect. People with ADHD require *immediate* short-term rewards rather than making themselves wait for a big reward on completion of a long project. For example, some would rather self-reward with left-over pizza than celebrate the completion of a project by going out to a great restaurant. Once small rewards have been incorporated in the time plan, then a system can be introduced whereby small rewards count towards obtaining a greater reward in the long term. Thus, the client needs to learn to organise a system whereby several small rewards count towards a bigger one in the long term, for example, completion of all tasks during the day (including pleasurable reward tasks) results in a 'larger' reward that evening, such as giving themselves a 'self-indulgent' hour that evening.

In sessions, David identified his short-term rewards as telephoning a friend, organising an evening out, coffee breaks and listening to music. His longer-term rewards were to look at vans and play football. He therefore organised his days so that there were regular short-term rewards and more intermittent longer-term rewards when he had achieved certain key tasks.

REVIEW AND EVALUATION

It is imperative that sessions include regular reviews of progress and evaluation of success. This can be achieved by re-administering the diary activity log, the time estimation exercise and reviewing the progress made towards obtaining goals. It is important to give clients positive feedback to encourage them, and improve self-efficacy and confidence. Clients should be encouraged to self-reward by crossing off tasks on their lists as this additionally provides a visual reinforcement system.

TIME-WASTING TRAPS

There are many time-wasting traps in which the client may become involved and these include the switching/diversion of attention, engagement in sensation-seeking behaviour, procrastination and 'false busyness'.

1. Switching Attention

Time wasting traps are not just excuses to avoid completing certain tasks. These may also be due to a momentary loss of concentration or distraction, causing the individual to lose focus and become preoccupied either externally (i.e. with a different

Table 5.8 Example of diary activity plan

Time	Monday	Tuesday	Wednesday	Thursday	Friday	Saturday	Sunday
7–8am	Sleep	Sleep	Sleep	Sleep	Sleep	Sleep	Sleep
8–9am	Get up, Shower Breakfast	Get up, Shower Breakfast	Get up, Shower Breakfast	Get up, Shower Breakfast	Get up, Shower Breakfast	Sleep	Sleep
9–10am	TAKE MEDICATION Go to job centre	TAKE MEDICATION Work on budget	TAKE MEDICATION Go to GP to collect prescription and go to pharmacy	TAKE MEDICATION Go to library	TAKE MEDICATION	Get up shower Breakfast	Get up Shower Breakfast
10–11am	Have cup of coffee Back to job centre	Have cup of coffee Work on budget	Pay outstanding bills	Research plastering courses	Go to college to enroll	TAKE MEDICATION Go to visit sister	TAKE MEDICATION
11–12am	Contact GP CONTINGENCY TIME	Phone friend about work	Application forms – personal details	Find out how to enroll – contact colleges	Visit bank manager	Go through application forms with sister	Tidy flat
12–1pm	Buy newspapers Go home	Get application forms	Application forms	CONTINGENCY TIME	CONTINGENCY TIME	Go through application forms with sister	Drive to parent's
1–2pm	Lunch	Lunch	Lunch	Lunch	Lunch	Lunch	Lunch
2–3pm	Look in newspaper	Drive van to local garage	Buy stamps from post office CONTINGENCY TIME	Application forms – employment history	Application forms – extra information	Meet friends to play football	Stay to chat
3–4pm	Phone friend CONTINGENCY TIME	Visit another garage	Look in newspaper	Application forms – employment history	Application forms – extra information	Football	Go home

4–5pm	Look in newspaper	Go to supermarket	Look in newspaper	Look in newspaper	Go to garage to investigate vans	Football	Make changes to forms
5–6pm	Look in newspaper	Drive home and unpack shopping	Look in newspaper	Go to gym	Free time	Football	Make changes to forms
6–7pm	Prepare meal	Prepare meal	Prepare meal	Gym	Out with friends	Out to pub	Watch DVD
7–8pm	Watch TV	Phone friend	Watch TV	Go home for food	Out with friends	Out to pub	Make food
8–9pm	Watch TV	Free time	Watch TV	Prepare meal	Out with friends	Out to pub	Free time
9–10pm	Watch TV	Free time	Watch TV	Meet friend	Out with friends	Out to pub	Free time
10–11pm	Watch TV	Free time	Watch TV	Quick drink	Out with friends	Out to pub	Free time
11–12pm	Get ready for bed	Get ready for bed	Get ready for bed	Get ready for bed	Get ready for bed	Out to pub	Get ready for bed
12–1am	Go to bed	Go to bed	Go to bed	Go to bed	Go to bed	Go to bed	Go to bed
1–2am	Sleep	Sleep	Sleep	Sleep	Sleep	Sleep	Sleep
2–3am	Sleep	Sleep	Sleep	Sleep	Sleep	Sleep	Sleep
3–4am	Sleep	Sleep	Sleep	Sleep	Sleep	Sleep	Sleep
4–5am	Sleep	Sleep	Sleep	Sleep	Sleep	Sleep	Sleep
5–6am	Sleep	Sleep	Sleep	Sleep	Sleep	Sleep	Sleep
6–7am	Sleep	Sleep	Sleep	Sleep	Sleep	Sleep	Sleep

task) or internally (i.e. by daydreaming). This often causes adults with ADHD to jump from one task to another before they have finished the current one and means that tasks will take longer to complete. The task may never be revisited and is often left unfinished. Incomplete tasks will remain on the client's mind and can cause feelings of anger, anxiety and frustration. For this reason, they are likely to interfere with their concentration on the novel task.

In order to prevent this dysfunctional set, when individuals have intrusive thoughts or ideas, they must be encouraged to make a note of these so they can return to them at a later time rather than acting immediately and embarking on a new set of activities. Usually the idea can wait and be accommodated in future schedules.

2. Delay Aversion

As mentioned previously, and related to attention switching and distractability, is the issue of delay aversion (e.g. Sonuga-Barke, Taylor, Sembi & Smith, 1992). People with ADHD have been shown to have difficulty in delaying gratification in order to achieve a longer-term goal. This means that they are more likely to opt for a shorter-term, sometimes smaller reward than be motivated to wait for a long-term reward. This systematic bias in the relationship between reward value and time can lead to time management difficulties as the individual is easily tempted to deviate from their original plan by the lure of an immediate reward albeit at the expense of achieving a longer-term goal. For this reason, people with ADHD may be more likely to give up on a task, such as completing a longer piece of work that takes 10 hours for which they will be paid £100 and become distracted by a more immediate reward such as being paid £10 for three hours worth of work.

In order to circumvent delay aversion, the therapist needs to determine whether the reward is highly motivating as well as being proportionate to the amount of time spent on a task. For example, they need to check whether a coffee break is an appropriate reward for an hour's work and whether it is sufficiently motivating for the client to continue working for the rest of the day. For some individuals, a coffee break may be an excuse to stay off-task by becoming distracted. The reward of taking a short walk may motivate them better.

3. Sensation-seeking Behaviour

Some clients complain that scheduling activities causes their day to lack spontaneity and excitement. In such cases, there is even greater need to plan constructive time breaks (for either planned rewards or free time for 'spontaneous' activities) into the time plan. Goals are the client's servant, not their master. Rewards must therefore meet the client's physical and psychological needs. This means incorporating exceptionally creative and stimulating pre-determined prosocial rewards in the time plan. This should not be of concern as the rewards are usually determined by the client relatively easily. Longer-term rewards of this type may include competitive sports and/or constructive venturesome activities (e.g. bungee jumping, go-karting, visiting fun fairs).

4. Procrastination

People with ADHD are extremely adept at procrastination. They are skilled at rationalising dysfunctional beliefs, intellectualising and playing 'devil's advocate'. This usually fulfils a functional role as it wastes time and serves to avoid an undesired task. However, it may also be due to a lack of confidence because individuals have set themselves too high a standard or have been unrealistic about what they can achieve. This is a particular problem for perfectionistic individuals who can never attain their own expectations. In such cases, perspective taking can help as individuals rarely expect the same standards in others that they apply to themselves. Individuals need to 'let themselves off the hook' and recognise that, by setting stringent standards of achievement, they set themselves up to fail. Avoidance of routine (but often necessary) tasks can also become a problem as these are perceived as boring. The client should consider whether seemingly insurmountable dull tasks need to be done all in one go or whether it is possible to break such tasks down into smaller parts to make them less of a chore.

5. False Busyness

A primary time-wasting trap is what can be termed 'false busyness'. This is when a person flutters about, usually looking very occupied (and pre-occupied) when in fact this 'busy bee' is wasting a lot of time by engaging in non-constructive activities. The entire day can be filled up by chatting at the coffee machine, making phone calls, surfing the internet, responding to junk email, window shopping, etc. False busyness can be determined by examining the diary activity log recorded prior to the time-management interventions outlined in this chapter. This needs to be addressed and discussed in sessions and a 'relapse prevention plan' agreed to avoid falling into this trap by recognising when they engage in these behaviours and the (dys)function they serve.

TIME MANAGEMENT IN PRACTICE/TIME KEEPING

Some of our clients describe how, even when they have carefully made their plans regarding what they are aiming to do for a day, they still have great difficulty in achieving this as they forget what they are supposed to be doing and end up being late for appointments and forget tasks. Some individuals overcompensate and arrive unnecessarily early for important events in order to make sure they do not miss out. In such cases, they inevitably then waste time waiting for the appointment, which could have been used more productively.

These problems with time management are due to prospective memory difficulties; that is, the ability to remember to do something in the future. This can be regarded as a deficit in executive functioning as it is closely linked to planning ability, which has been shown to be impaired in adults with ADHD (e.g. Young et al., in submission). Once a mental plan has been made, certain points in time are 'tagged' or marked by an executive functioning process such that the person is alerted at approximately the right moment that they should be performing a certain activity, such as turning down the boiling milk (e.g. Burgess, Veitch, de Lacy Costello & Shallice, 2000). For people with ADHD, this 'alerting system' could be seen to be working suboptimally such that they are either reminded at the wrong time that they are supposed to be doing something, which then becomes a distraction, or they are not internally reminded until it is too late and they have missed the event.

The best method for people with ADHD to keep time is to rely on external aids such as alarm clocks, digital watches and mobile phone alarms, etc. These alarms can be set at a regular time every day, for example, the night before, and be integrated into a routine. Some personal organiser systems or mobile phones can be programmed to make different tones according to the activity. Clients should be encouraged not just to set an alarm for an event beginning, such as a driving lesson beginning at 1.00 pm, but they should work out the time they need to begin getting ready for the lesson, e.g. start packing their bag at 12.00, catch the bus at 12.30, etc. Such an 'early warning system' can also improve attention as it can increase arousal, which is an interrelated system (see Chapter 4)

TIME KEEPING

Often, people with ADHD develop a sense of 'learned helplessness' regarding their timekeeping such that they assume they will always be late and others come to expect very little of them. A motivating method for improving time keeping is by asking the individual to rate the importance of punctuality and evaluate the impact of their lateness for different situations. An example is given in Table 5.9 for Chloe, a mother of two boys who also have ADHD (a blank form is included on the Companion Website for use in sessions).

By performing the evaluation in Table 5.9, Chloe was able to determine which events were absolutely crucial for her to be on time in order to avoid disadvantaging her children and damaging her reputation. Previously, she had shrugged off the implications of regularly being late, and assumed that others would just think she was 'scatty'. However, she was more motivated to prioritise events and be on time when she had explicitly thought through the consequences of poor punctuality.

Table 5.9   Evaluating the importance of punctuality

Situation	Importance of punctuality (0–10)	Potential impact/outcome of being late
Arriving late at work	8	Looks unprofessional People may think I'm uncommitted Other people have to cover for me until I arrive Would get more work done and not have to stay late
Late for parents' evening	9	Might miss out on hearing what teachers recommend Teachers may assume I'm a bad mother Sons' education may be affected
Late to pick up the boys from school	7	The boys may become unnecessarily worried that I won't come The boys need routine too Other mothers may think I'm neglectful
Late for hairdressers appointment	4	It may delay every appointment that follows mine They might turn me away and then I'd have to rebook
Late for lunch at parents' house	2	The food may be ruined It's not fair on mum who likes to be organised about when we eat. She may be upset They might worry I've had a car crash on the way
Late for doctor's appointment for repeat prescription	6	I may miss the appointment and have to wait until the end of surgery Other more ill people might have less time at the end of the day because all the appointments will become delayed I might not get the prescription, so run out of medication and then I'd be even less able to manage my time
Late to meet a friend for a drink	3	My friend may feel anxious or embarrassed about waiting alone It may look like my friend has been stood up It's wasting their time My friend may be in a bad mood by the time I get there. It may spoil the evening

CONCLUSIONS

Time passes quickly for people with ADHD resulting in them having difficulties with time estimation. This often means they are late for appointments and do not achieve objectives and goals.

By encouraging individuals with ADHD to make a time plan of progressive steps towards set goals, they will learn what it feels like to complete and achieve tasks. This in itself is positively reinforcing but, additionally, a reward system must be incorporated into the time plan process.

Time wasting activities trap the individual into engaging in distracting activities that serve as obstacles to achievement. Sticking to a time management plan can be further hampered by timekeeping difficulties and poor punctuality. By developing external strategies to compensate for prospective memory problems and examining the consequences of lateness in more detail, the individual can learn to improve their time keeping.

For the therapist, the goal is to help the individual learn that life is not an obstacle course but to teach the client to navigate their way through a pathway of the difficulties and challenges they are bound to encounter. Aside from the time management and organisational skills outlined in this chapter, this will also involve the problem-solving skills discussed in the next chapter.

6

PROBLEM-SOLVING

People with ADHD have difficulty solving problems for many reasons. They may respond impulsively, rather than think through a solution and its potential outcomes. They may worry unnecessarily about minor, more immediate issues and lose sight of the whole picture, in other words 'they can't see the wood for the trees'. This means that they may find it hard to generate solution options. Past experience means they may tend to focus on negative outcomes as these are what they have come to expect. However, by learning to adopt a methodical approach to solving problems, more optimal outcomes can be reached.

A 'problem' can be defined as any life situation or task that requires something to be changed or resolved. In order to allow the person to function adaptively. The problem may be explicit (for example, needing accommodation) or intrinsic (for example, feeling unattractive). Obstacles such as novelty, ambiguity, conflicts of interest, or lack of resources may prevent an immediate response or solution from being effective. Sometimes people may only begin to realise that a problem exists when they have failed to achieve a desired goal on several occasions, for example getting a job.

A 'solution' is a response or pattern of responses that can be cognitive or behavioural. A solution arises through the problem-solving process and achieves a problem-solving goal (D'Zurilla & Nezu, 1999). Implementation of a solution is an important part of the problem-solving process as this involves carrying out the solution in specific situations. Finally, solutions need to be evaluated as to their level of success in reaching the set goals.

For individuals with ADHD, their problem-solving abilities are often affected by executive functioning difficulties, e.g. a difficulty organising and sequencing information, and/or a difficulty inhibiting a prepotent response. Thus, their problem-solving abilities are hindered by core cognitive impairments, such as deficits in response inhibition, working memory and/or attention. It is important to assess the coping styles of clients, both adaptive and maladaptive, as these will determine appropriate problem-solving techniques, the hurdles they will face implementing them, and their potential success. This chapter examines the problem-solving difficulties commonly reported by people with ADHD, what is known about their adaptive functioning and coping mechanisms and the stages involved in successful problem solving. The model presented is a five-stage process that involves identifying and defining the problem, generating solutions, evaluating solutions, implementing the chosen solution and evaluating success.

PROBLEM-SOLVING DIFFICULTIES

Specific problem-solving deficits have been investigated using neuropsychological measures in order to establish their cognitive basis in ADHD (e.g. the Tower of Hanoi and Tower of London tasks) (Riccio, Wolfe, Romine, Davis & Sullivan, 2004; Young et al., in submission). There are several relevant areas of difficulty including response inhibition, working memory and attention (see Chapter 4 on inattention and memory).

Failure in inhibitory control when confronted with a problem may lead an individual with ADHD to respond before the optimal solution has been generated. A difficulty in delaying gratification may also lead ADHD adults to opt for a 'short-cut'; that is, an immediately rewarding solution, rather than implementing a longer-term solution that requires waiting and more effort but with a greater reward. Young et al. (in submission) explored these concepts using a Three Dimensional Computerised Tower of London task where 'discs' and 'rods' are presented on a computer screen. The participant is required to solve problems of varying difficulty by rearranging a set of discs in order to make them match a goal arrangement. It was found that people with ADHD did not increase their planning time and were less accurate as task difficulty increased. Failure to increase planning time with increasing problem difficulty was associated with elevated levels of impulsivity. This suggests that impairment in response inhibition, or a tendency to act with less prior thought, can lead to problem-solving failure.

Working memory difficulties and attentional impairment can affect problem solving at several stages for individuals with ADHD. There can be difficulties in generating solutions, as the individual may be liable to lose sight of previously suggested ideas and/or become distracted. They may find it difficult to hold in mind the advantages and disadvantages of solutions in order to weigh up which is most likely to be successful. In addition, working memory impairments may cause difficulties for individuals with ADHD implementing solutions as they may miss out crucial components or muddle up a sequence of events. For example, when solving the problem of getting a vehicle license renewed, they may go to the post office without organising the papers and find that they have left behind an important document.

Young et al. (2006) used an ecologically valid measure of spatial working memory, which involved a computerised simulated golf task – 'The Executive Golf' (Morris, Downes, Sahakian, Evenden, Heald & Robbins, 1988). This involves the participant predicting into which hole the 'golfer' will putt a ball. The participant is given feedback as to whether their selection is correct or not. The aim is to avoid returning to any holes previously selected. Performance can be improved by the participant developing a search sequence, however ADHD participants tended not to adopt any strategy at all, resulting in a significantly impaired performance. Furthermore, the deficit became more evident with task difficulty; that is, when they were required to process a larger array of holes in their spatial working memory.

These specific cognitive difficulties should be borne in mind when developing a problem-solving intervention for a client with ADHD. Their strengths and weaknesses may guide the therapist regarding the areas that may require more attention. For example, for more impulsive individuals, it may be necessary to focus on strategies that involve generation of multiple solutions in order to avoid them lunging at the first idea which comes to mind to resolve a situation. Alternatively, for people with inattentive difficulties, they may require more assistance in devising strategies for carrying out solutions without deviating from their planned and desired course.

COPING STRATEGIES IN ADULT ADHD

Adults with ADHD have been shown to use maladaptive coping strategies, such as confrontation, escape-avoidance and less planned problem-solving than individuals without ADHD (Young, 2005). This study also found that the way ADHD adults coped with stressful situations was determined by their cognitive ability. Indeed, impairment in executive function may lead an individual to lack flexibility in their ability to access and utilise a repertoire of appropriate coping strategies. For example, difficulties with impulse control may lead clients to cope with problems by responding rapidly and without thinking; this may mean they react in an aggressive or defensive way. They may find it difficult to employ problem-focused strategies if they feel emotionally overwhelmed by anger or anxiety, which in turn drives them to act out their feelings. Alternatively, due to previous adverse experiences and attentional difficulties, some individuals with ADHD may respond to stress or problems by not acknowledging the problem or actively avoiding dealing with it.

The coping strategies employed by adults with ADHD may also be affected by a lack of intimate, confiding, relationships as social support can act as a stress-buffer. Close, supportive interpersonal relationships provide the opportunity to consult about problems, gain helpful advice, benefit from the experience of others, and learn from the modelling of successful and unsuccessful coping mechanisms. However, 'words of wisdom' and the observation of adaptive functioning may be less accessible to individuals who experience multiple short-term interpersonal relationships, find it difficult to sustain relationships with acquaintances and old friends and may have strained relations with family members.

The individual's style of adaptive functioning will determine the outcome of a problem solution, in other words, its success and viability. A functional coping style provides the context for the generation and implementation of optimal solutions. A dysfunctional coping style can negatively affect the quality and suitability of solutions generated and may lead to inappropriate decision making. According to the Lazarus and Folkman (1984) model of coping, stress depends on a person's cognitive appraisal of a situation and their perceptions of their resources to deal with it. They suggest that feelings of stress can be relieved through both emotion-focused coping and instrumental problem-solving. Emotion-focused coping is used when the aim is to manage the emotions that are generated by a situation, for example, a death in the family or the end of a relationship. Problem-solving is used as a general coping strategy in situations that are perceived as changeable or controllable. Problem solving can affect a person's sense of control and change their negative appraisal of situations. A functional response to stress involves the ability to use emotion-focused coping and problem-solving in the appropriate situations.

There are gender differences in the likelihood of whether emotion-focused or problem-focused coping strategies are employed. Females are more likely to engage in emotion-focused coping, whereas men are more likely to use problem-focused coping. However, when people have ADHD, it seems that these are the exact areas in which the individuals of different genders need the most help. Females with ADHD often have emotion-related difficulties, such as anxiety and mood lability, which can impact on their ability to cope with stressful situations. Additionally, adolescent females have been shown to be less likely to confide in peers and use social support, which is a common resource used by young people (Young et al., 2005b). On the other hand, males with ADHD are more likely to externalise their distress and respond impulsively with aggressive or antisocial behaviour, rather than engaging in adaptive problem-solving. For these reasons, it is important to begin treatment with psychoeducation regarding when each type of coping may be more appropriate, and follow this through with teaching effective skills and techniques.

If a client is in a situation that is entirely beyond their control (and the therapist needs to check whether this perception is prone to cognitive distortion, such as catastrophising the problem), then emotion-focused strategies may be most suitable to help the client manage their feelings. These may include simple counselling or sharing of a difficulty with a friend, but may extend to mood-focused strategies such as those provided in Chapters 9 (Anxiety), 10 (Frustration and Anger) and 11 (Low Mood). However, situations that are within the control of the individual can be addressed using the five-stage model of problem solving provided below.

FIVE STAGES OF PROBLEM-SOLVING

Individuals of both genders can benefit from learning to apply an instrumental and structured method of analysing and resolving their problems. This involves adopting a five-stage process:

1. identifying and defining the specific problem
2. generating various solutions to the problem
3. evaluating each solution
4. implementing the chosen solution
5. evaluating success.

Stage 1: Identifying and Defining the Problem

Problems may creep up on individuals with ADHD or suddenly occur unexpectedly. They may be external obstacles to a goal that arise as part of a natural process (e.g. being unable to purchase materials to complete a task as the shop is out of stock); they may be the result of actions or interference by others, both positive and negative (e.g. a work colleague is off sick for a week and the client has to cover his work-load); they may also be self-generated and build up through worry (e.g. 'my boss hates me', 'I'm hopeless at parties'). Common areas for problems for people with ADHD are given in Table 6.1.

However, the client may need some prompting and assistance in teasing out the presenting problem. This can be achieved by asking four main questions in order to determine whether the individual has a 'solvable' problem or more general worries and anxieties. These questions have been included in an exercise format on the

Table 6.1   Common domains of problems in ADHD

Work	Underachievement at work, being passed over for promotion, not meeting sales targets
Transport	Missing trains, buses, being late, taxing, insuring and organising MOT for a car
Financial	Debts due to not paying bills on time, impulsive spending
Lack of support	Gaining appropriate support, e.g. setting up childcare arrangements, not accessing appropriate benefits
Household chores	Incomplete DIY tasks, putting off cleaning and laundry
Relationships	Difficulty making or maintaining relationships, argumentative with friends
Low self-esteem	Feeling like a failure, expectancy of failure
Sleep	Restlessness, insomnia, difficulty geting out of bed on time
Disorganisation	Disorganisation of time, time-wasting traps, day lacking structure, poor work–leisure time balance
Substance misuse	Drug and alcohol addictions, use of substances as a maladaptive coping strategy
Trouble with police	Opportunistic crime, aggressive outbursts, damage to property

Companion Website (Exercise 6.1). The questions will help determine whether the problem really needs tackling. If the problem derives more from a client's general attitude or anxious response-style, then the techniques outlined in Chapter 9 on coping with anxiety will be of help.

1. *Why* it is a problem?
2. *How* does it affect the client?
3. Does the situation have *potential for change*?
4. What could happen if it is *not solved*?

For example, take the case of Alex, a client with ADHD. Alex started a new relationship and was unsure whether to tell his girlfriend, Joanne, that he had ADHD.

1. *Why was it a problem?* Alex often had to take medication when he was with Joanne and did this in secret. If they were together when his medication wore off, he sometimes felt a bit 'ragged' and irritable.
2. *How did it affect the client?* Alex was worried about how Joanne would react if she knew. He didn't want to lie to her but he was worried that she would think he was crazy and/or be embarrassed by him taking medication.
3. *Did the situation have potential for change?* If Joanne knew about Alex having ADHD and was OK about it, Alex would feel very relieved. Alex believed they would have a firmer, more honest foundation on which to build their relationship. The downside was that they might split up if Joanne wasn't OK with it.
4. *What could happen if the problem was not solved?* The relationship would not have an open and honest foundation. If Joanne found out by someone else telling her, she might feel angry with Alex and feel that he cannot be trusted.

This example illustrates that problems are often complex. They are not straightforward or simple to resolve. If they were, they would not be a problem! Thus, part of the problem-solving process is investigation. Finding out as much as possible about the problem and how it has arisen will provide the client with the knowledge to find the appropriate solution and give them the self-confidence to implement it. This involves not only gathering facts related to the task itself but also examination of personal information, for example self-expectations and demands. Hence, if a person sets unrealistic, unachievable goals, then the problem is not the failure to achieve set goals, but the inability to realistically acknowledge their capabilities and skills, time-management problems, perfectionist attitude, etc.

Three questions can be asked in order to assist with understanding the problem:

1. What is the problem or situation?
2. What do I want?
3. What are the obstacles to getting what I want?

An example is provided in Table 6.2, which demonstrates how, by adopting this systematic methodology, problems may become more clearly defined and easier to understand. A blank version is on the Companion Website.

Table 6.2   Understanding the problem

	Problem list			
	I am unsure whether to tell girlfriend about ADHD	I am often late for work	I have been given notice to move out of my flat	I have fallen out with a friend
1. What is the problem/ situation?	Whether or not to disclose	Usually 20–30 minutes late	Need to find somewhere to live within one month	My friend has stopped contacting me since I blurted out a confidence
2. What do I want?	That she knows and feels comfortable/ accepts my diagnosis	On time or 10 minutes early	Find new accommodation in next fortnight	Being in touch with my friend again
3. What are the obstacles to getting what I want?	Finding the right moment Finding the right way to say it She may reject me	Difficulty getting up early Transport delays	Going away for weekend next week Raising deposit Worries about having to live with strangers	Pride Fear of rejection

Stage 2: Generating Solutions

The best way of generating solutions is to brainstorm all the possible ways of solving the problem. There are three basic rules for generating alternative solutions through brainstorming (D'Zurilla & Nezu, 1999):

1. Quantity leads to quality, i.e. the more solutions that are produced, the more good quality ideas there will be.
2. Deferment of judgement, i.e. the person needs to wait to choose a solution in order to generate better quality solutions at this stage.
3. Variety, i.e. the greater the range of solutions, the more likely a good solution will be generated. Thinking more laterally may prevent the person from choosing a well-tried but unsuccessful approach.

Thus the client should be encouraged to produce ideas including extreme solutions ranging from the sublime to the ridiculous. Figure 6.1 shows the solutions

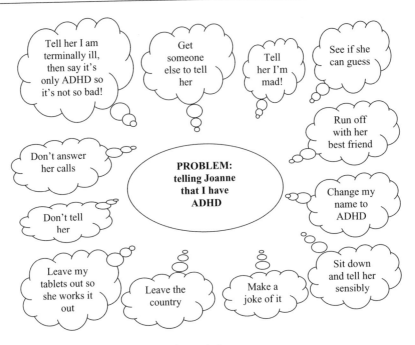

Figure 6.1   Example of brainstorming solutions

generated by Alex when he was brainstorming ideas regarding whether to tell his girlfriend that he has ADHD. A common obstacle to generating creative solutions is 'habits' (Parnes, Noller & Biondi, 1977). Habits hinder problem solving by causing clients to respond automatically and in a way to which they have become accustomed. Individuals with ADHD may well have a history of habitual and impulsive responding resulting in the development of 'maladaptive habits'. These become maladaptive coping strategies. For example, a client may habitually respond to a situation that is perceived to be threatening in some way by storming out and failing to address the problem.

Whenever Alex prepared himself to tell his girlfriend he had ADHD, he would become anxious and start an argument. The argument distracted him from following through his intention to disclose to her his ADHD status. Such habits may be helpfully identified collaboratively in sessions so that the client may recognise them when they occur and resist the impulse to automatically respond in a predetermined pattern of thinking or behaving.

One of the most helpful methods in solving problems, and one which is often overlooked by adults with ADHD, is simply reviewing the previous solutions they have applied to similar problems. The client should be encouraged to think about how they usually tackle problems and what has worked (or not worked) in the past. They should also evaluate the methods by which they have success-fully avoided problems in the past. This will involve engaging the client in a cost-benefit analysis of previous decision-making processes. Clients should be encouraged to think not only about what and who helped in the past, but also what made things worse. They need to identify the *process*, how they arrived at the decision, and whether this had a positive or negative outcome. They may also seek the advice of someone who has known them encounter similar situations in the past who may be more objective regarding what worked and what was less helpful.

For example, Alex was asked to consider what had happened in the past when he had told friends and girlfriends that he has ADHD. When he told his first girlfriend and their friends in the pub, they had laughed and thanked him for letting them know. His best friend asked if there was anything he could do to help. His friend asked him a lot of questions about the disorder. A few weeks later he and his girlfriend split up as she was due to go travelling. His mother told family members that he had ADHD, some of whom did not seem to grasp the nature of the disorder. One aunt sent him a 'Get Well Soon' card. From this experience, Alex decided that it would be better if he provided his own explanation of his condition.

Stage 3: Evaluating Solutions

So far the client will have learnt to identify and define problems and generate multiple alternative solutions. Once several solutions have been generated, these should be assessed according to the degree of satisfaction the client would feel with the outcome of each solution. Several methods are recommended to assist with this process, including evaluating effort, examining alternatives, rehearsal of the solu-tion, role-play and challenging cognitive distortions.

Evaluating effort

People with ADHD may avoid adaptive problem-solving when the effort involved in carrying out a solution is perceived to be too great. A desire for immediate gratifica-tion means that a short cut may be more rewarding than the alternative of expending more effort to achieve a greater goal. Motivational interviewing techniques will help the individual focus on the goal or task to be achieved and motivate them to stay on task, avoid distractors and achieve it.

For example, in order for Alex to achieve a successful relationship, effort needed to be expended in planning how to explain to Joanne about having ADHD. The alternative short cut, which did not require effort, was not tell her and to continue the relationship on the basis of dishonesty. The latter course may have provided immediate relief from the anxiety aroused in Alex whenever he contemplated disclosure to Joanne, but the problem remained unresolved. Indeed, it may even have become worse if, say, Joanne had observed Alex surreptitiously taking tablets and then ended the relationship on the assumption that he was taking illicit drugs. Alex examined his motivation to change the situation and achieve a better relationship by discussing his readiness to engage in change by formulating his position in the 'Stages of Change' model (Prochaska & DiClemente, 1982). Alex identified that he had been oscillating between the precontemplation and contemplation state. His ambivalence was expressed by him attempting to find some 'middle ground' by arguing that he should wait to tell Joanne about his ADHD ('I'll do it next week'). In Alex's case, this was a delaying tactic, which was challenged in the sessions. However, in some cases it may be sensible for clients to be encouraged to avoid premature disclosure in new relationships or less close relationships (e.g. acquaintances, working associates). It is all about doing what is right for the client and getting the balance right. This will inevitably involve encouraging the client to plan ahead and think about the consequences of their actions. As a therapist, the primary task is to help the client to learn to think before they speak and act, or react impulsively on the spur of the moment. Blurting out his medication history at a party is unlikely to be helpful in resolving Alex's problem. Alex determined to progress onto a stage of preparation by examining alternative solutions, rehearsal and role-play of favoured solutions in preparation of the action stage.

Examining alternatives

After eliminating all the ridiculous and least likely options, the client will usually be left with two or three possible 'realistic' solutions. These often have very different courses of action. This is the time to make a 'pros and cons' list for each – often the advantages of one solution are the disadvantages of another. Weightings can be given according to how important each 'pro' or 'con' is for the client. These may depend on the likelihood of achieving the goal, emotional well-being, time and effort.

Alex decided that he should choose between telling Joanne himself ('sit down and tell her sensibly') and not telling her, but continuing the relationship. Alex's pros and cons for telling Joanne that he had ADHD are given in Table 6.3. A blank version can be found on the Companion Website for use with clients.

Next Alex was asked to rank the five most important issues identified in the pros and cons list. He chose:

1. It would help Joanne understand why I am the way I am (pro)
2. It's being honest (pro)
3. It might freak her out (con)
4. She could find out anyway, and might be angry that I didn't tell her (pro)
5. She may leave me (con)

Table 6.3   Example of a pros and cons list

Pros of telling	Cons of telling
It's being honest	It might freak her out
She may not mind	She may leave me
She could find out anyway, and might be cross that I didn't tell her	I don't want to worry her
It would help her understand why I am the way I am	The relationship may not last
The longer I leave it, the harder it will be to tell her	She may laugh at me and tell other people

It then became clearer to Alex that, not only did he choose more pros than cons in his importance list, but he also ranked them higher. Therefore, he decided to tell Joanne that he had ADHD. The next stage for him was to work out exactly how best to do this.

Rehearsal

Rehearsal is an effective way of preparing for a difficult conversation or situation. The client should be taken into an imaginal mode by asking them to imagine the anticipated situation and see themselves acting out the chosen solution. The client can be oriented to the situation by being cued to imagine and describe the surroundings in detail, for example colour of curtains, type of flooring, cooking smells. At first, some clients may have difficulty engaging in an imaginal mode, but with practice this will become easier. In such cases, it may be helpful for the therapist to initially talk the client through the specific steps that may be taken to solve the problem whilst the client is in the imaginal mode. However, it is important that the client progresses to rehearsal of the solution unaided. In addition, they should try to identify possible pitfalls to success that were not immediately obvious and determine collaboratively how these may be overcome and/or constructively managed. The client should also consider how they feel during the process and at the outcome.

For example, Alex was asked to imagine the situation carefully. He thought it would be better to tell Joanne at her house, when they were relaxing watching television. However, when this was rehearsed in the imaginal mode, Alex discovered that the TV distracted him. Alex then decided to tell Joanne in the kitchen over a cup of coffee. Alex rehearsed what he would say to Joanne and, by using this technique, he felt more confident in his ability to see the task through to fruition and to achieve the outcome he desired.

Prior to working in imaginal mode it is very important to determine a calm, happy imaginal state that the client relates to positively. Sometimes the client may become distressed when working in imaginal mode and they may imagine alternative consequences, which may be negative. In such an event, the client should signal feelings of distress to the therapist using a predetermined code (e.g. by lifting a finger in the air) and the therapist then verbally directs the client to imagine a neutral, calm scene and focus on breathing exercises (see Chapter 9 on Anxiety).

Perspective taking role-play

The next stage involved Alex role-playing the scenario with his therapist. A role-play method is particularly useful for rehearsing problem solutions involving other people such as giving notice at work and ending a relationship. In the case of Alex, the role-play was reversed so that the therapist pretended to be Alex (the client), and Alex role-played his girlfriend Joanne (the person receiving the information). This helped Alex think about the likely impact of his problem solution on Joanne and amend his plans accordingly, such as by using more sensitive wording to explain about ADHD, having some written information to hand to her that would help dispel any inaccurate stereotypical lay beliefs she may have. Alex was able to think about the questions that Joanne might ask (for which he could then prepare answers and rehearse either in imaginal mode or by further role-play in sessions).

Practicing such situations in this way will make individuals feel less nervous when the situation actually happens and they will feel more prepared. This will improve their sense of self-efficacy and belief that problems are solvable and change is possible.

Challenging cognitive distortions

It is likely that at some stage during treatment distorted thinking will handicap the problem-solving process, particularly when maladaptive habitual responses are favoured ('I'm no good at it', 'I'll fail', 'I'm stupid', 'They don't like me'). The client needs to learn how to check that their ideas about various solutions are productive and viable. Cognitive distorted thinking is likely to sabotage helpful solutions in favour of ones that add little to resolving the problem, and/or may make it worse (for more help with cognitive distortions, see Chapter 11 on Low mood and Depression). In such circumstances, potentially helpful solutions may be discarded erroneously due to 'faulty thinking' processes resulting in:

- Overgeneralisation, e.g. 'everything I do always goes wrong, so why bother trying'.
- Black-and-white thinking, e.g. 'if I can't get it 100% right, there's no point in doing it at all'.
- Jumping to conclusions, e.g. 'I only just managed to complete Part 1, so I'll never get Part 4 finished'.

Alex tended to jump to conclusions and overgeneralise. In fact, his first girlfriend had ended their relationship before she went travelling around Europe with a friend. This occurred just after he had disclosed to her about him having ADHD. It may have been a matter of bad timing. Alex had formed the belief that future relationships would end if he told his friends and girlfriends about having ADHD. He felt very anxious about it. However, Alex had never considered alternative possibilities, such as his ex-girlfriend had wanted to go travelling for years, it had been arranged for a long time and it had nothing to do with him disclosing to her that he had the disorder. In fact, Alex had ignored evidence to the contrary, as his ex-girlfriend had said that she wanted to stay friends. She had stayed in touch and had sent him post cards from various countries. Additionally, Alex tended not to focus on the fact that his friends had not responded in a similar way. He still met them regularly in the pub and his best friend had obtained an information leaflet about adult ADHD.

Stage 4: Implementing the Chosen Solution

The client should have become motivated to effect change and resolve problems, and they will have generated multiple solutions to their problem and chosen the best. The client will have been prepared by rehearsal in sessions and have role-played potential outcomes. The next stage is to plan and implement the solution. Once an appropriate solution has been determined and rehearsed, the client is encouraged to implement this, taking care to avoid procrastination and time-wasting traps. For example, say the problem is debt and the target is to pay off £200 of a credit card bill by the end of the year. The solution implemented is putting aside £5 each week. This illustrates how steps to achieve the target should be planned by breaking down the goal into smaller achievable steps.

However, the process is often more complex, especially when problem-solving difficulties involve interpersonal relationships. This involves thinking about the best time and situation in which to address the problem, and if possible 'set the scene'. Depending on the problem, the time management principles set out in Chapter 6 may also be helpful if ultimate resolution and goal achievement requires the individual to create small achievable steps or tasks that lead to success. Tasks must be clearly defined and goals realistic. In the case of Alex, he was encouraged to work out a specific evening and place most suited to disclosing his ADHD status to his new girlfriend. This was then reviewed in the following session.

Step 5: Evaluating Success

Following the implementation of a solution, the client should evaluate their success. Did they achieve the desired result? Positive feedback by the therapist is a powerful reward! It is important that the client feels proud of their achievement and focuses on the benefits of success. They should reflect on the impact of success on their self-confidence, their mood and also their understanding of the original presenting problem (was it as life-threatening as they first thought?). Positive feedback will increase the likelihood of the client engaging in a problem-solving process without delay (or procrastination) in the future and motivate them to pursue further goals.

For example, Alex told his girlfriend and she was very pleased that he had trusted her and told her. Joanne told Alex that she had diabetes and had to inject insulin every day. She had been worried about how to tell him. In future, Alex adopted a similar model of disclosure to friends at the appropriate time. Both Alex and Joanne felt more confident about their relationship.

In case of partial or no success, the therapist must systematically evaluate all the obstacles and difficulties that arose and recommence the problem-solving process to explore how these may be better dealt with. Useful areas to explore include the client's feelings about successful resolution, such as fearing the consequences, anxiety about change or uncertainty. It may be that the problem needs to be re-evaluated and resolved in a different way. For example, if Alex had been unable to raise the issue of ADHD with Joanne, the therapist could examine where the obstacles lay. Had there been an external distraction that prevented him (e.g. other people nearby) or had Alex been thinking negatively about his solution plan?

Rewards are crucial to encourage the client and provide motivation. The reward system should include rewards for attempting resolution of the problem and one greater reward for successful resolution of the problem. Alex and Joanne went out for dinner to a romantic restaurant.

POSITIVE REAPPRAISAL

Despite the many pitfalls experienced by adults with ADHD in solving problems, they have been shown to reappraise stressful situations in a positive way (Young, 2005). This may mean that they are more resilient to disappointments and better able to 'bounce back' from difficulties. This trait has been found to be positively associated with impulsivity. This may indicate that more impulsive individuals may be less prone to dwell on their difficulties and attempt to get on with life. This can be hugely advantageous and may underpin many ADHD individuals' creative and entrepreneurial personality characteristics and successes.

CONCLUSIONS

People with ADHD are often faced with multiple problems that require solving. Their difficulty is in coping with problems adaptively and finding appropriate solutions. All too often, people with ADHD respond to the problems in their daily lives in a disadvantageous way, for example putting off targets, avoiding situations or people, responding in an irrational or impulsive manner. This is likely to be due to cognitive deficits and maladaptive coping styles that can hinder their problem-solving abilities. When small problems mount up, these become great problems. People with ADHD respond in much the same way to great problems or life events. It is at this point that the psychological problems such as depression and anxiety may develop when individuals feel overwhelmed by stressful problematic situations. It is therefore important that the individual with ADHD learns to encounter and resolve problems in a timely and appropriate way. It is important, however, to recognise that individuals with ADHD often have a predisposition to reappraise stressful situations in a positive light, which may be a protective factor for future problem solving and strengthen their resilience.

This chapter has reviewed the main stages involved in solving problems. These include identifying and defining problems, and generating alternative solutions. The implementation of a solution must always be followed by analysis and evaluation of success, and reward for success. This provides a constructive feedback loop to inform earlier stages of the future problem-solving process.

7

IMPULSIVITY

Behavioural and cognitive disinhibition are characteristics of ADHD associated with the lack of ability to control either behaviour, speech or certain thought processes. This means that someone with ADHD is likely to say the first thing that comes into their head, such as expressing feelings, thoughts and opinions without weighing up the consequences. They may also act without considering the consequences of their behaviour. In a way, they do not have an internal 'brake' that allows them to sift out inappropriate responses or behaviours. This is sometimes referred to as having poor 'response inhibition'; that is, they are unable to inhibit a prepotent response. Poor impulse control can cause problems for ADHD individuals in their social interactions. They may blurt out inappropriate comments and inadvertently offend people. Nevertheless in some circumstances the tendency to act on the 'spur-of-the-moment' can be advantageous as it means individuals are willing to take risks that may pay off, whereas someone without ADHD is likely to be more cautious and perhaps miss out on opportunities. Impulsivity or a lack of inhibition can also lead to an increase in divergent or lateral thinking, which allows people with ADHD to be creative. Indeed, there are several successful entrepreneurs and celebrities in the arts and music industries who have disclosed their ADHD and attribute their success in part to having the disorder.

However, the tendency to act and think in an impulsive way can also bring great disadvantages. People with ADHD tend not to engage in a systematic decision-making process or consider alternative perspectives. The need for immediate gratification may make individuals seem demanding, exhausting and tactless and they may be perceived as antisocial and irritating company. They may also seem inconsiderate and fickle as they can become impulsively enthusiastic about doing something but then quickly lose interest in favour of something new. They may be viewed as self-centred individuals who lack consideration for the feelings and needs of others. This presentation is likely to have negative social consequences resulting in the clients themselves feeling misunderstood and socially isolated.

This chapter examines the nature of the deficit that underpins impulsive behaviour in adults with ADHD. The current theoretical explanations are discussed along with a description of the typical impulse control problems that may be exhibited. The relevance of impulsivity to antisocial, delinquent and criminal behaviour is considered, particularly with regard to the interaction of comorbid conduct disorder and ADHD. Methods are provided for assisting individuals in identifying situations in which they may be vulnerable to responding in an impulsive way and determine appropriate control and coping strategies. Various cognitive-behavioural self-monitoring and self-restraint strategies are presented within the chapter. These include techniques to improve control, including the use of self-talk, distraction and self-instructional training.

THEORETICAL EXPLANATIONS

There are two competing explanations for why impulsivity arises in the disorder of ADHD. One is that there is a primary executive functioning deficit in inhibitory control mechanisms (e.g. Barkley & Biederman, 1997), such as the mechanisms that stop a person from running out across a busy road, or stop someone from blurting out a tactless comment. The probability of successful inhibition seems to relate directly to the length of the 'stopping' interval; that is, when people with ADHD are under pressure to inhibit a response in a short space of time, they are more likely to make mistakes. However, if they are given longer to inhibit a response, they are more accurate and hence less 'impulsive'. This concept has strong implications for intervention, as ADHD clients must learn to schedule time and be encouraged to 'stop and think' in order to reduce failures through impulsive mistakes.

An alternative theory is that the disinhibition or impulsivity associated with ADHD is due to aversion to delay (e.g. Sonuga-Barke et al., 1992). According to this perspective, impulsive behaviour is due to a choice to avoid delay, which people with ADHD find aversive. The theory considers that impulsivity is underpinned by a preference for immediate or short-term rewards and an inability to delay gratification in the longer term. This means that individuals are more motivated to receive a current reward even if it is less valuable than a more valuable longer-term reward. This has implications for everyday functioning where much of our behaviour, particularly in adult life, is governed by the principle of 'good things come to those who wait'. For example, most people find that the prospect of a salary at the end of the week or month is sufficient to keep them adequately motivated at work each day. However, for someone with ADHD, if they have become dissatisfied and/or irritated at work for some reason (e.g. bored with the work; annoyed with a colleague), they may be inclined to quit their job, feeling that the short-term reward of getting out of a situation is worth more to them than the long-term reward of being paid. Unfortunately the prospect of immediate reward and temptation may lure some individuals into delinquent and/or criminal behaviour. The implications for treatment strategies are to work with the need for immediate gratification by breaking down tasks into smaller stages and providing short-term goals that can be rewarded.

THE NATURE OF THE DEFICIT

There are several ways in which impulsivity is manifested in ADHD adults. People can seem to be too 'quick off the mark'; that is, individuals tend to respond before instructions have been completed or before they have acquired all the information necessary for starting a task. There are also difficulties when ADHD adults 'act without thinking', where individuals respond without first considering all the possible response options and their implications. Alternatively, a person may verbally or physically lash out at someone who has upset them without considering the social and/or legal implications. They focus on short-term rewards as opposed to long-term rewards, for example students may have difficulty resisting a readily available reward, such as an evening out, which may prevent them from achieving a longer-term goal, such as submitting their coursework on time.

Impulsivity can be conceptualised in two ways: 'behavioural impulsivity' and 'cognitive impulsivity'. *Behavioural impulsivity* refers to the inability to inhibit physical or verbal actions due to premature and/or over-rapid responsiveness. This is manifested as an inability to resist doing or saying inappropriate things, for example ADHD individuals may hit out at someone or something in a fit of temper and/or make hurtful comments. Behavioural impulsivity is associated with excessive attraction to immediate reward.

Cognitive impulsivity relates to disorganised behaviour associated with problems of executive function. This underpins forgetfulness, poor planning and poor time management. For example, clients may misappraise a situation or the intentions of others and make rash important decisions based on inadequate information.

Neuropsychological measures are available to help distinguish between the two concepts. Behavioural impulsivity is commonly measured using tasks assessing response inhibition; that is, the ability to inhibit a salient response when it is inappropriate. People with ADHD have been shown to exhibit impaired performance on such tasks, for example 'stop' tasks and 'go-no-go' tasks (Rubia, Oosterlaan, Sergeant, Brandeis & Leeuwen, 1998; Rubia et al., 1999, 2000). 'Stop' tasks typically involve responding according to certain contingencies, for example pressing a key on a computer in response to identifying cued target items. Hence, the individual is required to press a button every time they see a target on the screen. However, on occasions the testee is instructed to do the opposite, in other words, to stop responding in this way (by withholding their response), and this can be challenging for a person with ADHD who is likely to respond in the cued way and make lots of errors. Similarly, for 'go-no-go' tasks, the individual is typically required to respond to certain targets (i.e. 'go'), but not respond if they are preceded or followed by another 'no-go' target. For example, the individual is required to press a button every time they see a target on the screen, but if the target is presented with a second aural or visual cue (e.g. a 'bleep', or the target is a different colour), then the individual is required to withhold their response. In such cases, individuals with ADHD have particular difficulty co-ordinating their response pattern and make errors by 'misfiring' at the wrong time (i.e. they have difficulty withholding their response). However, performance may improve if individuals are provided with an increase in time between stimuli as this gives them more time in which to respond.

Behavioural impulsivity is also assessed using a task called the Matching Familiar Figures Test (Cairnes & Cammock, 1978), which assesses impulsiveness versus re-flectiveness in cognitive style. The test involves identifying target pictures among five distractors with both speed and accuracy. It is similar to playing 'spot the dif-ference' between pictures. Compared with people without ADHD, individuals with ADHD tend to respond rapidly and make an increased number of errors by selecting incorrect responses. This means that they tend to favour speed over accuracy and adopt a 'trial and error' approach to problem solving.

Cognitive impulsivity can be assessed neuropsychologically with various executive functioning paradigms as well as through careful observations and anecdotal reports of behaviour. The ability to co-ordinate a series of tasks and form a strategy can be assessed using the Modified Six Elements subtest of the Behavioural Assessment of Dysexecutive Syndrome (Wilson et al., 1996). Individuals with ADHD are more likely to break rules by impulsively changing task without planning a sequence. Another test from the same battery that can be used to assess planning skills is the Zoo Map task. This task requires the individual to assimilate information from rules and instructions about how they should organise a visit to the zoo and form a plan before plotting their route on a map. People with ADHD typically do not take the time to plan and impul-sively begin the route without formulating an effective sequence. This difficulty with planning was also found by Young et al. (in submission) where ADHD participants were less likely to adjust their planning time according to task difficulty for the Tower of London, a test of problem-solving.

It is important to bear in mind that, whilst deficits of cognitive impulsivity may be exhibited on some neuropsychological measures, they are most likely to be ex-tremely debilitating in everyday life. Thus, it is very important to question the client carefully about how they cope with completing chores and tasks on a daily basis, especially those that require sustained effort and concentration, or those in which the client lacks interest or motivation to complete. Indeed, one advantage of the Behavioural Assessment of Dysexecutive Syndrome (Wilson et al., 1996) is that it is an ecologically valid battery of executive functioning tests which translate relatively well from the artificial testing room into real life. Nevertheless, some individuals are still able to perform in an assessment setting, in other words control their cognitive impulsivity when effectively forced to do so, but have extreme difficulty in doing this on a day-to-day basis.

Table 7.1 provides a summary of the typical impulse control behaviours (and associ-ated problems) that are commonly reported by people with ADHD, or their friends and family.

Table 7.1   Typical impulse control problems experienced by people with ADHD

Consequence 'blindness'	People with ADHD find it difficult to consider the consequences of their behaviour before acting. For example, the social consequence of blurting out gossip or interrupting people
Difficulty waiting	ADHD can greatly affect someone's ability to queue or wait for their turn. This is particularly prominent in shopping queues when there is a delay
Motivation for immediate gratification	People with ADHD are more prone to opt for a short-term reward that involves less effort than working for longer periods and applying more effort for a larger reward
Taking short cuts	Individuals with ADHD are notorious for taking 'short cuts', which may lead to reduced accuracy or a lower quality of outcome
Demanding behaviour	People with ADHD may seem demanding and self-centred if someone else controls access to what they are wanting
Lack of insight	Situations in which they are likely to be impulsive may not be immediately obvious to someone with ADHD
Abrupt movements	Motor movements can be affected by impulsivity, such as getting up out of a chair suddenly, or snatching items from another person
Reckless driving	Driving can cause problems for an individual with ADHD who has difficulty waiting at traffic lights, or driving patiently behind slower drivers. Poor impulse control on the road can lead to many driving violations, commonly including speeding, jumping lights, but also may be more serious when greater risks are taken, such as overtaking when it is unsafe to do so
Rule breaking	Behavioural impulsivity may often present as disobedience or deliberate violation of instructions
Recklessness	Impulsivity can also manifest itself as recklessness due to the tendency to engage in dangerous activities without considering possible consequences
Jumping to conclusions	Jumping to conclusions is a general problem for individuals with ADHD. They may be more likely to misinterpret ambiguous situations, make assumptions based on very little information and also catastrophise
Incurring debts	Impulsive spending may lead individuals to buy items without considering whether they can afford them or whether they are necessary
Novelty seeking behaviour	A search for thrills and novelty may stem from an excessive attraction to immediate reward
Anxiety	Anxiety may lead to impulsive avoidance of aversive situations or exacerbate impulse control difficulties

The common theme for all these behaviours is that such individuals do not think ahead or consider the consequences of their actions. It is not that they are unaware of the difference between appropriate and inappropriate behaviour or that one solution/ response to a problem is better than another. The difficulty arises because they do not think or consider every option. Their decision-making processes may be impulse driven, resulting in a tendency to make important choices rapidly and without careful consideration or planning (also see Chapter 6 on Problem-Solving). A model of therapy should therefore aim to teach self-monitoring and self-regulation skills (e.g. 'to stop and think'), train the individual to consider consequences of action and generate appropriate and constructive alternatives.

ANTISOCIAL, DELINQUENT AND CRIMINAL BEHAVIOUR

Childhood ADHD is frequently associated with conduct problems and just as the developmental trajectory of ADHD symptomatology is heterogeneous, so is the developmental trajectory of children with ADHD and Conduct Disorder. Moffitt (1993) has theorised that there are two fundamentally divergent categories of delinquent adolescents. The 'adolescence-limited' group is characterised by noteworthy criminal activity that arises for the first time in early to mid-adolescence and features non-aggressive behaviour that typically desists by late adolescence. The 'life-course persistent' antisocial group is characterised by overt aggression in adolescence, typified by marked defiant and aggressive behaviour from a young age. Moffitt suggests that the delinquency of this group is associated with pre-existing cognitive and/or behavioural deficits, including neuropsychological dysfunction, family disharmony and attention deficits/hyperactivity. Indeed, a longitudinal epidemiological study of young hyperactive boys into young adulthood showed that hyperactivity was a risk factor in young men for later antisocial problems including violence, even after the coexistence of initial conduct problems was taken into account (Taylor et al., 1996). This may reflect that young children grow up with a 'double dose' of risk, characterised by both cognitive and conduct problems. Indeed there is some evidence that co-occurring ADHD and Conduct Disorder is a clinically and genetically more severe variant of the independent disorders (Thapar, Harrington & McGuffin, 2001).

Irrespective of the additional risk of ADHD, examination of the 'conduct problem route' into criminal behaviour portrays a pathway that often begins with truancy, bullying, vandalism, verbal and physical aggression. Conduct problems may escalate in adolescence to become oppositional defiant problems, juvenile delinquency and criminal behaviour. For adults with ADHD, this delinquent pathway may be further complicated by the addition of the development of personality problems.

The cognitive deficits of young persons with ADHD may therefore lead them to progress along increasingly antisocial trajectory. Symptoms may remit far too late for young people to break out of indoctrination in an antisocial peer group and culture, and/or purposefully break out of established antisocial patterns of behaviour. Court records suggest that ADHD is a great risk for juvenile contact with the criminal justice system (Satterfield, Swanson, Schell & Lee, 1994) and prison studies suggest that about two-thirds of inmates had childhood ADHD and up to 30% of them continue to be symptomatic in adulthood (Eyestone & Howell, 1994; Dalteg, Lindgren & Levander, 1999; Rasmussen, Almik & Levander, 2001; Retz et al., 2004; Rosler et al., 2004). This association may be explained by poor response inhibition in ADHD individuals resulting in a lack of self-control. Thus, recidivism is likely to be high and their offending behaviour typified by impetuous, novelty seeking behaviour, which leads to opportunistic crimes for which they are apprehended.

Such individuals require specialised group treatment programmes that focus on their criminogenic needs and labile temperament. There is a lack, however, of structured, manualised programmes available for an ADHD client group. The R&R2 for ADHD Youths and Adults (Young & Ross, 2007), which is a new edition of the original Reasoning and Rehabilitation programme (Ross, Fabiano & Ross, 1986), is designed to yield programmes that have an evidence-base in the reduction of antisocial behaviour of youths, juvenile delinquents and adult offenders. The R&R2 for ADHD Youths and Adults programme not only teaches symptom control, skills development and prosocial attitudes, but also involves the training of cognitive processes involved in problem solving. This group programme provides the opportunity to assess whether an individual has specific skills deficits or needs that will benefit from individual attention such as interventions outlined in the Young–Bramham Programme modules.

IDENTIFYING THE PROBLEM

So far, the two main aspects of impulsivity have been described; cognitive and behavioural impulsivity. Clients will readily relate to behavioural impulsivity as this is what they perceive as impeding their performance on a day-to-day basis, such as going 'off-task' and never finishing anything; jumping to the wrong conclusions; and losing their temper. The therapist should direct the client to identify *specific* situations when they are likely to respond in an impulsive manner. This should not present a great problem but if it seems difficult, the client should start by looking back at times or behaviours that they regret in retrospect. In particular they should identify problems that have occurred on a regular basis as these may be used to monitor progress in treatment. Through discussion, exploration and Socratic questioning regarding these situations (as well as observation of the client's behaviour in sessions), target behaviours may be determined that are suitable for treatment. As with all behavioural measurements however, the target behaviour must be specific and clearly defined by the client and therapist. The frequency of the target behaviour can then be measured either in the course of a session (e.g. number of interruptions) or outside of the session by the client, friend, partner or family member (e.g. shouting at motorists whilst driving), or by using an objective measure (e.g. a record of weekly shopping purchases).

The ultimate aim is for the client to take responsibility for monitoring their own impulsive behaviour. As individuals develop greater self-awareness of their behaviour, learning to self-monitor in this way may in itself act as a reduction strategy. Specific interventions should be discussed collaboratively, selected strategies implemented, reviewed and evaluated. This process is called the IMPULSE method of self-monitoring and regulating poor impulse control. Table 7.2 describes the IMPULSE method applied to the problem a client had with making shopping purchases on impulse. This happened so frequently that the client was getting into debt. A version of Table 7.2 that is suitable for use in sessions is provided on the Companion Web-site. Once clients have successfully mastered the IMPULSE system they should be encouraged to apply it to a range of problem behaviours (including those identified by others).

COGNITIVE BEHAVIOURAL TREATMENT STRATEGIES

Whilst behavioural management plans are helpful to adapt specific behaviours that occur on a frequent basis, the primary objective of treatment is for the individual to develop and maintain their management plan in order that in time this may become more generalised. The aim is for the individual to begin to cope more generally with impulsive responding. This involves learning techniques to monitor and control impulsive behaviour. There are several techniques, all of which encourage the individual to 'stop and think'. These include learning to apply cognitive strategies, such as self-talk, self-instructional training, double-checks and distraction techniques. Not all strategies will be helpful, but it is likely that the client will find some of these methods of benefit. This can only be determined by trying them out and evaluating progress.

Wherever possible, appropriate behaviour should be modelled. In addition, some individuals may benefit from watching recordings of themselves acting in role plays that require them to behave in an appropriate manner as well as in an inappropriate manner. When playing back the recording, the client should be encouraged to take a different perspective of their behaviour by imagining a friend or family member observing them. What would be going through their mind? Alternatively, the client could be asked to imagine that they are observing the behaviour of a friend or family member. What would they make of it? Would they view the interaction differently? Role-plays are particularly helpful in perspective taking as this gives the client the opportunity of considering the personal and social consequences of behaviour.

Be wary of cognitive avoidance, which may present as a lack of motivation. It may well be distressing for the individual to develop better insight into their own behaviour and its impact on others. This may cause clients to avoid facing up to past mistakes, which have been financially and/or emotionally costly, and/or painful memories. If this occurs, it may hamper progress in treatment. In some cases, individuals may deliberately attempt to sabotage treatment by disengagement (this representing a 'secondary gain' as it provides the short-term reward of removing themselves from anxiety-provoking treatment). Being sensitive to the client's feelings and acknowledging their difficulty by taking a non-judgemental and open approach is likely to be helpful.

Table 7.2 The IMPULSE method for identifying and monitoring behaviours

I: identify the behaviour For example: *Impulsive spending on credit cards*	The target behaviour should be chosen by the client. Not all impulsivity is problematic to the individual. It is important that they identify and target areas that they are motivated to change. For example, interrupting others and not taking turns appropriately in conversation may lead to problems with relationships and isolation
M: make the behaviour explicit For example: *Buying CDs and clothes when the client does not have the money*	Developing a clear definition of the problem is crucial if change is to be usefully measured. Vague targets such as 'stop being impulsive' are both difficult to measure and difficult to achieve. It is more sensible to use operationalised behaviours such as 'driving over the speed limit' or 'interrupting others'
P: Peer/partner monitoring For example: *Credit card bills brought to the session. Partner can monitor new purchases being brought into the house*	It may be possible for the therapist to monitor some behaviours such as interruptions in a therapy session. However, other behaviours may be less easy to assess. Video cameras might be usefully employed to monitor some behaviours. In some situations it may be possible to enrol the help of a partner, friend or family member, who can count behaviours such as changing the television channel or staying seated at mealtimes
U: Understanding and self-monitoring For example: *For all items purchased, evaluation of whether they were planned and whether the client could afford them*	If the IMPULSE method has been monitored by a person other than the client, the responsibility for monitoring should next be passed to the client. It may be helpful to compare reports of behaviour in order to check that the client is able to recognise the target behaviours appropriately. Self-monitoring can serve as an intervention in itself as it may encourage recognition of triggers or antecedents to behaviour
L: List plans to tackle the problem For example: *Planning a weekly budget*	Once the behaviour has been monitored and a baseline rate has been established, the client and the therapist collaborate to form an intervention plan (see strategies section below)
S: Strategy implementation For example: *Carrying out budget*	The client applies the agreed strategy

E: Evaluation of strategy
For example:
  1. *Feedback from client, particularly regarding times when they have resisted temptation*
  2. *Count of number of unplanned purchases*
	Evaluation of the strategy success is performed via two methods: (1) the client should be invited to give feedback about the strategy – what has been helpful/unhelpful, etc; and (2) there is a repeat monitoring period in order to establish the frequency of target behaviours. This is compared to the original baseline measure

Self-talk

Self-talk is essentially proactive thinking. To a certain extent, everyone engages in self-talk, sometimes even out loud. People often think through plans in their heads for various situational outcomes and rehearse potential responses. The client can be taught to apply self-talk as a cognitive technique to interrupt an automatic dysfunctional thinking process, for example by saying words like 'Stop', 'Control', 'Look before you leap', 'Think before you speak'. If the client is in a state of high emotional arousal then this will exacerbate cognitive deficits resulting in them feeling overwhelmed and confused. Self-talk, such as 'stay calm', 'I can do this', at the same time as visualising (pre-determined) calming images is likely to help the individual to feel more in control. Potential calming images should be discussed and tried out in sessions in order that the client may develop a repertoire of helpful and restful visual images that can be accessed and cued as necessary (e.g. a Caribbean beach; sitting on top of a mountain; an English garden; an evening sunset). Once thinking has been interrupted in this way, the client should be encouraged to stand back and take a different perspective, such as 'Is there another way I can think about this and resolve this problem?'; 'What would my mother, brother, friends say?'

Self-talk must be tailored to individual needs by identifying what the client finds helpful. This needs to be achieved collaboratively in sessions and tested out and evaluated in 'real life' settings, such as by setting up 'mini-experiments'. Once useful self-talk has been identified, this should be practised when an individual is not acting on an impulse, but is carrying out day-to-day activities that do not require decision making. For example, the self-talk can be rehearsed when driving on a clear road. The more experience an individual has using self-talk, the more likely they will apply it in the heat of the moment.

Self-instructional Training

A second step towards 'taking the heat out of an impulse' is self-instructional training. Self-talk interrupts a dysfunctional thinking process and, once this has been achieved, the individual must then learn to direct themselves towards more positive functional thinking. Self-instructional training helps the client to stand back from a situation, appraise it from different perspectives, evaluate possible responses and outcomes, re-appraise and select an appropriate response. This is achieved by teaching the client to engage in self-directed purposeful instructions. Until the client becomes used to this process it should be enacted out loud in sessions. For example, Julie, a client with ADHD, has difficulty waiting in line to pay for groceries in a supermarket. If the line is very long she invariably gets irritated and restless and walks out of the shop leaving her shopping behind. In this case, the therapist and client devised the following management plan:

1. Whenever possible, Julie did her shopping at more quiet periods during the day.
2. When she had to wait in line and began to feel restless and irritated and had thoughts that she should leave the shop, she employed self-talk by saying to herself 'stop', 'calm down'.

3. Next Julie evaluated her options in a self-directed thought process, e.g. 'if I walk out of the shop I will not have achieved my goal of getting the shopping done; that means that I will have to make time to come back to the shop at a later time and I will have to change my plans for this evening; the shop may still be busy later on and I may not get my shopping today; I have run out of cereal so I will have to go to work without eating breakfast. If I stay, I can cope with feelings of irritation by occupying my thoughts using a distraction technique; I will have my shopping and can have what I want for breakfast; I can meet my friends this evening'.
4. Julie then applied selected distraction techniques (see Table 7.4).
5. Once the shopping had been completed, Julie rewarded herself for achieving her goal, e.g. by having a chocolate bar when she leaves the supermarket.

The most common obstacle to success is the ADHD individual's desire and motivation for immediate gratification. An immediate or short-term reward, such as leaving the shop to avoid feelings of irritability and restlessness, is preferred over the longer-term reward of purchasing the shopping. Thus, consequential thinking (i.e. evaluating potential outcomes, their merits and disadvantages) is an important component to any management plan. This may be introduced to the client by encouraging them to rehearse a strategy in sessions called CONTROL (see Table 7.3). CONTROL is a process in which the client engages in self-talk to stop dysfunctional thinking, makes self-directed statements and/or instructions and considers options and alternatives. The CONTROL

Table 7.3 The process of CONTROL

C: Control	In order to interrupt a dysfunctional thinking process, the person should say (either aloud or to themselves) 'CONTROL' as a thought-stopping technique. In addition, they may benefit from temporarily removing themselves from the situation
O: 'Off-line' processing	Self-talk and self-instructions are applied to anchor attention to calmer images and an emotionally neutral state
N: New solutions	Alternative solutions are generated by using self-directed statements. Rationalisation and problem-solving techniques will additionally be helpful (see Chapter 6)
T: Test solutions	Solutions can be tested through mental rehearsal, and predicting outcomes, e.g. I can (1) buy the new TV now on credit but have less money each month for a year, (2) save to buy the TV and have it in six month's time, (3) buy a cheaper one, etc.
R: Re-evaluation	Once the options have been considered, the most preferable can be chosen by reviewing the client's goals
O: 'On-line' processing	Once a decision has been made, this should be carried out, i.e. the solution becomes 'on-line'. Determine and include a reward for successful engagement of the CONTROL process
L: Look for benefits	In order to further positively reinforce the CONTROL process, evaluate outcome by examining advantages and positive outcome

process is achieved by teaching the client to interrupt their dysfunctional thoughts (which triggers them to go 'off-line') and engage in a sequential thinking process whereby they employ techniques to lessen emotional arousal, generate alternative options and evaluate these options before going back 'on-line' to carry out a solution. Consequential thinking is a particularly powerful tool if the client is able to write down the advantages and disadvantages of potential outcomes, although in some situations this will not be possible. The most important aspect of this technique, however, is that the client learns to introduce an additional feedback loop or circuit in their thinking process, i.e. the 'off-line' stage. In order to facilitate the introduction of the process of CONTROL to the client, the client could be provided with cue cards to carry in their wallet or purse, which can be used to prompt the individual components of the process. This information has been included on the Companion Website in a format that could be used for this purpose. The CONTROL process has also been provided on the Companion Website in a format for use in sessions whereby the client can write out and test methods to interrupt dysfunctional thoughts. With practice the client will be able to successfully engage in this process without prompting.

Double Checks

As self-talk and self-instructional training techniques become a more automatic process; the client should be encouraged to incorporate a system of 'double check-ing' information, assumptions, beliefs, etc. This involves a decision-making process whereby clients can be encouraged to 'double-check' or review decisions by asking themselves the five questions given in Table 7.4.

It is important that the individual keeps in mind the objective or goal to be achieved. For example, a common problem for people with ADHD is that they make impulse purchases. This inclination is not helped by the practice of stores to actively encour-age impulse buying by displaying small relatively cheap 'luxury' products by check-out cash registers. However, many clients have additionally made relatively large purchases on impulse, many of which are costly mistakes. It is not uncommon for ADHD adults to report the presence of numerous unworn unsuitable clothes and/or unused DIY accessories in their homes.

Learning to postpone decision making, albeit briefly, is thus a good 'safety guard' for adults with ADHD. Treatment should focus on getting the person to 'stop and think'. Individuals should go through the 'double-check' system outlined above and

Table 7.4 'Double-check' questions

---

1. Is this what I really want to happen?
2. For how long have I wanted to do this?
3. What will happen if I do this?
4. What will happen if I don't do this?
5. What are the longer-term consequences?

---

it may be helpful for them to have these questions written down on a small card that they carry around in their purse or wallet. (These are presented on the Companion Website in a suitable format.) The client should also determine a management plan in sessions that they then apply 'in vivo', for example, leave the shop without making the purchase; walk about for five minutes and go through the questions on a card, before deciding whether to return to the shop to make the purchase or not. It is important to measure and evaluate outcome in order to demonstrate success. In this case, keeping a record of purchases and 'near purchases' would reinforce success by highlighting potential savings from the latter over a set period of time.

Distraction Techniques

One of the most common times that impulsive behaviour is expressed by people with ADHD is in situations that require a person to wait or queue. An aversion to delay and lack of tolerance causes individuals to feel bored, frustrated and/or irritated. Every minute seems like ten and individuals will often favour the short-term reward of giving up and leaving the queue altogether, or deciding not to wait any longer but demand instant attention instead. The problem with the former scenario is that this means they will not achieve their objective. The problem with the latter scenario is that they are very likely to provoke a confrontation. In such situations, the individual could apply distraction techniques to develop better self-control (by distracting themselves from ruminating over their negative thoughts and feelings about the situation). These techniques can be practised either in advance of difficult situations that are anticipated, or practised in the imagination. Table 7.5 outlines a variety of distraction techniques which may be helpful. This table is also provided in handout form on the Companion Website.

Table 7.5   Distraction techniques

Object focus	Focus on an object and describe it in detail
Person focus	Look at the person in front of you in the queue – imagine what they might be called, what they do for a living, where they live, what sort of character they might play in a film, etc. (Be careful not to stare as this may be perceived as confrontational or provocative)
Sensory awareness	Focus on each sense in turn and make a mental list using sight, hearing, taste, touch and smell
Counting	Complicated counting tasks, such as backwards in 7s, can provide good distraction
Word generation	Try to think of as many animals/countries/towns/girls names/ boys names beginning with each letter of the alphabet.
Fantasies	Imagining where you would rather be – on a beach, in the mountains, swimming…
Winning the lottery	How would you spend a million pounds?
Puzzles	Crosswords, word-searches, etc., can assist with waiting, although attentional problems may lead to distractibility

External Strategies

It may be helpful if the client invites parents, partners and/or a good friend to attend some of the sessions (if appropriate) as this provides an opportunity for techniques to be observed and reinforced outside of the session. Friends or family can support the client by reminding them of techniques learned in the session, rehearsing the techniques and providing cues when appropriate for these to be applied 'in vivo', for example by cueing the client to engage in a process of CONTROL, and/or monitor progress and change in behaviour. Positive feedback by others may also be an important component of a 'reward system' as praise will reinforce successful and/or appropriate behaviour. Inappropriate or unacceptable behaviour should never be reinforced. Exceptions or making allowances, such as 'oh that's Steve, he's a bit crazy', must be avoided. It is very important that feedback is consistent and constructive and the individual does not feel personally criticised.

CONCLUSIONS

Learning to develop better impulse control involves the recognition of situations in which a person is vulnerable to acting without thinking, applying various cognitive behaviour techniques to cope with that situation, obtaining and rewarding successful outcome. Once a dysfunctional thinking process has been interrupted, other more positive or neutral beliefs can be recruited and reviewed to develop a more balanced view of a situation and the potential methods for dealing with it. Situations can be rehearsed in order for the client to become accustomed to utilising self-control techniques and potential outcomes evaluated.

PART III

COMORBID AND ASSOCIATED PROBLEMS

8

SOCIAL RELATIONSHIPS

It is common for people with ADHD to feel they have difficulties in their interpersonal relationships, whether these are friendships, romantic relationships, working relationships or family relationships. Negotiating social relationships can be just as difficult with people they know well, with close acquaintances and with strangers. Most teenagers form and develop social relationships from their immediate environment, such as at school and colleges. However, young people with ADHD tend to make relationships from the local neighbourhood, for example through parental associates, or by 'hanging out' in the street. This perhaps reflects a need for individuals to draw on wider social networks and sometimes make friends with peers who are excluded from school or unemployed (Young et al., 2005a).

Children with ADHD often grow up believing that they are misunderstood or that they are 'different' from others in some way. No matter how much they try, relationships tend to go wrong, and they do not develop as intended or expected. Anger management and impulse control problems may lead people with ADHD to have volatile relationships, which break down easily. In the end, they stop trying and lack the confidence to initiate friendships and more general social behaviour. Self-awareness of their social difficulties causes distress and, at times, a defensive attitude. Sometimes these feelings are taken out on loved ones, such as parents or partners. They may respond in an 'unnatural' way or attempt to overcompensate. For example, often people with ADHD will report feeling that they need to 'play the clown' in social situations in order to mask anxiety or attentional problems. Being the centre of attention reduces the need for them to focus attention on others. They may also feel that by being funny and amusing they will be more attractive to others. However, despite being the 'life and soul' of the party, many people with ADHD report feeling very isolated generally. They find it difficult to form meaningful and lasting relationships because of low self-esteem and a history of being rejected or let down by others. They may find others are intolerant of their ADHD symptoms. Some individuals may be vulnerable to exploitation by others because of their motivation to be liked and ingratiate themselves in a peer group. They may become part of a 'bad crowd', believing that bad friends are better than no friends. Others may be encouraged to engage in antisocial behaviours for the benefit of others, for example, by delivering drugs, or through, theft from shops. Females, in particular, may try to compensate by engaging in promiscuous behaviour in an attempt to develop meaningful relationships. Some people are vulnerable to inappropriate self-disclosure in an attempt to 'fast-track' friendships. Sadly, disruption to social relationships is an experience often learned at a young age.

It is important for individuals with ADHD to recognise that the way they present themselves to others can influence the way others interact with them. This includes the way they talk to others and express themselves (verbal communication), their non-verbal posture and actions (body language), and the general impression they give of themselves (emotional expressions, ADHD features). This involves raising awareness of social behaviour and examining the effect that some or all of these be-haviours have on influencing other people's perceptions. For example, inattention in ADHD may be misinterpreted by another person as the individual lacking interest in what they are saying. An adult with ADHD may be perceived as fickle because they flit from one person to another, or from one topic of conversation to another. This may be perceived by others as lacking sincerity. Due to impulsivity, individuals with ADHD may also be prone to making snap decisions and jumping to conclusions. This means they may take things at face value, based on first impressions and stereo-typied influences. For example, if an acquaintance walks down a corridor and does not acknowledge them, they may immediately assume that that person does not like them and behave in a way which reflects this, thus leading to a self-fulfilled proph-ecy. They may not consider other explanations for the lack of acknowledgement, for example the person being in a hurry and preoccupied with an urgent matter.

The skills covered in this chapter refer to 'appropriate' behaviours as determined by prosocial rules and norms. These should be selected and adapted in a 'pick and mix' fashion according to the needs of the client. However, it is worth noting that different cultures have different social rules. For example, loud and boisterous behaviour may be viewed as a sign of being social/friendly/happy in some cultures, whilst in others it may be viewed as rude and obnoxious. Therefore, it is necessary for the therapist to consider cultural issues. Similarly, the client must think about the social circum-stances and the expectations of those around them as this will guide them as to how they should behave. Different social situations have a range of expectations regard-ing how individuals should present themselves. For example, the social demands of an interview are very different from the requirements of being with a group of friends at a party. It may be more difficult for people with ADHD to be adaptive to the changing social demands of situations and they may rely on a social repertoire that has worked well in one setting, but is totally inadequate or inappropriate for another.

Treatment sessions should be structured to include aspects important for the develop-ment of both micro-skills and macro-skills. Micro-skills include the adoption of specific social skills training techniques to encourage skills such as appropriate eye contact, voice volume and tone, body positioning. Macro-skills encompass more complex interactions, such as giving compliments, constructive feedback, turn-taking and listening skills.

This chapter describes methods to help the therapist facilitate identification of social skills deficits in adults with ADHD and outlines techniques for improvement. Sessions have a skills development focus and include aspects of verbal communication (e.g. conversation and listening skills); non-verbal communication (e.g. body language, gestures and posture); emotion recognition; and the modification and regulation of social behaviour in different social settings (e.g. at work, at parties). The chapter pays particular attention to difficult situations that individuals may face. This includes coping with rejection, as many individuals with ADHD experience rejection frequently more than most. This is encountered early in school when children report feeling socially isolated and recall times when they played alone in the playground, being the last to be picked for team activities, not having anyone to sit next to on school trips and not being invited to tea. These early experiences mean that as they grow up and can exercise greater choice and control over how and with whom they spend their time, they may avoid social situations. However, individuals with ADHD are not naturally reclusive as they are enthusiastic, social and friendly people. Thus, the paradox is that they desire and strive for social acceptance, but feel anxious when in company or in social situations, and uncertain about how to behave. It also means they are unsure and nervous about disclosing their ADHD status in new relationships. This latter issue is one of the most hotly debated issues discussed at our clinic in group treatment sessions.

IDENTIFICATION OF SOCIAL PROBLEMS

Some clients may report 'hundreds' of good friends but on closer questioning these turn out to be casual acquaintances with the other 'friend' probably holding an entirely different perspective of the relationship. It is extremely important to overcome defensiveness and embarrassment about social relationship difficulties as it is clearly difficult for the therapist to help unless the client recognises and acknowledges the problem. Thus, the first step to improving social relationships is through self-evaluation and identification of target areas for treatment that the client may wish to build on to give more confidence and proficiency when interacting with others. Table 8.1 presents a social skills questionnaire completed by a client who lacked confidence socialising in large groups, such as at parties. The questionnaire may be self-rated or completed by friends/family. The aim is for clients to identify their areas of weakness that become treatment targets for skills development. If the client rates a high number of 'I don't know' responses, then it may be helpful for clients to ask family and/or friends to complete a questionnaire. However, people with ADHD may lack insight into their social problems, in which case this is a useful exercise to compare their own perspective with that of others. Discrepancies can be used as a basis for further discussion and treatment to help them develop a more accurate interpretation of intentions and emotions signalled by others.

Table 8.1   Social skills questionnaire

How good are you at...	Never good	Rarely good	Sometimes good	Mostly good	Always good	I don't know
1. Interacting with friends					✓	
2. Interacting with strangers		✓				
3. Talking to strangers at parties	✓					
4. Going to parties		✓				
5. Meeting a friend in the pub				✓		
6. Listening to people				✓		
7. Starting a conversation			✓			
8. Asking questions			✓			
9. Answering questions			✓			
10. Admitting if something has not been understood		✓				
11. Looking at people when talking to them		✓				
12. Not fidgeting			✓			
13. Speaking clearly		✓				
14. Recognising how others are feeling		✓				
15. Explaining to others about your ADHD diagnosis	✓					

VERBAL COMMUNICATION SKILLS

The way we present ourselves verbally (aspects of our voice, speech and conversation) informs others of how pleasant or easy it is to interact with us. Too little or too much talking can cause difficulties in how well others are able to listen to or understand us. People with ADHD often interrupt or butt into other people's conversations. They may switch topics of conversation or 'go off at a tangent' and this can be difficult for the listener to understand or follow what they are saying. People with ADHD often report a feeling of ceaseless mental activity, which can be exhausting for both the individual themselves and the people with whom they communicate. They can be particularly excitable by novelty and high stimulation, and may have a tendency to speak rapidly, too loudly and too much when they get excited. At such times, they may experience a 'flood' of ideas and thoughts, which, although enthusiastically expressed, are hard for the listener to keep up with and follow. The listener may be overwhelmed or bored if they do not share the same interest. Thus it

Table 8.2   Characteristics of ADHD speech and suggestions for improvement

Feature	ADHD characteristic	Perceived by others	Skill development
Rate	Speaking too quickly; others are unable to keep up	Intense personality, a person who is 'hard work'	Slowing down and taking breaths between sentences
Clarity	Mumbling	Lacking in confidence	Speaking clearly, articulating each word
Intonation	Speaking at a high pitch	Overexcitable personality, irrational, histrionic	Lowering the tone of the voice
Fluency	Becoming distracted and going off at a tangent	Disinterested in others and lacking in sincerity	Keeping track and structuring what is being said
Volume	Speaking loudly	Aggressive and intimidating	Quietening to a moderate volume
Amount	Talking too much	Superficial and narcissistic	Being more succinct, learning to summarise information or get to the point more quickly

is important for individuals with ADHD to increase their awareness of times when they are speaking too quickly and making people feel pressured or rushed. At such times, the response of the listener may be to withdraw.

Rate of Speech

Clients may benefit from using self-talk to encourage themselves to 'slow down'. By practising this skill, they can appear calmer, more collected, confident and in control when talking to others. Clients should also learn to attend to physiological changes in the body, for example, as they become excited and aroused about a subject, they may feel hot, or notice their heart beating faster. Identifying physical changes will allow them to consider that they may be speaking too fast or overly passionately about a topic. Rehearsal is another useful method of improving rate and volume of verbal communication and this may be done initially through reading passages or repeating what the therapist says. The client should then move on to role-playing situations and it is especially helpful if this can be recorded and discussed in sessions. By playback of the recording, the client becomes the observer or listener in the interaction and is better able to take an alternative perspective. Performance may be self-rated (or informant-rated) according to each of the variables in Tables 8.2, 8.3 and 8.4 (see, also, the Companion Website).

Table 8.3 Conversational skills

Feature	ADHD characteristic	Skill development
Turn-taking	Not giving the other person the opportunity to talk	Allowing equal talking times
Interruptions	Butting into conversations	Timing speech appropriately, i.e. waiting for others to finish
Multiple questioning	Interrogating other people	Asking questions to stimulate conversation
Latency	Delaying after someone has asked a question	Giving a prompt response
Being relevant	Wandering off the topic and confusing people	Keeping the conversation relevant and to the point
Interesting content	Conversation is motivated by ADHD individual's interest	Making it of interest to other people to maintain their attention
Repairing	Being offended by mistakes, e.g. if other person calls you by the wrong name	Correcting them politely
Overenthusiasm	Dominating the conversation. Not asking questions or opinion of others. Talking about yourself all the time	Develop listening skills. Ask questions

Conversational Skills

People with ADHD have a tendency to dominate and monopolise conversation, with little recognition of turn-taking or the level of interest the listener has in a topic. They also have difficulty attending to what others are saying, drift off, and lose the thread of the conversation. This may lead them to butt in and make inappropriate comments. Conversations may appear very 'one-sided' and the client must learn to balance talking and listening. Putting questions to another person indicates interest in that person, such as in their life and in what they have to say and contribute to a conversation.

Recording sessions and/or role-play interactions are helpful techniques to demonstrate appropriate and inappropriate skills. These should be discussed from the perspective of each person in the dyad. Improvements in some of the common problem areas outlined in Table 8.3 can be rated on a Likert scale (see Companion Website) – either by self-evaluation of progress, self-ratings of observed recordings, or informant-evaluation of progress.

Listening Skills

It is clear from the foregoing that listening skills are a big problem for people with ADHD and a primary target for intervention. Clients may not have adequate listening

Table 8.4 Listening skills

Feature	ADHD characteristic	Skill development
Attending	Not maintaining focus on what is being said	See Chapter 4
Acknowledgement	Seeming not to listen	Responding as though you have heard what has been said, e.g. 'mm', 'yes' or nodding head
Responding	Not noticing a question, or saying 'I don't know'	Acknowledgements, e.g. nodding, saying 'oh right'. Sharing your opinion or giving question-type feedback, e.g. 'did you really?'
Personal self-disclosure	Fear of people prying into their private life	Sharing information can put others at ease
Reflecting	Forgetting what someone has said	Repeating them means that you have more chance of remembering and makes the other person feel that you are listening to what they are saying

skills for two reasons. First, they do not give the person an opportunity to speak, thus appearing uninterested in their point of view. This occurs when they become overly aroused (either by anxiety or enthusiasm) and they are motivated to fill the gap by talking, or their thoughts tumble out in an incoherent jumbled manner. Second, they do not adequately attend to what the person is saying, perhaps because they are distracted by noise or activities going on around them or because they are focusing on what they are going to say next (or perhaps internally distracted by lots of thoughts and ideas springing to mind). Specific listening skills are outlined in Table 8.4 (see the Companion Website for this in a format suitable for use in sessions).

NON-VERBAL COMMUNICATION SKILLS

Non-verbal communication can express thoughts and feelings without the use of spoken language. A great deal of information is conveyed non-verbally. A useful exercise is to watch a television programme with the sound turned down, and ask the client what they think is being said and how the speaker/recipient feels. Ask the client why they have come to their view and guide them to think about subtle indicators by body language. This will increase awareness of how individuals communicate non-verbally and how they are perceived by others. It will also improve their ability to correctly 'read' the non-verbal cues of behaviour.

ADHD symptoms themselves may convey inaccurate information about the individual, for example attentional deficits may be interpreted as lack of interest. A tapping foot may be misinterpreted as impatience and rudeness rather than as a restless symptom of ADHD or anxiety. Impulsive interruptions or gestures may seem discourteous or abrupt by listeners and perceived by the listeners to be insulting.

Non-verbal cues serve a very important function in social interaction and by explaining the rationale of certain non-verbal cues to clients, they will be more inclined to introduce these more frequently in their social interactions.

Making Eye Contact

This informs others they are being listened to and are interesting. Clients should try to look people in the eye intermittently, as avoiding eye contact may be interpreted as them feeling bored with the conversation, lacking interest in the conversation and/or not listening. Staring people straight in the eye without looking away may be interpreted as aggression and/or intimidation.

Facial Expression

Facial expressions inform others of feelings, such as smiling when happy, scowling when dissatisfied. Some facial expressions may evoke undesirable responses from others, for example, failing to smile when greeted may be interpreted as being unfriendly. It may be helpful to look at magazine photographs together and using the list of possible feelings, outlined in Table 8.5, see how well the client and therapist agree about facial expressions and their portrayal of the feelings of the person in the picture. Emotions can be role-played using facial expressions only. Then subsequent introduction of body posture and language in these role-plays will help the client build up a repertoire of social cues. Table 8.5 (available on the Companion Website) provides a suggested 'emotion list' from which the therapist and/or client may select an emotion to act out a situation or guess the emotion portrayed (for example the therapist may role-play eating a meal and act out a feeling of satisfaction and the client has to guess the feeling 'satisfaction').

Table 8.5   Emotions and facial expressions

Positive emotions	Negative emotions
Calm	Disappointed
Happy	Frustrated
Excited	Ashamed
Satisfied	Bored
Relaxed	Restless
Sexy	Tired
Loving	Sad
Proud	Angry
Attentive	Frightened
Important	Confused

Posture

This informs others of attitude, for example slouching may be interpreted as laziness/disinterest. An upright body posture can inform others that attention is being paid. Magazine photographs can also be discussed from this perspective.

Body Movements

Body movements add emphasis to what is being said. However, excessive use may be annoying to others, such as fiddling or fidgeting. Pointing a finger at someone may be perceived as intimidating or provocative. Nodding your head when someone is talking shows that they have been understood, and that you are in agreement with them and supportive.

Physical Proximity

This informs others of familiarity as well as intention. Distance and 'personal space' will be different with different people, for example, you stand closer to a friend than to a stranger. Personal boundaries are usually invaded when a person behaves in an aggressive and provocative manner.

Figure 8.1 summarises some useful 'do's' and 'don'ts' with regard to social communication (see Companion Website for the figure in handout format).

EMOTION RECOGNITION

Misappraisal of social situations may arise from misinterpretation of social cues. These basic social perception skills are crucial for recognising and engaging in appropriate social behaviour. These can be rehearsed in role play and modelling an appropriate response. In particular, people with ADHD may be less able to recognise emotional cues due to poor attentional control. This means they are disadvantaged through an inability to adapt their behaviour appropriately in response to another's mood state. Social information drawing on verbal and non-verbal cues constantly requires reading and integration. It is important that responses can be shifted according to changing cues and emotion recognition is an important aspect of the process. To be able to better understand others, clients with ADHD need to be encouraged to look out for 'clues' or indicators (some of which may be subtle) about how that person may be feeling, i.e. what kind of mood they may be in. Emotional cues can be perceived from several sources and are presented on the Companion Website in a format that can be used as a source for discussion in treatment, including facial expressions, posture, gesture and voice quality (see Table 8.6 below).

Figure 8.1   How to communicate effectively

Table 8.6 Emotion recognition

Facial expression		Happy = eyebrows neutral, eyes screwed up, mouth elongated and corners up
		Sad = eyebrows down, eyes lower, corners of mouth down
		Angry = eyebrows lowered, eyes wide open, mouth tense, nostrils flaring
Posture		Happy = hands in the air, waving, hands outspread – 'open' presentation
		Sad = body bent up, head down, hands to face – 'closed' presentation
		Angry = fist up and clenched, leaning forward
Gestures		Happy = waving arms about, clapping hands together
		Sad = restricted, hands in pocket, shoulders slumped
		Angry = fist shaking, finger wagging, pointing, foot stamping
Voice quality		Happy = loud, high and variable pitch, fast
		Sad = soft, slow, low
		Angry = loud, high, harsh

Facial Expression

The key is to focus on the different movements and patterns of a person's *eyebrows, eyes and mouth* for cues on how someone is feeling. It is possible that some individuals with ADHD mistake a happy face, with eyes slightly scrunched up and teeth showing, for an angry face. They can also miss facial cues due to poor attention and thus not pick up on someone's altered mood state. Examples of typical emotion states include:

Happy = eyebrows neutral, eyes screwed up, mouth elongated and corners up
Sad = eyebrows down, eyes lower, corners of mouth down
Angry = eyebrows lowered, eyes wide open, mouth tense, nostrils flaring

Posture

Positioning of different *parts of the body* produces an overall pattern, which can convey emotions to others. People with ADHD can often forget that their posture can be read, and enter situations with an anxious and tense posture, which can override all their efforts to make appropriate conversation. They can also misinterpret others' postures as aggressive if someone is standing in an assertive way. Examples of postural emotion expressions include:

☺ Happy = hands in the air, waving, hands outspread – 'open' presentation

☹ Sad = body bent up, head down, hands to face – 'closed' presentation

😠 Angry = fist up and clenched, leaning forward

Gestures

The pattern of movements of a person's *hands, arms and shoulders* can reveal a great deal about how they are feeling. Since people with ADHD tend to fidget and make rapid movements, this can be misinterpreted by others as threatening or distracting. Furthermore, fidgeting can make others feel irritable and annoyed, wishing that the person would stop fiddling, and lead them to terminate the conversation early. People with ADHD can also misperceive emotional gestures or find sudden movements unsettling when they have lost attention in a conversation, leading them to react inappropriately. For example:

☺ Happy = waving arms about, clapping hands together

☹ Sad = restricted, hands in pocket, shoulders slumped

😠 Angry = fist shaking, finger wagging, pointing, foot stamping

A fun way of learning to display and read social behaviour and emotions is to role-play feelings in the session with the client. The client and therapist take it in turns to select emotions listed in Table 8.5 and instead of just relying on facial expressions as previously outlined, the speaker and the observer have to guess the emotion expressed drawing also on gestures.

Voice Quality

The pattern of *tone, speed and loudness* of speech usually varies with emotions. Someone's mood state can be clear from the quality of someone's voice without any recognition of the content. If people with ADHD have become distracted, a route back into a conversation can be for them to establish the tone of the topic before interrupting inappropriately, for example, with a cheery flippant remark when someone is explaining how unhappy they have become. Other examples of the way voice quality can express emotions are:

☺ Happy = loud, high and variable pitch, fast

☹ Sad = soft, slow, low

😠 Angry = loud, high, harsh

A useful exercise with clients is to watch video recordings of social behaviour (soap television programmes are particularly good for this purpose) and analyse the emotions presented together. Through positive reinforcement of the client's judgements, they will develop greater confidence about interpreting social situations correctly. It may also be helpful to develop the theme further by pausing the video and discussing the consequences of the behaviour/interaction, in other words, how they think the other person will respond. This will encourage the ADHD person to think about the consequences of behaviour and consider alternative possibilities rather than jumping in with both feet and making snap decisions or incorrect assumptions based on inadequate information.

MODIFICATION AND REGULATION OF SOCIAL BEHAVIOUR IN DIFFERENT SOCIAL SETTINGS

So far social skills training techniques have been discussed, which the individual may employ to improve verbal and non-verbal methods of communication. However, social interaction is a dynamic process, which usually involves rapid shifts in the appraisal of a situation and the ability to respond in an appropriate way. A particular difficulty of individuals with ADHD is self-regulation. This means they may not be good at modifying their behaviour in complex social situations, just as they may have difficulty determining subtle shifts in the attitude of others. Responding to the variable demands in social situations becomes a problem as they develop a set way of behaving, such as being jovial, which works in one setting but may not be portable. It can therefore be helpful to role-play changing social demands and look for shifts in behaviour patterns.

The type of social situations that can be problematic for people with ADHD include making and maintaining friends, talking to members of the opposite sex, not knowing many people in a social situation, maintaining important and/or formal conversations, refusing unreasonable requests, dealing with criticism, apologising and/or admitting mistakes, and disclosure of ADHD status.

Making and Maintaining New Friends

Although some people with ADHD may appear to be the centre of attention and the 'life of the party', they may actually lack many meaningful relationships or true friendships. Recognising that interpersonal relationships require mutual effort and input is a good starting point. However, for people with ADHD, it is much more difficult to maintain friendships in adulthood than childhood. In adulthood there are fewer 'enforced' social opportunities than those experienced in childhood, such as playtimes at school. Thus, children with ADHD at least have a peer set to refer to for reinforcement (both positive and negative) of their social behaviours. Nevertheless making friends and maintaining friends is a long-standing problem. This causes some adults to have a propensity to impulsively curtail relationships early, for example, when someone lets them down or cancels arrangements at the last minute. It is therefore important to reinforce the idea that relationships require persistence and flexibility, but they need to learn to read social situations accurately. Attentional problems may mean that individuals forget arrangements or fail to keep in touch. Time management strategies (see Chapter 5) will help individuals make plans to meet up with friends, remind them of the appointment and remember important dates such as birthdays. Telephone and information technology is becoming increasingly sophisticated in helping us plan and organise our time and individuals should be encouraged to incorporate strategies such as text messages and emails in their daily routine.

Talking to Members of the Opposite/Same Sex

Individuals with ADHD have a natural enthusiasm but this may result in them becoming excited and overeffusive when meeting someone to whom they are attracted. This may be perceived as boisterousness or 'showing off'. Their eagerness may lead them to push limits and seek to escalate intimate relationships at a faster pace than is anticipated or acceptable to the other party. Role-plays designed to encourage the individuals to note the behaviour and body language of the person of interest, and then match and mirror this can be a useful exercise for the individual with ADHD. It teaches them to focus their attention and inhibit impulsive responses and/or assumptions.

Not Knowing Many People in a Social Situation

Whilst most people experience some anxiety about entering social situations in which they do not know anyone or very few people, people with ADHD are often acutely anxious about their ability to cope in such social settings. This is because they have often received negative feedback in the past when they have said the wrong thing, drawn unwanted attention to themselves, felt foolish or perceived disinterest or rejection by others (see Chapter 9 on Anxiety for further information). Social events can be intimidating and the client may be helped by carefully planning and rehearsing appropriate social behaviour beforehand. The therapist should review strategies that the client has found helpful in the past, along with techniques that they have successfully used to resolve problems in previous sessions that may be adapted for this purpose, for example, distracting or challenging negative thoughts. In sessions topical news items that are of interest to the client can be rehearsed in conversation (e.g. from newspapers or magazine articles). The client should be guided to observe the 'rules' of interaction, such as turn-taking, body posture, etc. In preparation for a social event in advance, the client can choose three current news items and/or choose to recount interesting details regarding a recent personal event. This will 'arm' the client with something to talk about if they are worried that they may run out of things to say and/or blurt out something inappropriate and look stupid. Whilst this preparatory work in sessions may increase the client's confidence in social settings, they should be discouraged from talking about themselves all the time or monopolising the conversation. An important technique to teach the client is to get the other person to talk about themselves by encouraging the client to ask questions and *listening* to the answers. The target person should not feel they are under interrogation but that the person they are talking to is really interested in what they have to say. Role-plays in sessions will be helpful for the client to get the balance right.

Maintaining Important and/or Formal Conversations

People with ADHD can sometimes appear overfamiliar due to a lack of formality, poor impulse control and/or anxiety. This is very likely to be perceived by others as them not taking the matter or situation seriously. They may be viewed as superficial, uncaring and/or irresponsible. It is extremely important that individuals respond appropriately to the formality of a situation. For example, when interacting with individuals in authority, such as in a police interview, people with ADHD should be advised that being overly formal is better received than informality. Using titles can increase the sense of respect, so clients should be discouraged from using first names. In the workplace, they need to adopt a level of professionality when interacting with colleagues and line management. The client may need to develop various impression management techniques, such as the manner of addressing authority figures (e.g. the police or occupational managers); to review the use of slang and swear words commonly used by the client for acceptability as some words are unsuitable for formal occasions and may even cause offence; and to pace speech differently as serious and important conversations are more likely to be paced more slowly.

One of the most frequently experienced 'formal settings' is that of the job interview. People with ADHD are often disadvantaged at interview by their ADHD symptoms, which are exacerbated in this situation by anxiety, causing them to become distracted, to not listen fully to questions, give impulsive responses and fidget in their seat. It is particularly important for people with ADHD to prepare well for such events. The first step is to work out a route to the destination with a time plan. Arriving late, hot and flushed is not a good start and will unnecessarily increase anxiety! Practising asking for questions to be repeated or rephrased can be a useful skill to develop and rehearse in therapy. The introduction of anxiety management techniques may also help empower the individual (see Chapter 9 on Anxiety).

Refusing Unreasonable Requests

People with ADHD are often motivated to forge interpersonal relationships by a need to be liked, as they have difficulty getting along with others for any length of time. This means they may at times accede to unreasonable demands as they are eager to please others. Some individuals may be vulnerable to exploitation by others. This may mean they put pressure on themselves to fulfill certain roles or functions to a standard that they cannot achieve and they let down the person they are seeking to ingratiate or impress. They may behave in a way that is hurtful to other people who love them. The client needs to recognise this pattern of interaction, acknowledge it and resolve it. Sessions that focus on social perspective taking (by challenging negative thoughts and assumptions; identifying dysfunctional assumptions about weakness and failure; and acting out different roles of a dyad), rehearsing situations that acknowledge mistakes and apologising for them will prepare the client to put this into practice 'in vivo'. Some individuals may be asked to comply with illegal requests, for example, to steal items, deliver drugs. They may come under peer pressure to take risks and engage in dangerous or reckless behaviour, such as driving a car whilst drunk. Challenging negative thoughts about what it means to be a 'dissenter' may be a useful exercise.

Assertiveness techniques, described in Chapter 10, will be helpful for the client to improve their ability to assert themselves with confidence, reduce feelings of inadequacy and choose a course of prosocial behaviour. The therapist can teach the client to evaluate the feasibility of requests by creating a list of advantages and disadvantages of complying with a request. It is recommended that initially these are set out in writing. Of course, this is not possible *during* a social interaction and strategies for postponing decisions should be role-played with the therapist, for example the client may be helped by rehearsing making a statement such as 'OK, I'll give it some thought and come back to you' or 'I can't talk about this right now as I have to go, but I'll phone you about it later'. Once the client has got used to applying the technique, they should be encouraged to learn to apply it as a cognitive process so they can respond immediately. The written word, however, is powerful and should not be underestimated. Important choices should *always* be made by writing down advantages and disadvantages of options. Strategies for refusing to take on additional responsibilities or demands may be developed by the client and therapist role-playing scenarios in which the client rehearses saying 'no' and refusing to comply with a request.

Dealing with Criticism

People with ADHD are used to being criticised. They have been criticised by their parents at home, by teachers at school, and by youth workers in social settings. To name a few, they may have been labelled obstinate, hyperactive, unruly, disruptive, oppositional, aggressive, rude, disobedient, unhelpful or lazy. Adults are taught that criticism should always be constructive but this technique of delivering criticism is not always applied. Even when it is, what the child or young person with ADHD hears is only the criticism. ADHD children have tried to do better, they have tried to improve and please their mother, teacher, youth worker, neighbours and friends but it never quite comes out right. Their intentions are good but are often not achieved because something gets in the way or distracts them from their course of action. But just because they have always been criticised and are used to it, does not mean that it no longer hurts. As time passes, individuals learn to put up a 'front' that defends them from critical onslaughts. This may be perceived as a lack of interest in the impact of their behaviour or attitude towards family and friends. The more criticism they receive, the more they protect themselves by disregarding it. This means that helpful feedback may be ignored. Clients will know about criticism as they have grown up with it. What they need to learn is the cycle of negativity outlined above, and how a negative attitude – which is their protective mechanism – provides a feedback loop that induces negative behaviour and critical attitudes from others. They need to learn to *listen* to the 'constructive' part of feedback, as this may provide important advice, and to become less hypersensitive to just one part of the message. Specific techniques for dealing with criticism are outlined in Chapter 10 on anger management.

Apologising and/or Admitting Mistakes

Saying sorry is a difficult skill as it involves admitting an error. This makes some people feel exposed. As children, people with ADHD have often felt blamed or held responsible for things for which they should not have been. They have often apologised for misdemeanours they have not fully understood, for example they cannot think through the outcome of a given situation and this has not been explicitly explained to them, such as drawing their attention to the potential dangers of playing with matches, or playing 'chicken' across roads and railway tracks. In adulthood, some individuals are frequently pedantic and argumentative. They are more motivated to explain their point and be 'right', than think about an issue from a different perspective. It is not possible to be right all the time and the ability to compromise is important in negotiating interpersonal relationships. The therapist must help the client to find common ground and compromise, even if this means agreeing that a difference of opinion exists. However, because some adults with ADHD have a defensive attitude and are intolerant of attitudes that are not similar to their own, they may behave in a way that is hurtful towards others. This means they need to recognise this pattern of interaction, acknowledge it and resolve it. Sessions that focus on social perspective taking (e.g. by challenging negative thoughts and assumptions, which may identify dysfunctional assumptions about weakness and failure; and acting out different roles of a dyad), rehearsing situations that acknowledge mistakes and apologising for them will make it easier for the client to put this into practice 'in vivo'. Possibilities will probably present themselves that can be modelled in treatment sessions. For example, if a client forgets to do their homework or arrives late for a session, the therapist should express their own thoughts and feelings, for example, by saying that they felt annoyed that the client had arrived late for the session; that this had made them feel the treatment was a low priority. If a client misses a session the therapist should express deep concern about the welfare of the client, for example, they may have had an accident. It is important that the therapist expresses their concern and/or distress *and* goes on to explicitly outline what the client may have done to reduce this, such as by telephoning to say they are late because of traffic.

Disclosure of ADHD Status

One of the most challenging social issues for people with ADHD is whether to reveal that they have the disorder to acquaintances, colleagues, friends and family. If they decide to make this disclosure, they need to evaluate at what stage in their relationship to do so and/or the most appropriate time. This is a very important issue for adults with ADHD and a great source of anxiety that is hotly debated during the group treatment sessions run at our service. This topic has therefore been expanded in Chapter 6 on problem-solving techniques. Some individuals resolve the issue by telling everyone they meet, irrespective of the anticipated outcome. Other people are very circumspect and do not even tell close members of their family.

A primary concern seems to be related to anxiety about how other people will respond/react to them if they know they have the disorder. They worry about possible stigma or inaccurate understanding about the disorder and believe this will affect them in the future, for example, through discrimination in the workplace. This was a particular concern for one client who worked as a manager in a supermarket and was terrified that his boss would find out that he had ADHD and that he took medication. Although he did well in his job and had been promoted, he thought this would prevent future promotions as he would be perceived as an individual unable to cope with greater managerial responsibility. This client was also very concerned that the staff he managed would discover that he had ADHD, as he believed he would become a source of ridicule and be defined as a 'nut' who needed psychiatric medication. This caused him to feel anxious and stressed as it took effort to 'hide' the disorder. The client felt he could not be himself and he felt isolated, which reinforced childhood feelings of being misunderstood, alone and set apart from others.

Other people with ADHD respond in quite a different way. They act indiscriminately by being overtly open towards people they do not know very well and by giving them a lot of personal information and unnecessary detail about themselves, including their ADHD status. This causes people to feel uncomfortable and withdraw, which is perceived by the individual with ADHD as rejection. Alternatively, other people may take advantage of the person with ADHD by viewing their social insecurities as an opportunity to exploit them (e.g. encouraging them to become involved in antisocial or criminal activities).

ADHD individuals report that they spend a lot of time trying to tease apart 'what is me' and 'what is ADHD', but very few come to any conclusions. This process is most likely to occur following diagnosis and treatment with medication. Indeed, this process may become a source of distress as people feel that their personality is only associated with the ADHD disorder and not 'owned' by them as individuals. Following treatment, this preoccupation seems to become more marked and it is helpful to improve self-awareness by outlining a story or description of 'what I am like as a person'. Of course, this will include characteristics that are generally associated with ADHD, but will also include case-specific characteristics that relate personally to the individual. When completing this task, the client should be encouraged to include as many positive aspects about themselves as possible. They should then imagine that they spend six months on a desert island and consider what other people (friends, family, work colleagues, partners) would miss about them during this period. By increasing an awareness of self – both the positive and negative – the client will be more able to improve the way in which they interact with others. This means they will have greater confidence about how to explain to others about their ADHD condition and how it affects them personally, to whom they give their explanation and when.

Many members of the public have misconceptions about ADHD. The client themselves is often the best source of information about what it is like to have ADHD. Once the client has decided to disclose to someone that they have ADHD, it will be helpful if they can give that person some written information about ADHD and/or explain first-hand ways in which they can be helped and/or changes that can be made to the environment that will optimise performance. For example, by being precise and succinct in instructions and in their interactions, such as by feeding back (constructively) if they are getting overenthusiastic, interrupting others, standing too close, talking too loud, etc. Instead of being expected to remember lots of information, they can write it down, for example having a 'things to do' list, shopping lists, etc. Nevertheless, some people prefer not to disclose their ADHD to anyone and hold their diagnosis as a safely guarded secret. Seeking social support is a constructive coping strategy and if individuals do not wish to 'come out' publicly they may find it helpful to link with ADHD support services. Often these groups have internet chat rooms, which are an important source of practical information and emotional support, and which can be accessed anonymously.

Once they have disclosed that they have ADHD, some people will undoubtedly feel that they are being judged in some way and possibly experience rejection (real or perceived). This perception is likely to be stable in spite of the fact that several factors may have influenced the disclosure. The therapist can help the client examine whether this is an accurate perception and determine the dysfunctional assumptions that arise from (or result from) their thoughts.

CONCLUSIONS

Social relationship difficulties can be the source of many problems associated with ADHD, including anxiety, depression, low self-esteem and substance misuse. Moreover, these comorbid difficulties, in addition to the core symptoms of ADHD themselves, can impact on social behaviour, through inattention, poor impulse control and restlessness or fidgeting. A common theme for individuals with ADHD is feeling isolated and misunderstood, despite paradoxically often seeming gregarious and self-assured in social situations. Clients' confidence in their social abilities can be improved through psychoeducation techniques regarding verbal and non-verbal communication. Several exercises have been suggested in the chapter to help individuals to determine their own social strengths and weaknesses, with strategies to develop both self-awareness and recognition of others' social intent. In particular, the chapter has introduced techniques to improve the ability to recognise emotion by accurately identifying facial expressions, posture and gestures. Social situations are often transitory and variable in nature requiring swift responses and rapid change in social discourse. This is a considerable challenge for individuals who have developed a set of maladaptive social repertoires.

9

ANXIETY

Anxiety is a common condition in the normal population but its prevalence is increased in individuals with ADHD for whom comorbidity rates are reported to be around 25% (e.g. Biederman et al., 1993). Nevertheless, these rates suggest that the majority of adults with ADHD do not have comorbid anxiety problems, but this is not our clinical impression. Studies usually apply stringent cut-offs that place an individual either in or out of a given category, and the studies are helpful in ascertaining the individuals who have a comorbid anxiety problem at a level of functional impairment. However, there are many clients who may not formally meet a category of disorder, yet present with anxiety problems that usually stem from past experience and lack of confidence, and which may hamper their progress in treatment.

It could be argued that comorbidity rates of ADHD and anxiety are artefacts of a similarity between ADHD symptoms and anxiety symptoms (e.g. restlessness, inattention, ceaseless mental energy). However, a 25% overlap has been reported in both community and clinic studies (Anderson, Williams, McGee & Silva, 1987; Biederman, Faraone, Keenan, Steingard & Tsuang, 1991; Millstein, Wilens, Biederman & Spencer, 1997), suggesting that it is unlikely that comorbidity rates simply reflect symptoms being 'counted' twice in about one-quarter of cases. In some cases, anxiety has been reported as a side effect of stimulant medication and, when this appears to occur following treatment, then it may be helpful to recommend a psychiatric review and possible change of medication to non-stimulant treatment.

Predisposing factors for comorbid ADHD and anxiety are reported to be perinatal complications, such as late pregnancy difficulties, problems in delivery and the neonatal period, particularly in those without a familial history of ADHD (Sprich-Buchminster, Biederman, Milberger, Faraone & Lehman, 1993). Thus, many individuals enter the world with a predisposition to develop anxious and dysfunctional coping strategies. These usually become expressed following persistent demoralisation and criticism from others (both real and perceived), causing individuals to become nervous about performing tasks or entering situations. Disadvantages regarding academic attainment, experience of failure in the workplace and difficulty getting along with others can lead adults with ADHD to develop 'anticipatory anxiety' regarding events in which they have previously experienced disappointment and/or failure. In addition to worries about future events and interpersonal performance, people with anxiety and ADHD may also become preoccupied with their past behaviours and/or performance. In such cases, individuals may re-live negative experiences, for example, when they believe they have performed badly; when they believe that people have judged them to be 'below standard' compared with others; and times of embarrassment regarding errors of judgement and/or inappropriate behaviour.

For ADHD adults, anxiety is likely to be expressed in multiple ways. People with ADHD are more likely to suffer from marked self-consciousness or susceptibility to embarrassment or humiliation stemming from childhood (Keller et al., 1992). For most people with ADHD, anxiety starts in school as 'performance anxiety', for example, when they have to stand up in class and read out loud. They make mistakes and miss out words, or even skip whole lines. Their peers tease them or bully them; they get laughed at and called names. In such situations, they may either withdraw or impulsively lash out. Either way, this has negative social consequences and ADHD children begin to lack the ability to interact confidently with their peers. Some children over-compensate by trying to overly please others, or by bullying other children. Others compensate by 'acting the clown'. They may seek friendships at school from children outside of their peer set, in other words children older or younger than themselves, or by preferring the company of adults. With the passing of time, small anxieties become greater anxieties; this is especially exacerbated as they progress through education into young adulthood when greater academic and social demands are encountered. Before they know where they are, the young anxious ADHD child has developed a way of interacting with the world that is based on uncertainty and insecurity. Anxiety becomes generalised, affecting their beliefs and confidence regarding whether they will achieve in just about anything that they attempt to do. This often results in a preoccupation or over-concern about their level of competence to fulfil various roles and domains of function.

In today's society, people are evaluated by success, by the job they do, the house they live in, the car they drive. These icons represent achievement. There are multiple demands to fulfil, requiring an ability to multi-task and take on multiple responsibilities and roles. Mother, father, wife, husband, daughter, son, friend, congregation member, youth leader, mentor, manager, employee, executive: these roles have to be juggled and it can feel as though there are many plates in the air, which have to be kept spinning. Society is fast and busy, and people with ADHD favour speed over accuracy, so when they work at a rapid pace they make errors and they fail.

Feeling anxious makes everything else that one has to think or do much harder. Anxiety affects cognitive processes by affecting appraisal and evaluation of situations, causing a shift of focus internally to exaggerated self-monitoring and self-regulating. Anxiety increases attentional difficulties and impulsivity. It can inhibit the ability to reason in a rational way. Thus ADHD individuals, who already have cognitive vulnerabilities, will become even more vulnerable in an anxiety-provoking situation by performing less competently. For an individual with, say, generalised anxiety disorder, this means that they have a 'double dose' of cognitive impairments due to ADHD symptoms becoming much more pronounced at times when they probably need to focus the most.

This causes a difficulty with the neuropsychological assessment of ADHD symptoms (attention and impulsivity) as clients may become very anxious in the testing environment. In order to evaluate individual differences in strengths and weaknesses, many cognitive tests start with very easy items and become progressively more difficult. This means that an individual will consistently reach a stage when they are unable to answer a question or resolve a problem or puzzle. This highlights their difficulties and the testing procedure may reinforce underlying beliefs that they are 'stupid' and/or remind them of negative school experiences. If individuals become very anxious they are unlikely to do well and give up easily on tasks, causing them not to reach their potential and the tester to underestime their level of performance. Children with comorbid anxiety and ADHD have shown greater impairment on tasks that put demand on short-term or working memory (Pliszka, 1989); that is, tasks that involve both active processing and transient storage of information (Baddeley, 1986). It is possible that anxiety diverts some resources away from processing and storage within the working memory system. However, it has also been suggested that anxiety has a motivational function as it increases arousal, which may in turn improve attentional control. This is likely to occur in tasks that do not require retention of information (i.e. memory processing) but require the individual to inhibit a response, for example, continuous performance or stop tasks. On such tasks, children with ADHD and comorbid anxiety may perform better (Pliszka, Hatch, Borcherding & Rogeness, 1993). Unfortunately, such studies have not been conducted with adults with comorbid ADHD and anxiety.

Anxiety disorders present in several forms; for example, generalised anxiety, social phobia, simple phobia, agoraphobia, panic disorder, obsessive-compulsive disorder and post-traumatic stress disorder. Our clinical impression is that people with ADHD are more likely to have generalised anxiety, but social phobia, panic disorder and obsessive-compulsive disorder have also been reported by our clients at the clinic. Of course, these are not mutually exclusive categories and ADHD adults may have problems associated with one or more of these disorders. Difficulties may be more prominent according to the social, academic or occupational demands and/or their life course at the time. For example, an individual may have generalised anxiety problems and social phobia depending on the presenting situation, and in times of great stress they may additionally experience symptoms of panic.

A generally anxious disposition about everything and everyone they encounter may become more specifically focused as social anxiety for people with ADHD. Feeling different from their peers leads some individuals to compare themselves regularly and unfavourably to others, resulting in their selectively attending to their own perceived negative features and the positive characteristics of others. Some people may frequently require reassurance in social situations, for example 'Did I come across ok? I wasn't tactless, was I?'. They worry that they are being observed by others in social gatherings and become self-conscious and clumsy. Some people try to overcompensate by acting the fool and being the 'life and soul of the party'. In such cases, a target of anxiety treatments should focus not only on reducing anxious cognitions, feelings and behaviour, but also aim to calm down the individual so that they do not respond in an overly excited manner, drawing undue attention to themselves by behaving in a bizarre and/or inappropriate manner (sometimes perceived by others as childish). This is not to dampen down the natural creativity and enthusiasm of people with ADHD but to encourage the individual to behave with more control and maturity.

The increased prevalence of obsessive-compulsive disorder (OCD) in individuals with ADHD may be mediated by its links with Tourette's syndrome (Pauls & Leckman, 1986), since the rate of ADHD is higher among those with Tourette's syndrome and the rate of Tourette's is elevated among those with ADHD. OCD symptoms are also likely to worsen attentional difficulties by diverting functional resources to the obsessive thoughts. However, symptoms that appear to be associated with OCD may be strategies developed by people with ADHD to compensate for an attention deficit by regularly checking for errors or things they may have forgotten. Nevertheless, as a person becomes increasingly anxious, this checking behaviour may become more ritualistic and obsessive. Clients may be embarrassed by their private obsessions and/or compulsions and this may cause them to avoid mentioning them to clinicians particularly during their assessment. They may hope that by having their ADHD treated, their OCD symptoms may also disappear. Over-focusing in an obsessive or perseverative fashion can lead to failure to complete tasks, due to concentrating on a minor aspect of a task to excess. Some individuals with these difficulties may prefer not to do a task at all, rather than risk doing it incorrectly. Exploration and challenging thoughts are useful treatment strategies, in addition to systematic desensitisation to reduce ritualistic checking behaviours.

Due to the overlap between ADHD symptoms and anxiety symptoms, it is important to conduct a thorough and comprehensive assessment of the anxiety-related presenting problem, and ascertain the relationship between the thoughts, beliefs, feelings and behaviours of the individual about their ability to complete a task or perform competently in a situation. As in the usual cognitive behavioural treatment of anxiety, it is important to provide a psychoeducational component, outlining the anxiety model and the relationship between cognitions and behaviour.

ASSESSMENT

The Companion Website provides a questionnaire, the Anxiety Checklist, that will help the therapist determine and classify the type of anxiety-related problems

Table 9.1   Anxiety checklist

In the past week, rate how often you have experienced the following symptoms	Never	Occasionally	Sometimes	Often	Very often	Always
Generalised anxiety						
I have worried about money, e.g. being able to pay bills, debts					✓	
I have worried about not coping at work/school				✓		
I have worried about my health						✓
I have worried that things will go wrong in the future, anticipating disappointment/failure					✓	
I have worried that I am not capable of being a good parent, employee, son/daughter						✓
Social anxiety						
I felt self-consciousness			✓			
I avoided social events, e.g. parties		✓				
I avoided crowds	✓					
I was concerned about performance				✓		
I was worried about meeting new people		✓				
Panic						
I felt constriction in my chest						✓
I felt heart palpitations						✓
I thought I was having a heart attack						✓
I felt dizzy and faint					✓	
I felt the blood rushing around my head				✓		
Obsessive-compulsive disorder						
I felt uncomfortable if the house was not clean and tidy	✓					
I needed to check everything several times before I was confident that it was right		✓				
I had to do things in routines otherwise I worried	✓					
I had intrusive thoughts	✓					
I tended to over-focus		✓				

experienced by the client in the past week. The Anxiety Checklist is presented in Table 9.1 and is designed around themes that are regularly discussed by our clients at the clinic as sources of anxiety (e.g. generalised anxiety, social anxiety, panic, obsessive-compulsive problems), in order to help the client and therapist to identify the subtype of the comorbid presenting problem of anxiety. Table 9.1 gives an example of a completed Anxiety Checklist for a client with generalised anxiety, who had experienced an acute panic attack relating to feeling overwhelmed by pressure to meet a deadline at work. Thus, the Anxiety Checklist provides a helpful guide for identifying whether anxiety problems are general or more specified, and forms a basis for discussion and exploration, in order that the therapist may take an adaptive approach to treatment and conceptually plan and frame treatment, although it should be borne in mind that categories of anxiety are not mutually exclusive.

The Anxiety Checklist provided on the Companion Website deliberately excludes the names of categories (i.e. generalised anxiety disorder; social anxiety; panic disorder; obsessive-compulsive disorder) in order that the client's responses are not biased. These categories are included in Table 9.1 for illustrative purposes only.

TREATMENT

There are two primary differences when treating adults with ADHD and comorbid anxiety compared with treating adults without ADHD who have anxiety:

1. It is important to acknowledge the overlap in anxiety and ADHD symptoms and attempt to disentangle symptoms that are better addressed by the techniques discussed in the sessions to improve attention and reduce impulsivity (e.g. in Chapters 4 and 7).
2. Since ADHD adults have difficulty in delaying gratification, it is important to introduce an immediate reward system to positively reinforce success and achievement on a much more frequent basis than that usually applied.

The CBT model of treatment proposed is adapted from four fundamental stages to the treatment process: psychoeducation about the anxiety model from a cognitive-behavioural perspective; learning to cope with negative thoughts; the development of self-control; and changing behaviour.

Psychoeducation

Psychoeducation is an important part of the treatment process. It is important to explain to the client what happens to them when they become anxious or worried and apply this to the anxiety-provoking experiences of the client. This includes teaching the client how their anxiety impacts on their thoughts, feelings and behaviour, and explaining that there is an interrelationship between these factors. To a certain extent, this also means normalising anxiety as a functional process. Everybody becomes anxious or worried at some point in their lives. It is a normal and healthy reaction. Anxiety or worry usually arises during times of stress or danger. It allows preparation for fight or flight, in other words whether to stand one's ground or whether to run away. People understand that if they were to be put into a cage with tigers then they would feel anxious. Their anxiety would cause them to have a sharpened awareness of pending danger, and prepare to protect themselves. Anxiety causes the body's systems to speed up, which affects emotions, thoughts, feelings and behaviour. Anxiety is dysfunctional if this process is activated when the person is not in the tigers' cage, but when they are going to miss a deadline, because they have not finished a task or because they have to go to their sister's birthday party. This explanation will usually make perfect sense to the client.

The Companion Website contains an Anxiety Chart called 'What happens to you when you become anxious?'. This introduces the client to the core components that develop and maintain anxiety – thoughts, feelings, physical reactions and behaviour. Encouraging the client to complete the chart by separating out these factors will be helpful when the model of anxiety is introduced as the client will be able to theoretically relate the model to their own experience. An example of a completed Anxiety Chart for a person with anxiety about completing a project on time for work is presented in Table 9.2. A blank copy is provided on the Companion Website.

Explaining the cognitive-behavioural model of anxiety, that is, the interrelationship between thoughts, feelings and behaviour in the development and maintenance of anxiety, usually makes complete sense to the client on an intellectual level. For example, explaining that feeling anxious about a missing pending deadline set by their manager at work may influence *thoughts* (e.g. by thinking 'I'm useless, I never get it right. I won't get promoted'), which may lead to *physical reactions* of nervousness

Table 9.2 Anxiety chart: What happens to you when you become anxious?

Thoughts	*Feelings*
• I can't focus • I'm going to lose concentration • There must be something seriously wrong with me if I can't do this • Everyone else will criticise me • I'm going mad • I can't manage this • I'm useless	• I feel frightened • I feel panicky • I feel like I've lost control • I feel that 'fear is going to take over' • I feel on edge and irritable • I feel uncomfortable
Physical reactions	*Behaviour*
• Increased fidgeting • Sweaty palms • Increased heart rate • Going pale as blood rushes to major organs • Stammering • Restless pacing • 'Butterflies' in stomach	• Not wanting to go out • Avoiding social situations • Making excuses not to do things • Using tobacco, alcohol, drugs, comfort foods, etc. to calm nerves • Only going out when someone else is there • Overcompensating by being outgoing and/or overwhelming • Playing the fool or behaving in a reckless manner

(e.g. nausea and dry mouth and *feelings* of irritability and rising panic). This in turn influences *behaviour* (e.g. give up trying, making excuses, avoiding the situation and stay at home).

Apart from learning about the interrelationships between thoughts, feelings and behaviour, the client must also understand how these factors are dynamic and how they work together to cause deterioration in functioning. This becomes a cycle or a downward negative spiral of increasing anxiety, with thoughts, feelings and behaviours fuelling each other as they become more severe. Figure 9.1 gives a visual representation of the 'anxiety spiral' and this is also included on the Companion Website in handout format. Figure 9.2 shows a completed 'thought bubble anxiety spiral', and a blank version of this is on the Companion Website, which may be completed in sessions with the client.

Anxiety can be described as a three-legged table (see Figure 9.3). If one of the legs is knocked out, then the anxiety table will be unstable, fall over and be eliminated. Anxiety exacerbates cognitive deficits and if the client can learn to reduce their anxiety then they are more likely to cope in settings and situations perceived as anxiety-provoking. The 'legs' of the table are thoughts, feelings and behaviour, and these will be discussed in the following sections. The client should be advised that you are going to teach them ways to knock out each of these legs; that is, by using a 'three-pronged attack'.

Coping with Negative Thoughts

Anxiety is associated with unpleasant negative thoughts. These are automatic and flash through the mind in situations that provoke anxiety. For example, if an individual worries about what other people think of them, then they may feel anxious when they are talking to people they wish to impress but do not know very well. This may mean that the individual will alter their behaviour in order to reduce feelings of anxiety, such as by not contributing to the conversation in order to avoid being evaluated by others. Common thoughts expressed by our clients include:

- thinking there must be something seriously wrong with them
- thinking that they are being foolish
- thinking that they are being criticised by others
- thinking that they are not mentally well
- thinking badly about themselves
- putting themselves down
- thinking that they are a failure

Clients need to learn how what they think and believe affects their feelings and behaviour. For example, if a person wakes up hearing a crash in the middle of the night and believes this is a burglar, they may feel frightened and call the police. If they believe it is because they have left a window open and the wind has blown

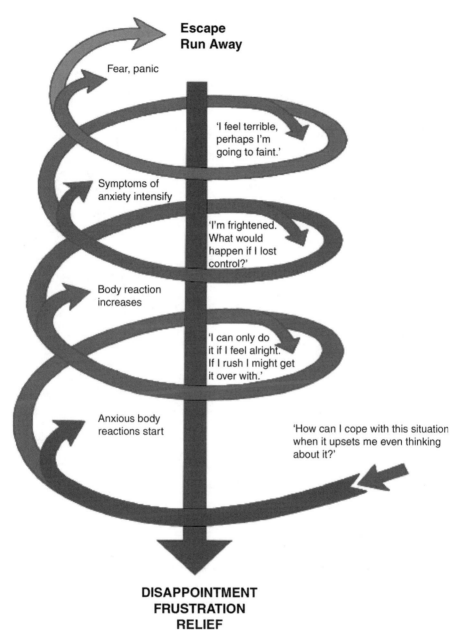

Escape
Run Away

Fear, panic

'I feel terrible, perhaps I'm going to faint.'

Symptoms of anxiety intensify

'I'm frightened. What would happen if I lost control?'

Body reaction increases

'I can only do it if I feel alright. If I rush I might get it over with.'

Anxious body reactions start

'How can I cope with this situation when it upsets me even thinking about it?'

DISAPPOINTMENT
FRUSTRATION
RELIEF

Figure 9.1   Anxiety spiral

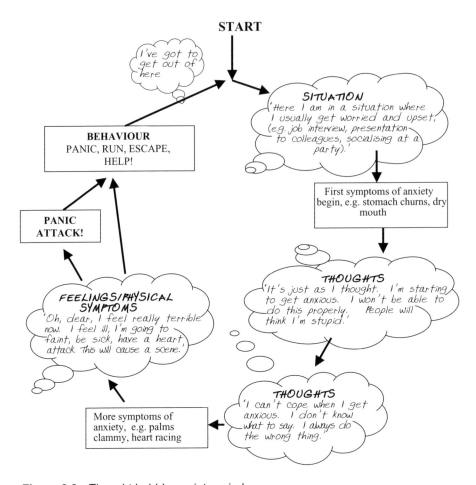

Figure 9.2 Thought bubble anxiety spiral

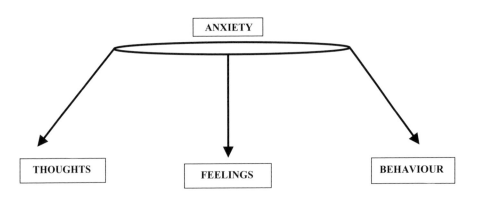

Figure 9.3 The three-legged anxiety table

something over which has created the crash, they may feel less frightened, go and pick up the object and go back to sleep. Thus, different thoughts in the same situation lead one to experience different feelings and to carry out different behaviours.

Negative, anxiety-provoking thoughts are difficult to identify for a number of reasons. They are habitual and flash through everyone's minds without us even realising. They are automatic and occur without effort, and some thoughts further perpetuate anxiety, for example:

- 'I'm going to make a fool of myself' (anticipation)
- 'I can't cope with this anymore' ('I-can't-stand-it-itis')
- 'I can't breathe, I'm choking' (misinterpretation of body reactions)
- 'I've got to get out of here' (thoughts of escape).

A common technique that has been shown to be useful to help clients identify negative thoughts is keeping a 'thought diary'. This is a record of the situation they were in, what was going through their mind at the time and how they were feeling. These feelings can then be rated for how much they believe in them. An example is provided in Table 9.3 for an individual who was having difficulties at work, who is feeling under pressure from their employer to meet a deadline and also having social anxiety regarding socialising with colleagues. A blank version is provided on the Companion Website.

Once the individual has learned to apply cognitive techniques to challenge negative thoughts, the diary can also be used to record the challenges and then re-rate how much they believe in them. Using this method, the client will be able to evaluate the success of their cognitive challenges demonstrated by a weakening in their belief system. Table 9.4 provides an example of negative challenges and a blank version is provided on the Companion Website.

Table 9.3 Example of a thought diary

Time and date	Situation	Feelings	Thoughts	How much do I believe this?
Mon 4th 8.15 am	Getting ready for work	Feeling jittery and a bit sick	I will never survive this week	40%
Mon 4th 10.15 am	Boss asks to see me in his office	Terrified	I'm going to be fired	50%
Tues 5th 6.15 pm	Going to pub with colleagues	Feeling out of place	I've got nothing to say	70%
Wed 6th 12.00 pm	Deadline is end of day	Complete panic	I can't do this. It's all over	50%

Table 9.4 Example of negative challenges in a thought diary

Time and date	Situation	Feelings	Thoughts	How much do I believe this?	Cognitive Challenge	How much do I believe the thought now?
Mon 4th 8.15 am	Getting ready for work	Feeling jittery and a bit sick	I will never survive this week.	40%	I felt like this last Monday and got through the week	20%
Mon 4th 10.15 am	Boss asks to see me in his office	Terrified	I'm going to be fired	50%	I don't know for sure I'll be fired. I was called in last Friday when the boss told me that my last project was now implemented and working very well	20%
Tues 5th 6.15 pm	Going to pub with colleagues	Feeling out of place	I've got nothing to say	70%	Of course I have something to say. I'm not mute....all I have to do is ask people about themselves. I'll ask what they are doing at the weekend	40%
Wed 6th 12.00 pm	Deadline is end of day	Complete panic	I can't do this. It's all over	50%	I can do this. I am catastrophising. I must relax and calm down. I have worked under pressure before	30%

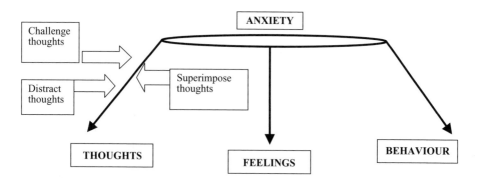

Figure 9.4 The three-legged anxiety table – coping with negative thoughts

Figure 9.4 shows the three techniques that can be used to cope with negative thoughts: (1) challenge negative thoughts – Tuesday 5th; (2) superimpose negative thoughts with more positive thoughts – Monday 4th; and (3) distraction from thinking negative thoughts – Wednesday 6th. In practice, the techniques applied by the client will depend much on the context and their personal preference. Figure 9.4 is included on the Companion Website in handout format.

In sessions, the therapist will need to teach the techniques, rehearse them with the client and determine what works best and when. For example, ruminative thoughts about future performance may be best dealt with by cognitive challenges; superimposing negative thoughts with positive thoughts may be helpful to motivate the client to finish a task; distracting themselves from negative cognitions may be more helpful when coping with social anxiety. Thus, experiencing anxiety is a *process* and techniques will vary in efficacy depending on at what point they are applied in the process. Table 9.5 outlines some suggestions for techniques that are appropriate for the different stages of anxiety.

Table 9.5 Cognitive techniques and the process of anxiety

Onset of anxiety	Identify negative automatic thoughts
	Cognitive challenges
	Identify thinking errors
Midst of anxiety	Coping self-statements
	Self-instructions
	Flashcards
	Distraction techniques
Decreasing anxiety	Self-praise
	Rewards

Challenging negative thoughts

Just as thoughts can increase anxiety and low mood, they can also decrease it. Different thoughts in the same situation lead people to experience different feelings and to carry out different behaviours. This means they can learn to change their behaviour by controlling their thoughts. This is a difficult skill to master. The therapist should begin by explaining to the client that when they feel anxious or distressed, then they are particularly vulnerable to 'thinking errors'. This essentially means that the client is viewing the world through glasses that distort what they see. Common thinking errors for people with ADHD are that an individual catastrophises and/or jumps to conclusions ('it's all completely hopeless, it will never work and I'll be ruined, no one will ever speak to me again'). Table 9.6 describes some common thinking errors and these are also provided on the Companion Website in Table 9.6a, together with an exercise in a format that can be given to the client and used as a basis of discussion. The most likely categories for thinking errors are provided in Table 9.6, but note that thinking-error categories are not mutually exclusive. Usually, by using these materials and by looking back over the thinking errors they have recorded in their thought diaries, the client will recognise the thinking errors common to them.

In order to break the cycle, the client must learn to change old ways of thinking, this means challenging their thoughts and assumptions. Assumptions are 'if … then …' statements such as 'if I don't do this report in time for the meeting, then I'm a complete failure'.

One way of encouraging the client to challenge their thinking is to get them to imagine that they are a skilled lawyer who is 'cross-examining' a thought. For example, they could ask themselves the following questions:

1. What evidence do I have for thinking in this way?
2. What is the evidence that I can't cope? Think of times when I have successfully coped in the past.
3. Am I overestimating the likelihood of this event happening?
4. What is the worst that could happen?
5. What can I do about it?

These questions are presented in a 'handout' format on the Companion Website (see Table 9.6b), together with the example of cognitive challenges that can be applied to challenge common negative thoughts shown in Table 9.7.

Fortunately, the ADHD personality seems to be predisposed to engage in a 'cognitive challenge process' as ADHD individuals have a tendency to positively reappraise stressful situations (Young, 2005). This means they seek to cognitively reframe situations and are receptive to thinking about their problems in a different way. This characteristic probably leads people with ADHD to face disappointments with resilience, and gives them the determination to try again.

Table 9.6 Thinking errors

Thinking errors	Definition
All or nothing	The client sees everything in black and white and cannot appreciate that there is any middle ground or 'grey areas', e.g. 'I can never concentrate on anything'
Overgeneralising	The client draws a general conclusion on the basis of a single event. They often assume that something will always happen even when this has occurred on one occasion, e.g. 'I will mess it up next time'
Catastrophising	Exaggerating or overestimating the likelihood of events can be due to catastrophising. The client often thinks that whatever can go wrong will go wrong, e.g. 'Because I didn't pay the gas bill on time, I'm going to be evicted'
Personalising	The client blames themselves for anything unpleasant. They believe everything people do or say is a reaction to them. They assume everything is their fault, e.g. 'She had left the room because I upset her'
Negative focus	Positive aspects of a situation are ignored or misinterpreted, so that the client tends to look on the 'dark side' and is pessimistic, e.g. 'At my work appraisal, they said I needed to learn a new skill, so I must be useless at my job'
Jumping to conclusions	The client has an automatic negative interpretation of events, even in absence of facts. This may mean that they tend to predict the future or read minds, when there is little evidence to support these predictions, e.g. 'I have been too slow, she thinks I cannot possibly do this'
Shoulds and oughts	The client believes they are failing to meet standards or expectations, without considering whether they are reasonable or realistic. They may believe they should always get everything right, e.g. 'I ought to always be on time'

Exercise

What are the following thinking errors?
1. 'I did that badly. What's the point in doing it again?'
   Answer: *Negative focus*
2. 'I upset her by blurting out gossip. I'm a terrible person.'
   Answer: *Overgeneralising*
3. 'I should have finished everything I planned to do.'
   Answer: *Shoulds and oughts*
4. 'Everything goes wrong.'
   Answer: *Catastrophising*

A second way of inducing clients to challenge thoughts is to teach them to take the perspective of another person. Social-perspective taking is a very helpful technique, as often clients expect something of themselves that they would not expect from others. The therapist should invite the client to imagine that a friend came to them

Table 9.7   Examples of negative thoughts and challenges

Negative thoughts	Examples of cognitive challenges
I am just not good enough	I am not perfect. Like everybody I am good at some things and not so good at others
What is the point in trying?	If I don't try, I won't know. Trying in itself will broaden my experience and skill. Nobody is expecting me to do it perfectly
What if I make a mistake – it would be awful	Everybody makes mistakes. It is good to make mistakes because that is the best way to learn
I have nothing to say – I'm boring	I have opinions, thoughts and feelings. I like reading and going out. Perhaps I need to improve my ability to express myself. I can practice
Nobody likes me	There are people who like me. I have had better relationships in the past and will in the future
Everybody else has a better time than I do – they're happy	I don't know this for a fact. Just because they seem busier doesn't mean they are more satisfied
It would be best if I stayed away from people, because I'm no good at relationships	If I stay away I don't give myself a chance. I'll probably be all right if I can just relax
I might break down emotionally in front of people and feel ridiculous	I have good reason to be upset. People are a lot more understanding than I think. It would not be the end of the world. What is wrong with showing emotion?
I'm hopeless at everything. I'll never sort myself out like this	Just take one step at a time. Totally condemning myself is nonsense. I've overcome more difficult problems than this

with the same problem, what would they tell them? Would they view it in the same way, in other words, believing that there are no solutions and they will fail? Techniques that look at alternative interpretations or alternative outcomes may be helpful, for example replacing thoughts like 'I can't cope' with 'This is difficult, but I can manage if I take it a step at a time'.

Superimposing positive thoughts

A problem for people with ADHD is that they often do not have a plethora of 'successful' experiences to counterbalance life's disappointments. The scales seem tipped against them and every idea they have or every project they start comes to nothing – usually because they do not stick to it and either become distracted by something else that takes their interest and so give up when it becomes more difficult, or it takes longer than anticipated to finish. This means that their negative automatic thoughts may have some evidence base, and this possibility makes it a more difficult task for the individual to challenge these as 'thinking errors'. One solution is to superimpose negative thoughts and assumptions with positive cognitions and beliefs, such as making positive and motivating self-statements.

Identifying and challenging negative thoughts is helpful to reduce the onset and escalation of anxiety. However, once a person is involved in a full blown anxiety attack, it is not always easy for them to apply cognitive challenges. In such cases, the client should be encouraged to list the cognitive challenges that have been particularly appropriate and efficacious and put these on small 'flashcards' and keep them in a wallet or purse. Then, if they become very anxious and cannot engage themselves in an alternative thinking process, all they have to remember is to look at the card, which will jolt them into engaging in the process.

Superimposing positive thoughts rather than challenging negative thoughts may be a more helpful technique for patients with ADHD because of their resilience and tendency not to give up. This may be a more 'natural' way for them to cope with negative thoughts, to identify them and immediately superimpose them with a more positive and motivating thought. For example, if the client thinks 'I can't cope with this situation, I am going to lose control', they replace the thought with 'I can cope, I am in control of this situation'.

'Coping self-talk' in the form of making positive self-statements and giving self-instructions to talk themselves through the anxiety process may be helpful strategies that are more accessible to the individual at a stage of advanced anxiety. However, replacing negative thoughts is also a process that takes practice and patience but with time it becomes easier as it becomes as automatic as 'old ways' of thinking.

There are many different positive statements that will help to replace negative thoughts. Some examples are shown in Table 9.8 (and are also on the Companion Website in 'wallet-size' handout form) and the client should note that some cue them to apply other techniques that will help 'knock out' other legs of the anxiety table.

Distraction from negative thoughts

A further cognitive technique that may be applied once the individual is in the midst of feeling acutely anxious, is that of cognitive distractions. This involves teaching the client to distract themselves from thinking negative and damaging thoughts that

Table 9.8 Positive self-statements

Anxiety is not harmful, it is a normal human response
I can cope with these feelings
There is no need to escape or avoid this situation, if I just carry on the anxiety will subside
As I relax the anxiety will begin to ease off
Relax, breathe gently and try to let go of the tension

serve to increase anxiety. To work, this must involve a specific and directed active process, such as making themselves engage in mental arithmetic or counting items, as opposed to reading a newspaper and relaxing. In the latter case, the client is likely to find that they have read a whole article but not taken in any of the information. The active process could be either cognitive or physical. If clients distract themselves from negative thinking by engaging in periods of intense physical activity (e.g. running, team sports), this is likely to not only reduce the negative thinking but relieve feelings of agitation and restlessness.

Controlling Feelings of Anxiety

To understand how anxiety affects us, it is necessary to be aware of the physical sensations it can produce. These include breathlessness, nausea, palpitations, dizziness, sweating and chest pains. Individuals with extreme anxiety may believe, or have believed in the past, that there is something seriously wrong with their health. For example, they may have interpreted these physical symptoms or signs as coronary heart failure and believe that they are having a heart attack. Common feelings expressed by our clients with ADHD include:

- feeling frightened and panicky
- feeling they are losing control
- feeling confused and having difficulty focusing on a task or on thoughts
- 'flooding' of thoughts and ideas
- ceaseless mental energy
- feeling irritable and/or aggressive
- feeling on edge and nervous
- feeling unhappy
- feeling over-emotional and labile

Figure 9.5 can be used to discuss common physical expressions of anxiety. A copy can be found on the Companion Website and it may be helpful for the client to determine the somatic symptoms they have experienced in the past and self-regulate for these early signs of anxiety. If the client can identify early indicators of anxiety, they can apply techniques to manage the anxiety at an early stage and increase the likelihood of them managing it successfully.

Body reactions to anxiety may be understood as a physical health problem and not recognised to be symptoms of an underlying psychological problem or disorder. In cases of acute anxiety leading to panic attacks, some clients are even admitted to hospital Accident and Emergency departments, as they believe they are having a heart attack. This may especially occur if the clients' problems are associated with work, stress and performance anxiety (such as not completing tasks on time and missing deadlines). Body reactions to anxiety, or somatic symptoms, are relatively easy to identify and clients should be taught to use somatic indicators to trigger the use of treatment options outlined in the chapter.

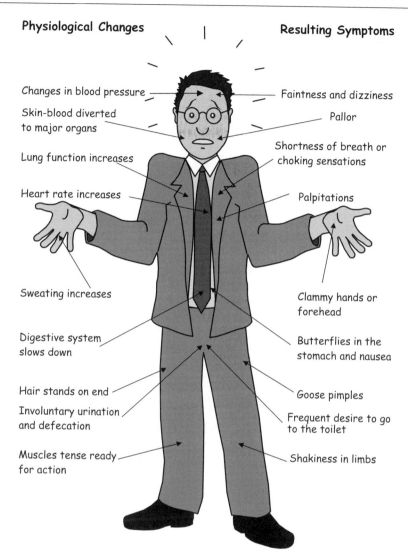

Physiological Changes

Changes in blood pressure

Skin-blood diverted to major organs

Lung function increases

Heart rate increases

Sweating increases

Digestive system slows down

Hair stands on end

Involuntary urination and defecation

Muscles tense ready for action

Resulting Symptoms

Faintness and dizziness

Pallor

Shortness of breath or choking sensations

Palpitations

Clammy hands or forehead

Butterflies in the stomach and nausea

Goose pimples

Frequent desire to go to the toilet

Shakiness in limbs

Figure 9.5 Bodily reactions to anxiety

A method of coping with feelings of panic is presented in Table 9.9 and this is also included on the Companion Website.

A paradoxical treatment technique will help the client learn that they can control feelings of panic by applying techniques to effectively cope with it. This is achieved by inducing hyperventilation by asking the client to take rapid and shallow breaths. After a few minutes the client will go red in the face, feel hot and flushed, their heart

Table 9.9   Ten rules for coping with panic

1. Feelings of panic are an exaggeration of the body's normal reaction to stress.
2. They are unpleasant but not harmful or dangerous. Nothing worse will happen.
3. Stop adding to panic with frightening thoughts about what is going to happen.
4. Concentrate on what is *really* happening in your body, not what you fear might happen.
5. Wait for the fear to pass. Accept it. Do not fight it or run away from it.
6. Notice that once you stop adding to thinking frightening thoughts, the fear starts to fade by itself.
7. The whole point of practice is to learn how to cope with fear – without avoiding it. This is an opportunity to make progress.
8. Think about the progress you have made. You are moving towards success.
9. When you feel better, start to plan what to do next.
10. When you are ready, start off slowly in an easy and relaxed way. There is no need for effort or hurry.

will start to palpitate and they will feel dizzy and sweaty. The client will recognise these symptoms as those they have experienced when in a state of panic. Once this has been achieved, it is necessary to reverse the state by asking the client to breath slowly and deeply, to close their eyes and concentrate on their breathing, and on the air filling their lungs. The therapist can then introduce calming self-talk by asking the client to say to themselves coping self-statements identified in earlier sessions; pointing out that if they can induce this state at will, then they can reduce it. This is an important lesson in self-control.

It is useful for the client to understand how their body feels when they are relaxed as this means they will better develop an awareness of signs of tension (i.e. that will flag up changes in the body and indicate the presence of a problem that they can treat). When in a relaxed state the body has a slow heart rate, breathing is slow and regular, and tension in the muscles is reduced. The client should feel calm and their body should feel 'quiet' as if they are gently ticking over rather than feeling revved up and active.

Controlling 'feelings' of anxiety means knocking out a 'leg' of the table using techniques that induce a sense of calm and wellbeing (see Figure 9.6). This can be achieved by relaxation techniques to reduce muscle tension and create a state of physical calmness. When clients learn to manage and reduce unpleasant feelings, they can adapt the method to help them feel more relaxed in anxiety-provoking situations. This means they will feel more in control. However, relaxation techniques need to be practised until they become an automatic process. In order to do this, the client needs to rehearse the relaxation techniques morning and evening, preferably before they go to bed. It will help if they find a quiet space somewhere, perhaps after a warm bath, to maximise the efficacy of the techniques. Gradually, the techniques should be introduced in a briefer form at times during the day when the client feels anxious, if appropriate.

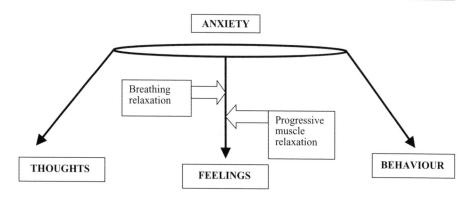

Figure 9.6   The three-legged table – controlling feelings of anxiety

There are different types of relaxation exercise, the most helpful for people with ADHD being breathing exercises and progressive muscle relaxation techniques. Both should be introduced to the client in sessions and practised at home. Initially, practice should be set as specific homework tasks but the aim is for clients to make relaxation a part of their daily routine. Progressive muscle relaxation techniques are particularly good for 'preventative' relaxation, to help the client induce and maintain a relaxed frame of mind. They are also helpfully applied in anxiety provoking situations, but may be inappropriate in some situations, such as staff meetings, as colleagues may wonder what they are doing. Breathing exercises can be more subtly applied in such situations and just as effective. The exercises outlined in this chapter are also presented on the Companion Website for the client to practise outside of sessions.

Relaxation strategies: breathing exercises

These are exercises that can help correct breathing. In order to learn the technique, breathing practice needs to be initially when the client feels reasonably calm and relaxed. Table 9.10 provides two exercises that can be used in treatment sessions and a handout of instructions is provided on the Companion Website for the client to use at home.

The client should be reminded that they are learning a new skill – at first it may feel strange, or difficult, to breathe like this. It is important to continue on with practising, despite these feelings, as gradually they will notice an improvement.

Relaxation strategies: progressive muscle relaxation

Alternatively, the therapist can teach the client to induce a state of total relaxation of mind and body by teaching progressive muscle relaxation techniques, breathing

Table 9.10   Breathing exercises

Exercise 1

1. Begin by lying quietly on your back, rest one hand on your stomach and the other on your upper chest.
2. Breathe in gently. Tell yourself to breathe IN and OUT, gently and rhythmically, aiming for 7–8 breaths per minute. Do not hold your breath for too long, just slowly IN and OUT. Concentrate on the breath filling your lungs and being expelled from them.
3. As you breathe out imagine your body relaxing, deeper and deeper. With each exhalation, your body is sinking further and further into a state of relaxation.
4. Practice this for 10 minutes everyday and, once it feels easy and natural to breathe like this, move to Exercise 2.

Exercise 2

1. Repeat the steps from Exercise 1, but this time in a sitting position, progressing to standing up. For at least 3 weeks, try to be aware of your breathing at different times during the day, and correct it if necessary.

techniques and mental imagery. Research has shown that, aside from treating anxiety, progressive muscle relaxation techniques reduce tension, headaches and migraine; lower blood pressure; relieve chronic pain and/or menstrual symptoms; and improve sleep (Roth & Fonagy, 1996).

Table 9.11 (also on the Companion Website) outlines the instructions for progressive muscle relaxation techniques, which require the individual to engage in a set of deep muscle relaxation procedures, whilst working through the body's muscle sets. The exercise can be completed in 10 minutes or extended for much longer.

The client can lie on a bed or sit up in a straight-backed chair. The client may start with the breathing techniques learned in the exercises in Table 9.10, proceed to the Progressive Muscle Relaxation procedure, then incorporate mental relaxation whereby the client is asked to focus mentally on different parts of the body and imagine them 'unwinding'. They can also use relaxing visual imagery, for example, by asking them to imagine being in a tranquil place. Clients often imagine being on a beautiful beach with white sand and palm trees. The client should be cued to see the colours, hear the wind rustling, and see the sun glinting on the water.

It can be difficult at first for clients to practise the progressive muscle relaxation technique on their own as they have to learn a sequence and remember what to do. This means they stop and start as they have to read the instructions, which interferes with the relaxation process. It is extremely helpful to make up a tape of the process in the session for the client to keep and use at home. This also means that it can be adapted to be personally appropriate, for example by introducing at the end visual imagery that has been previously successfully discussed and used in sessions.

Table 9.11   Progressive muscle relaxation

For each exercise, tense your muscles for about 5–7 seconds. Relax for about 30 seconds between each exercise. Practise in a quiet, comfortable environment whilst sitting on a chair.

1. Make a tight fist with your right hand, then relax.
2. Push your right elbow down into the chair while at the same time pulling your arm towards your chest. Then relax.
3. Make a fist with your left hand, then relax.
4. Push your left elbow down into the chair while at the same time pulling your arm towards your chest. Then relax.
5. Arch your eyebrows as high as you can, then relax.
6. Squint your eyes tightly together while wrinkling your nose, then relax it.
7. Clench your teeth together tightly while pulling back the corners of your mouth in an exaggerated smile. Then relax.
8. With your teeth separated, press your lips together while pressing your tongue against the roof of your mouth. Then relax.
9. Pull your chin down as if trying to touch it against your chest while at the same time pulling your head backwards. Then relax.
10. After taking a deep breath, press your shoulder blades together behind you as if you are trying to touch them together. Then relax.
11. After taking a deep breath, make the muscles of your stomach hard and taut (or make the muscles of your stomach tense by pulling them in or pushing them out). Then relax.
12. Press your heels into the ground, then relax.
13. Point your toes towards your head, then relax.
14. Point your feet downwards, while turning your feet inwards and curling your toes under. Then relax.

Changing Behaviour

The third leg of the table involves treating behavioural avoidance (see Figure 9.7). Avoidance is probably the greatest and most negative behavioural implication of anxiety. When we feel anxious we tend to want to avoid what we perceive as psychological threats. Our natural response is to avoid unpleasant situations.

Common feelings expressed by our clients include:

- not wanting to go out
- becoming distracted, losing concentration and going off task
- avoiding social situations
- making excuses not to do things
- not sticking up for themselves when they should

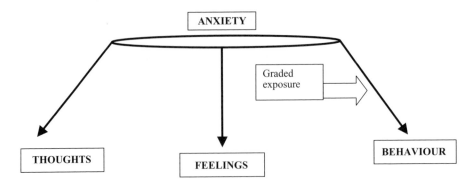

Figure 9.7 The three-legged table – changing behaviour

- calming their nerves by smoking, drinking alcohol, taking drugs, eating
- only going out when they have someone with them
- overexertion, overactive, 'high' energy
- preoccupation with thoughts, ideas and worries

On a short-term basis avoidance is useful as it is the quickest way for clients to protect themselves and alleviate their anxiety. Of course this is not functional, however, as it means that the client learns to cope by avoiding anxiety-provoking situations, such as going to work, going to parties, finishing important tasks. This adds to the vicious cycle of negative thoughts (see anxiety spiral in Figure 9.1). Unfortunately, this becomes habitual and the client engages in a process of avoidance whenever they face anxiety-provoking situations, for example by thinking: 'I can't do this; the last time I tried I couldn't do this and I gave up; I gave up and didn't do it.' Thus this cognitive and behavioural process is self-reinforcing. Instead of facing and resolving the problem, the client avoids it and makes the problem more daunting to face the next time. Fear leads to avoidance, which leads to more fear, which leads to more avoidance, and so on. The more the client avoids a situation the worse their anxiety becomes. It becomes gradually worse and the anxiety generalises to other situations and circumstances. In time, avoidance behaviour reduces confidence and self-esteem. Confidence is developed through achievement and an important part of managing anxiety is to start facing up to fears and to stop avoiding anxiety-provoking situations. This is a very difficult thing to do, so it is important that the client (and the therapist) does not expect too much too soon, or that unrealistic targets are set. The taste of success will involve the therapist structuring a hierarchical schedule of graded exposure to tasks that have become challenging to the client. Using this approach, the client will learn to plan a gradual way to develop confidence and reintroduce activities they have avoided and achieve them. Table 9.12 describes a set of incremental stages for the client to follow to build confidence and achieve tasks. This is also included on the Companion Website, in a format to hand out to clients.

Table 9.12 Overcoming avoidance and increasing confidence

1. Make a *list* of situations you avoid because of your feelings.
2. *Grade* each situation, using a scale of 0–10 (0 = no anxiety, 10 = severe anxiety).
3. List situations in *order* of difficulty – put the least difficult at the top of the list and the most difficult at the bottom.
4. *Take action* – tackle each situation in turn – begin with the least difficult first. Reward yourself for completing each stage. Succeeding in completing the least difficult task on the list will make it easier to face our other fears and help prepare us for the most difficult.
5. Keep a *record* of what happens and the progress you make, i.e. use a diary.
6. *Evaluate* how you coped. Congratulate yourself on what you have achieved. Initially, the most important aspect of success will be just 'facing' the situations. Gradually, you will be able to evaluate how well you are managing your feelings.
7. *Reward* with small rewards for each step and a greater reward for completion of the programme.
8. *Practise* – KEEP PRACTISING – the more you tackle a situation, the better it will become and the more confident you will grow. By tackling our fears a step at a time, we can gradually regain confidence and self-esteem.
Remember: do *not* expect too much too soon and be *proud* of whatever progress you do make!

For example, one of our clients, Sarah, was extremely anxious about going to the local shops as she had previously absent-mindedly walked out of a supermarket with her basket without paying. The security guards had stopped her and brought her for questioning, but not pressed charges. Sarah was anxious that people would recognise her and that they would embarrass her by escorting her off the premises. The situations she avoided were as shown in Table 9.13. Sarah then rated how difficult she thought each situation would be on a scale from 0–10 (see Table 9.14). These situations were then rearranged into the order of difficulty as shown in Table 9.15. (Blank versions of Tables 9.13, 9.14 and 9.15 are found on the Companion Website.)

Table 9.13 Example of stage 1: list of situations avoided

1. Make a list *of things you avoid because of your feelings*

Entering the supermarket past the security guards
Going around the supermarket with a basket
Paying the cashier
Going to the nearby newsagents
Going to the hairdressers next door
Walking down the road past the supermarket
Going to the chemists

Table 9.14   Example of stage 2: grading of list of situations avoided (0–10)

2. Grade *each situation, using a scale of* 0–10 (0 = *no anxiety,* 10 = *severe anxiety*)	
Entering the supermarket past the security guards (because they may grab me, or I might impulsively draw attention to myself)	10
Going around the supermarket with a basket (because they could spot me at any moment)	8
Paying the cashier (because she may recognise me from before and tell other people in the queue)	9
Going to the nearby newsagents (because they may have been told about me, but I know the shopkeeper from the past)	2
Going to the hairdressers next door (because staff from the supermarket may look at me through the window)	6
Walking down the road past the supermarket (because the security guards may think I've stolen something and follow me)	5
Going to the chemists (because they may have a 'wanted' list of potential shoplifters	3

Sarah and the therapist then planned each step of the hierarchy. They carefully discussed what could go wrong and how to plan around these difficulties. They role-played what Sarah might say to the security guards if they did stop her. She decided that after each stage she would reward herself by having a bar of chocolate from the newsagents, new shampoo from the chemists, a haircut, and a CD from the supermarket. ADHD clients are particularly motivated to work towards

Table 9.15   Example of stage 3: ranking list of situations avoided (0–10) and choosing rewards

3. List situations in order of difficulty – put the least difficult at the top of the list and the most difficult at the bottom	Grade	Reward
Going to the nearby newsagents	2	chocolate
Going to the chemists	3	shampoo
Walking down the road past the supermarket	5	magazine
Going to the hairdressers next door	6	haircut
Going around the supermarket with a basket	8	long bath
Paying the cashier	9	cake
Entering the supermarket past the security guards	10	CD

short-term rewards and, although anxiety reduction in itself can be an internal reward, motivation can be enhanced using external rewards in addition. Sarah found that she quickly progressed and once she had walked towards the supermarket, her anxiety was not as severe as she had anticipated.

CONCLUSIONS

Many individuals with ADHD present with some anxiety difficulties, even if they do not meet full criteria for a formal diagnosis. Anxiety can develop in many different ways in line with the main categories of disorder including panic disorder, social anxiety, generalised anxiety and obsessive-compulsive disorder. However, there may be some overlap in the phenomenology of anxiety symptoms and the core symptoms of ADHD, including feelings of restlessness and distractibility. It is therefore important to carefully assess for such difficulties and intervene as necessary using appropriate techniques. A CBT approach has been provided, which begins with psychoeducation regarding the disorder using the 'three-legged table analogy'. In order to tackle anxiety difficulties, the client and therapist can decide to 'knock out' each of the legs (thoughts, feelings, behaviours) in turn. Thoughts are addressed using challenging strategies and superimposing positive thoughts, or developing distraction techniques. Feelings of anxiety can be modified using a range of relaxation techniques and avoidance behaviours can benefit from using graded exposure. Whilst these strategies are well known to therapists who work with individuals with anxiety disorders, it is recommended that they are adapted in order to accommodate the idiosyncrasies of people with ADHD and the examples through the chapter illustrate how this may be achieved.

10

FRUSTRATION AND ANGER

Everyone gets angry sometimes, it is a natural emotion. Most people feel angry when they perceive injustice or feel that their rights have been violated. However, due to their symptoms, ADHD individuals may be predisposed to have a labile or explosive temperament. They may have developed maladaptive ways of coping with feelings of anger and express their feelings inappropriately. For people with ADHD, feelings of anger are more likely to be expressed outwardly than inwardly suppressed, due to their inability to inhibit a response and having a low threshold for irritability and boredom. However, denial of anger and suppression of angry feelings is not uncommon, especially in compliant individuals. When anger is expressed overtly, other people are likely to perceive this as a negative character trait, and view the person with ADHD as being unpredictable and, in some cases, frightening and dangerous. Tolerating frustration can be difficult for adults with ADHD and, in particular, they may become annoyed by their lack of achievement and failure to finish tasks. They also get annoyed when friends and family, meaning well, start telling them what to do, organise their life for them, complain about lack of commitment and motivation. This is perceived as 'nagging'. A cycle of negativity is commonly reported between parents (especially mothers) and children with ADHD (Barkley, 1998). Research into ADHD in childhood has shown that negative interactions are a reciprocal process, with ADHD affecting the manner in which the child responds with their parents and, hence, the way in which parents behave towards their children. These learned cycles of responding may well extend to adult close friendships and intimate relationships. People with ADHD may feel resentment towards other people who do not have ADHD and seem to have fewer difficulties and more successes in life. Thus, anger management difficulties can lead to numerous negative outcomes, including breakdown in relationships, termination of employment and involvement with the police.

It is not uncommon for people with ADHD to have accumulated feelings of anger towards psychiatric services. This is frequently expressed, following diagnosis and treatment, as dissatisfaction towards services for not meeting their needs.

People with ADHD usually have a long history of presenting to both child and adult psychiatric services (Young et al., 2003). They can feel that their problems have not been taken seriously by clinicians and also may feel misunderstood by partners and friends. Some individuals may have a propensity to blame others for not identifying the disorder in the first place and for not providing appropriate support. They may feel frustrated and angry if they believe that they have been previously misdiagnosed or labelled, or misjudged. It will not be easy for individuals with this type of experience to make a collaborative therapeutic alliance. Clinicians need to be aware of these issues and may need to sensitively introduce anger management techniques early in therapy, in order to develop rapport and gain trust.

This chapter explains how, in order to understand their anger, people with ADHD require education regarding its function as a normal emotion. Reasons for becoming angry are reviewed for people with ADHD, such as the need for immediate gratification. Dysfunctional ways of managing anger common in ADHD are discussed, including having too much control and having too little control. Treatment involves psychoeducation regarding the stages of anger, according to a cognitive behavioural model, focusing in particular on observing the physical signs of anger, such as body language. Ways of dealing with insults and criticisms are addressed, including recognising the difference, appreciating constructive criticism and learning to accept criticism. Similarly, developing assertive expression in the context of poor impulse control and recognising the difference between aggressive behaviour and assertive behaviour are covered.

WHAT IS ANGER?

Anger is a normal emotion experienced by everyone. The aim of treatment is, therefore, not to 'stop' anger, but to improve control and use anger adaptively. It can be particularly functional in motivating change. Anger is a healthy emotion that allows individuals to problem solve, to impose control and/or to change a situation. A second aspect of anger is that it has an alerting function. It signals potential danger and protects us from harm. It is not uncommon for anger to be triggered in situations where other emotions are activated, such as fear or sadness. Situations where there is a perceived or actual injustice are likely to trigger anger and it represents an adaptive response to dissatisfaction with the environment. Anger management is about identifying effective ways for the client to show their discontent without causing distress to themselves or others.

There are obviously many reasons why people become angry. The following themes seem to be shared by many people with ADHD:

1. *Taking things personally.* People with ADHD may be more likely to interpret any threat or blame as a personal slight, and become angry as a result of these feelings.

For example, if a family member has mislaid a belonging and asks whether other family members have seen it or used it, it might be presumed that they are being accused of something (borrowing it without asking, stealing the item). Because the person feels they are being (unjustifiably) blamed for something, they feel upset and angry.

2. *Losing control of a situation.* If someone with ADHD feels like they are not succeeding, they tend to give up easily. It is better to give up than plough on with a task, struggle alone with it and feel hopeless and stupid. Their inability to achieve may make them feel angry inside and giving up can compound frustration. It may also make other people annoyed with them and lead to confrontation. Feeling angry in such circumstances has a secondary function, as high emotional arousal is distracting. The individual focuses on their feelings, enabling them to escape or avoid the situation, such as the unfinished task.

3. *Feeling threatened.* Situations where an individual is being directly challenged or threatened can be difficult to manage for anyone. However, individuals with ADHD are more likely to catastrophise and overreact to criticism, even when this is constructive, due to their own learned sense of underachievement. If they do find themselves in a provocative situation when someone is bullying or intimidating them, they may act on impulse and respond aggressively without thinking about the consequences of their behaviour.

4. *Learned behaviour.* People with ADHD may have developed maladaptive response patterns over years for dealing with frustration and anger. It may be that they are not particularly angry, but behave in a way that suggests they are, because this is how they have learnt to behave. This will give the wrong impression of themselves to other people who perceive them as being 'prickly' and overly sensitive.

5. *Poor impulse control.* This core symptom can itself lead to an escalation of feelings of anger, whereby an individual may be more likely to act out on their anger either in an aggressive or violent way towards others, themselves or property. Thus, individuals are less likely to walk away from a severe verbal confrontation and more likely to respond with physical aggression. This may mean that they enter into many fights or destroy property. Some people may harm themselves impulsively and abuse substances.

6. *Feeling resentful.* Angry feelings may build up slowly, especially if the person feels that they are being judged or stigmatised by others. They may feel resentful of people who seem to have an easier life.

7. *Frustration with attentional difficulties.* It can be obvious when assessing someone with ADHD when they become annoyed with themselves for not being able to focus or sustain attention. They become angry when they make mistakes, forget instructions, or are slow to finish. Adults with ADHD have some insight into their difficulties, and they are often observed to give an incorrect response and then later correct themselves realising their mistake. However, anger can often compound attentional problems as individuals can become distracted by their angry thoughts and lose focus on the task in hand.

8. *Frustration with lack of services.* Adults with ADHD are likely to have experienced professionals who either dismiss the ADHD disorder as a clinically valid condition and/or who lack knowledge and understanding about the disorder and their special needs. This occurs in educational services, social services and health services. Often an individual has presented at multiple child and adult services and told their story over and over and over again. This can be a hurdle for a therapist to overcome and it may hinder progress.

9. *Anger as an avoidance mechanism to processing other emotions.* Feelings of anger may be expressed in preference to the expression of other emotions, such as distress and crying, in order to avoid the expression of what may be perceived as 'weaker' emotions. This is more likely to occur in males with ADHD.

10. *Stimuli for excitement.* Moving into a state of high arousal provides a state of high stimulus and, for some individuals, excitement. This may satisfy a desire to seek 'thrills' or 'sensation' and relieve feelings of boredom and monotony. For example, an aggressive argument with lots of drama, shouting, gesticulating, slamming doors and banging may provide an individual with an adrenalin rush. This acts as a positive reinforcement of the behaviour, with the adrenalin rush as the 'reward', thus increasing the likelihood of them repeating the behaviour. Anger can also be rewarding if the angry individual is able to avoid an uncomfortable or boring situation.

11. *A source of communication.* Many individuals have poor social skills and have difficulty communicating and expressing their thoughts and feelings. This may be due to a specific skills deficit and/or to a lack of confidence that has been negatively reinforced by a history of dysfunctional social interactions with peers and siblings. Individuals may respond with anger for two reasons, they may misappraise social situations and the intentions of others and respond aggressively (social skills deficit) and/or feel resentment and anger towards people with whom they interact in a world they perceive as harsh and biased against them.

12. *Establishment of superiority.* People with ADHD commonly develop low self-esteem, and this is probably established early in childhood. It becomes reinforced as they become older and failures become a self-fulfilling prophecy. In order to defend against feelings of vulnerability and cover them up, they may use aggression to convey the message, 'I'm better than you'. As the therapist will demonstrate to the individual in treatment, simply engaging in this process (even when feelings of anger are not actually present) will have an iatrogenic effect, resulting in 'real' feelings of anger.

13. *Road Rage.* There are many opportunities on our roads for drivers to build up feelings of anger: people driving too fast, too slow, cutting in, not indicating, not giving way, abruptly stopping, people flashing their lights, tooting their horns or making gestures. Driving on busy roads and at peak times is stressful at the best of times and everyone knows what it is like to be in a driving situation when they feel irritated and frustrated. However, there is an increased risk that people with ADHD will experience road rage and also have road traffic accidents (Barkley 2002; Barkley, Guevremont, Anastropoulos, DePaul & Shelton, 1993).

These occur because individuals drive without due care and attention; they may become distracted from their driving by talking to passengers or by scenery; they may drive recklessly. An alternative or additional possibility is that they may become wound up in situations that are common to most people, but where they are unable to self-regulate their feelings of anger and inhibit their responses. People with ADHD are therefore more likely to act in a provocative way on the roads, to jump out of their cars at traffic lights and threaten other drivers.

DYSFUNCTIONAL MANAGEMENT OF ANGER

There are two main ways in which people with ADHD may manage their anger maladaptively. The first is through escalation of a situation by an overt expression of aggression, and the second is by suppression of angry feelings.

Escalation

A person with a predisposition to 'escalation' is likely to explicitly express their feelings of anger and to make them well known to the people around them. Their threshold for revealing annoyance is much lower and they may be labile in temperament. Such individuals are likely to have many impulsive symptoms and their poor behavioural control and emotional regulation difficulties result in them being more likely to respond explosively in stressful and challenging situations. For example, if someone pushes in front of them in a queue, or if someone makes a personal remark, they are unlikely to inhibit the impulse to respond aggressively, by either making a remark verbally or through non-verbal expression (e.g. glaring or standing too close to the person). This can lead to either a subtle escalation of aggression or a rapid escalation, depending on the severity of response, the manner in which their feelings have been communicated and the response of the recipient. Some people feel a sense of power and excitement by deliberately provoking and intimidating other people, which has a reinforcing property by providing an immediate reward. It may also be functional, as it means the individual avoids displaying other emotions, such as their own fear and anxiety, and/or revealing feelings of vulnerability. There may also be positive reinforcement from the recipient backing down. Although this will often be a 'normal' way to respond to overt threat and provocation, the behaviour will be perceived as submissive and reinforce the fact that they can achieve this status through intimidation. Of course, the longer-term impact of this type of behaviour includes losing friendships, destroying objects, physical injury and criminal convictions.

Suppression

This second type of anger is latent or suppressed anger. When asked, individuals often deny feeling angry and do not admit to situations that have made them feel angry or upset. A person with a predisposition to suppress angry feelings expresses these covertly. They may be passive-aggressive and compliant. They may appear to be coping well with stressful situations but all the time feelings of resentment and anger are slowly building up inside. In such cases, individuals may suddenly explode, the trigger being seemingly innocent. Their response will be commented on by others as being disproportionate to the trigger. They may have a reputation for being unpredictable, a 'loose cannon'. Another way in which suppressed anger may be released is in circumstances when this has developed from experiences that remain unresolved, in other words that were not dealt with at the time. Anger that has been 'bottled up' may surface in seemingly unrelated situations, which remind the individual of the earlier experience and their feelings about it. It is thus misplaced anger and can cause great confusion to those around. In order to avoid the inappropriate expression of this type of anger, the client needs to develop an understanding about difficult situations they have experienced in their lives, relate these to their feelings and learn to express these appropriately and move on.

TREATMENT OF ANGER

When treating individuals with anger problems, the therapist needs to begin with psychoeducation. This is achieved within a CBT framework of teaching the individual to recognise feelings of anger, physiological responses, thoughts and behaviours. They are then encouraged to determine the stages of anger, the antecedents, behaviours and consequences of anger. Specific anger management techniques are then introduced, such as distraction techniques, self-talk and relaxation methods.

Psychoeducation

Recognition of Anger: As with other emotions, anger can be conceptualised as having three components that are interrelated: physical, cognitive and behavioural (see Figure 10.1 – also presented on the Companion Website in handout format). Clients should think about the last time they were angry. What parts of the body do they notice change when they are angry? Such changes are caused by increased adrenaline as the body is preparing to face a threat. After the physical symptoms, negative or aggressive thoughts occur automatically and can serve to increase the physical anger symptoms. Negative thoughts may be 'I hate this man', 'I'm going to kill him'. Negative thoughts can lead to angry behaviour, such as clenching fists, squaring up, invading personal space, which may similarly go unnoticed by the individual. Videoing role-plays may be a useful method to identify those behaviours that need to be the focus of intervention. However, negative thoughts occur so rapidly when anger takes hold, so it may mean that only identification of feelings or initial 'gut reactions' are possible. It is important to encourage the client, in such circumstances, to *stop* and not respond automatically. Simply encouraging the individual to stop and take stock; that is, to pause before acting, may be sufficient to prevent an escalation of anger into violence.

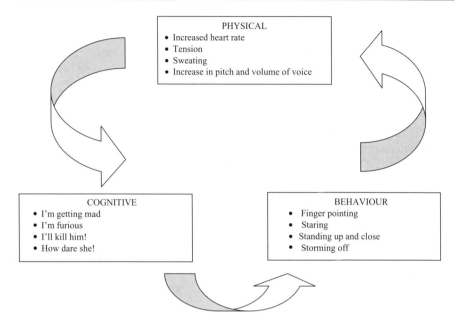

Figure 10.1   Physical, cognitive and behavioural aspects of anger

Body Language

Clients should be encouraged to pay particular attention to body language as it is an important and primary indicator of anger. They should be asked to identify the physical signs of anger, both their own non-verbal signs and those of other people. If individuals are more aware of their own anger signs, they are also more likely to be able to identify them in others. Early identification of a situation getting out of control means that the individual has a longer period to think rationally before high levels of arousal cause them to react. It also provides the opportunity to introduce techniques to de-escalate the situation and walk away.

Three Stages of Anger Expression

Anger can be understood as a three-stage 'ABC' process, involving antecedents to anger, behaviour during anger (anger expression) and consequences of anger. It is therefore useful to establish a personal pattern or 'blueprint' for the expression of inappropriate anger. For some people, rather than beginning with an examination of the client's own anger behaviour, it may be useful and less threatening for them to think about someone else whose anger they have recently observed, even a confrontation on television. Following this example, they may then feel more comfortable talking about the stages of their own anger.

1. Antecedents

There are often common triggers of anger, for example, being with certain people in certain places (e.g. family celebrations, job appraisals). Clients should be encouraged to look for commonalities in situations when they become angry. They may then develop strategies for either avoiding such situations or preparing themselves so that they can handle the situation more appropriately. This can include preparing self-statements to keep themselves calm, practising in advance what they could say, and also to determine which compromises they may be willing to make to diffuse the situation.

For example, Jonathan, who was an IT programmer, found that he was more likely to become angry when he was concentrating and people interrupted him at work. He had a tendency to be verbally aggressive to people who disturbed him. He often regretted being rude to colleagues immediately afterwards and spent the rest of the day worrying about what they thought of him and not managing to get his work done. Using problem-solving techniques, Jonathan developed a system to convey to colleagues that he could not be disturbed between certain times and was willing to act as a help-desk at certain times of day.

2. Behaviour

The client should learn to recognise their physical signs of anger and develop ways of behaving and thinking that allow them to display their anger appropriately, so that they do not lose control. Techniques are discussed in the anger management section to address these issues.

For example, Jonathan learned that an early indicator for him feeling angry was him becoming impatient with the approaches and requests of others. Usually he was very helpful and would take great care to explain a concept. He also noticed that his face started to feel hot and in his mind he started to swear at the people asking for help. By identifying these indicators, Jonathan was able to recognise his own signature early warning signs of anger and avoid losing control and upsetting colleagues.

3. Consequences

The client should be asked to reflect on how they behaved and coped with that situation. They can examine both the positive and negative consequences. For example, Maria often became angry in traffic jams and, instead of waiting, she responded by driving down side-roads even though she often did not know where they led. This relieved her feelings of tension but she often ended up lost and took longer to arrive at her destination. Having recorded the time it took her to make both journeys (taking alternative options) over a two-week period, Maria discovered that she actually saved more time, and arrived at her destination earlier by sticking to the main route (despite the traffic jams) than driving around back roads to avoid the queues. Sessions focused on establishing methods to support Maria in sticking to the main route, by making the back routes less attractive and finding a way to fill the time whilst she was in the traffic jam (see techniques below).

ANGER MANAGEMENT

It is not easy to learn to manage feelings of anger, especially when individuals are predisposed to impulsive responding, which may mean they make angry outbursts and cannot inhibit themselves from lashing out. It is one thing to practise anger management techniques within sessions and quite another to apply them when the individual feels upset and aroused. Together with a labile temperament, this can mean that individuals have considerable difficulty with anger control.

It is important to move away from the perception that it is the person that is the problem. It is a problem that the person has. Just as an individual can make themselves feel angry inside by thinking about situations and people who have caused them to become upset in the past, it is possible for them to make themselves feel less angry. It is a matter of anger control and the client needs to feel empowered. It may be helpful to actually demonstrate this process in sessions by asking the client to 're-live' and describe an anger-provoking scenario in an imaginal mode. When they start to feel angry, the client should be reminded that they have induced themselves to feel this way and that their physical and cognitive state has undergone some fundamental changes. The therapist should point out changes in the body, ask the client to write down what is happening to them (sweating palms, palpitating heart, face feeling hot). The client should also be asked to look in a mirror and describe what they see (red face, furrowed brow).

If the client cannot re-live a previous anger-provoking experience or can do so without inducing physical symptoms of anger, then it may be helpful to role-play a scenario that is meaningful and relevant to the client. For example, Mick was getting very upset with his housemate, Dave, who kept 'borrowing' his CD player to take to work each day. Dave was a car mechanic and his CD player at work had broken. On three occasions Dave had brought the CD player back with flat batteries. Mick had put in new batteries but Dave had made no comment. Mick liked to play his CD player when he had a bath in the evening as he found it helped him to relax and unwind. Mick was getting fed up with Dave's lack of consideration and he was feeling taken for granted. In the treatment session, the therapist role-played Dave and Mick role-played himself becoming extremely angry with Dave and said that he was inconsiderate and taking advantage of him. The therapist escalated the situation by shouting at Mick saying he was being petty and childish. The therapist used negative body language, by moving closer to Mick and pointing a finger at him. The therapist then called 'stop' and de-escalated the situation, reminding Mick that this was a role-play and they were in the treatment room. Mick was asked to say how he felt, to think about his own physiological arousal, look in the mirror and describe what he saw. He was asked to describe his thoughts, what was going on in his mind whilst the therapist had shouted back at him. He was asked to think about what he might have done next. Fight or flee? Mick was then taken through a relaxation technique that included him imagining a calming, positive image (see Chapter 9).

By engaging in the above process, clients can learn to recognise how they behave when they feel angry and how others perceive their body language. The role-play or 're-living experience' can be gone through frame by frame, like watching a video, and together the client and therapist can discuss the escalating and de-escalating factors. For example, how did the client feel when the therapist pointed their finger at them or stood closer to them? Did they notice facial and/or body changes in the therapist? Most important, however, is the lesson that if anger is induced deliberately within a session, then this is under the control of the client and therefore they also have the ability to control anger outside of the session.

Of course, the therapist needs to exercise their judgement before role-playing anger provoking scenarios within sessions. In some cases it may be wise to agree with the client that a third party is present who can help by participating in the role-play.

Once the client has learned to recognise their feelings of anger, and that they may exercise control over them, the next stage is to teach the client strategies to help them manage their feelings of anger. There are three basic techniques that may be useful, distraction, self-talk and relaxation.

Distraction Techniques

Recognising that a situation is escalating and becoming confrontational usually means that the individual has an option. The option is to decide to opt out of the situation by walking away. If the individual notices early signs of feeling angry then they can distract themselves by walking away from the situation and occupy themselves in a neutral, unrelated task. However, it does not help to walk away from the situation and then wind themselves up by talking about it to lots of people. Seeking social support and asking friends for a perspective is different from complaining to lots of people and directing their anger at them.

For example, if Mick had got into an argument and felt like hitting Dave but instead walked away, this would be a positive response. However, if he then went and telephoned all his friends to rant and rave about Dave, he would have continued to become increasingly more angry and distressed. He may have returned and acted provocatively towards Dave and escalated the situation further. Furthermore, he may have upset and irritated his friends. So when walking away, attention should be diverted to a positive or neutral occupation and not one that will fuel the person's anger further or direct it at someone else. This is destructive so the therapist must encourage the individual to be constructive when they have extracted themselves from an anger-provoking situation.

This is especially so in cases when the individual is unable to walk away from situations indefinitely, for example, in work situations. By distancing themselves from the situation, the physiological response will decrease, and the person will be able to think more rationally and calmly. The client can then figure out a constructive response and return to the situation in a better frame of mind.

Self-talk

Calming self-talk is about developing the ability to speak positively to ourselves. This is achieved by collaboratively devising phrases the client may say to themselves to help control feelings of anger. Some people call this 'positive thinking', but it is not just about thinking, it is a deliberate cognitive rehearsal of positive self-statements that encourage and reaffirm the individual's ability to get through the situation and exercise self-control. For each person, the statements will differ, but they may include statements such as 'I can get through this', 'I am not going to show this person that I am feeling angry', 'I am better than this'. This can be practised by re-living the angry experience or by role-playing it again and including calming self-talk statements.

When working in an imaginal mode, the client should imagine a past situation that made them feel angry and then imagine themselves talking to themselves and encouraging themselves to cope better with the situation and have a more positive ending. Self-talk statements may be cued by the therapist, but these should be rehearsed several times until the client is able to apply the technique themselves. It is very important that the client can imagine themselves coping constructively with the situation, that they imagine controlling their feelings and determining a positive outcome.

Relaxation

Relaxation techniques are described in detail in Chapter 9 on anxiety management. However, these techniques are very helpful for coping with feelings of anger as well as anxiety because the techniques make the individual focus on themselves. This not only means that clients learn to regulate their breathing, but that they concentrate on their internal state and distance themselves from external concerns. This has been practised for many years by cultures throughout the world in the form of meditation. Of course, relaxation techniques are not very helpful in controlling a reactive response to a provocative situation by a person with a labile temperament in vivo. However, these techniques will help people control feelings of resentment that are bubbling under the surface and are being suppressed. By applying the breathing exercises, inducing a state of relaxation, alternating tension and relaxation in the muscles of the body and engaging in calming mental imagery, the client can manage 'generalised' feelings of anger, such as the feelings of resentment and dissatisfaction that are present most of the time, but of which they are unsure why or where they come from. The client should be encouraged to practice relaxation techniques regularly and make them part of their daily/weekly routine as appropriate. It may be helpful for the client to listen to music that they find particularly calming.

Reframing the Situation

The client will begin to learn to recognise feelings of anger in themselves and in others, to identify signs or triggers that indicate a conflict or confrontation is getting out of control, to impose self-control and manage feelings of arousal and de-escalate the situation. A further way of managing conflict and confrontation is to teach the client to reduce the likelihood that a difficult situation will become threatening or anger-provoking. This involves cognitively reframing a situation and controlling the situation by improving the client's mode of communication. This means teaching the individual to apply the "ADHD Formula" (see Table 10.1).

A = Address the situation

First the client should state the facts of the situation. This is a simple appraisal of the problem stated briefly and neutrally.

> Mick: 'Dave, this evening when you returned my CD player the batteries were flat.'

D = Describe your feelings

Then the client describes how they are feeling. Again this should be factual and the client must only use 'I feel...' statements rather than 'You made me feel...' statements, which can antagonise and attribute blame.

Table 10.1   The ADHD formula

Address the situation
Describe your feelings
Help them understand
Define the consequence

Mick: 'I feel really annoyed about this.'

H = Help them understand

The third stage is for the client to help the (target) person understand how they can make the situation better. Again this is explicitly stated by providing a statement of the desired resolution or outcome. This is a very important stage, which is often left out of a process of resolution. It is very important to let the target person know what it is that is wanted, they are not 'mind readers'.

Mick: 'In future I'd appreciate it if you would replace the batteries if they are flat.'

D = Define the consequence

Finally, the client defines the consequence if the specified behaviour is not met. Again this must be pragmatic and explicit.

Mick: 'If you can't agree to this, then in future I won't lend you my CD player.'

By adopting the ADHD Formula, Dave learned how Mick was feeling, why he was feeling that way, how he could put it right and what would happen if he did not agree. It was simply but explicitly explained. Dave had been very busy at work. He had been very distracted and he had meant to replace the batteries but had forgotten. Dave realised that he had not thought about the situation from Mick's perspective or realised that his behaviour had caused ill-feeling. The position was clear and the situation was defused immediately by Dave apologising and replacing the batteries. Mick had the outcome he wanted, he did not get worked up inside with building feelings of resentment and thoughts that he was being taken advantage of by his friend.

DEALING WITH INSULTS AND CRITICISMS

People with ADHD are particularly susceptible to anger following both insults and criticisms. This is possibly because they are more likely to be defensive due to having received an accumulation of critical comments and feedback throughout their lives from parents, teachers, friends and siblings, and now wish to protect their self-esteem. They are also more likely to respond impulsively to criticism, without hearing the person out or fully understanding what has been said, without accurately appraising the intention of the other person and assuming malicious intent. However, if clients are able to learn to distinguish between insults and criticisms, they are more likely to be able to respond appropriately to both types of statements.

Insults

An insult is something that is said to cause annoyance whereas a criticism is something that is said about a behaviour. Insults are inherently designed to make a person feel bad and/or angry. In order to prepare themselves to deal with insults, a client should be asked to think of the worst insult someone has said to them that has made them feel angry. They should then be asked the following questions:

- Why did this make you feel bad? (e.g. was it threatening to your family, masculinity, etc.)
- What was it about the statement that made you upset? (e.g. was it just what was said or did the way it was said cause you to be upset also? Was it the tone of their voice? Was it the demeanour of the person? Was it a specific body language?)
- Why do you think the person said these things?

By taking a step back and being able to review an insult as a comment that was intended to cause upset, the client may be able to learn why it made them angry. However, more importantly, they will be able to speculate on the motivation behind the comment. This will help them to relocate the anger by understanding that this is an emotion within the other person that is being expressed inappropriately and unkindly towards others. This should help clients to see insults for what they are and reject them as a truth about themselves. If a client feels they are being insulted, self-talk in the form of calming statements will help them control their feelings and control the impulse to retort aggressively, for example:

- 'I know he is only saying this to wind me up, I won't give him the pleasure.'
- 'What do they know about my family anyway.'
- 'I know that I am a decent person and that is what matters.'

Criticisms

Criticism is a necessary, and often helpful, form of feedback. It is much better if it is presented constructively. However, it can be difficult for anyone to receive, particularly if it is framed negatively. An example of the difference between positive or constructive criticism and negative criticism is given below:

- Negative: This report is really difficult to read. It is so badly structured that it is difficult to follow what you are trying to say. You need to learn how to structure reports or you will never get a point across.
- Constructive: You have written a good report and made lots of interesting points. It could be made better if you structure it more by using sub-headings. Here is an example of a really good report, which may be helpful for you to look at.

Due to their history of failure and/or underachieving their potential, people with ADHD are used to being criticised and, unfortunately, insulted. This means that they find it hard to acknowledge any feedback that is not positive and rewarding because they are hypersensitive to perceived criticism, even when this is sensitively and constructively delivered. As soon as they perceive any form of critical feedback, they feel threatened and become irritated and/or angry. This means they are likely to disregard what is being said or interpret the comment in an overgeneralised way (usually without hearing it out or discussing the comment fully and appropriately). They may respond to the perceived criticism in one of two ways, both of which involve an overreaction; (1) by becoming angry and aggressive; or (2) by feeling excessively hurt and wounded. In the latter case, they may internalise the comment as a unchangeable personality flaw, rather than perceiving the criticism as relating to a behaviour that is changeable.

In order to deal with criticism, individuals with ADHD need to *listen* carefully to what is said to them and make sure they fully understand the problem. Attentional deficits may lead them to miss the earlier part of a statement and just catch the end, which means that their reaction will be based on missing information, an inaccurate appraisal and interpretation of what has been said. Constructive criticism usually begins with a positive comment, and, if this has been missed, they are more likely to interpret the comment or feedback as a personal insult. By now, the client should be self-monitoring their feelings and be more able to recognise signs of increasing feelings of irritability and anger that may trigger an inappropriate response and/or one they may regret. Thus, they will recognise 'warning signs' within themselves when they receive feedback, comments and/or criticism that they perceive as negative and/or threatening. At this point they need to be able to interrupt the anger process by asking the person to explain the problem or comment in more detail. Through repetition of the comment they may hear parts that had been previously missed. They will understand the issue better and establish the person's motivation. It may, of course, become clear that the person was being insulting, but equally it may become clear that the person who is criticising the client is trying to help by offering good advice and constructive feedback. Encourage the client to accept this gracefully even if they are still slightly aroused and irritated. Role-play in sessions both giving constructive criticism to others (avoiding rapid, blunt delivery of information) and receiving it. It is important to role-play both aspects because the giving and receiving of constructive criticism is a mutual process, and understanding the dynamics of both sides will help the individual to accept critical feedback better in future.

Giving constructive criticism means phrasing a criticism in a helpful way, through emphasising positive aspects, offering suggestions for improvements and supporting the individual to make changes or corrections. Receiving constructive criticism appropriately means making a statement of acknowledgement of the problem, clarifying any misunderstandings, outlining a shared understanding and plan for resolving the issue. In some circumstances, it may be appropriate to apologise for errors or mistakes.

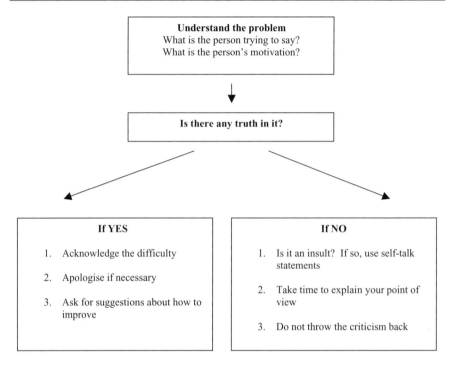

Figure 10.2   Dealing with insults and criticisms

Figure 10.2 is a flow chart which summarises ways of dealing with insults and criticisms. This is presented on the Companion Website in handout format.

ASSERTIVENESS

It has already been suggested that some people with ADHD suppress their anger. They can be compliant in demeanour and go along with the wishes and/or suggestions of others that they would normally reject. This means that over time they may build up strong feelings of resentment inside. For these individuals, it will be helpful for them to learn to become more assertive and to express their own wishes and needs rather than going along with an attitude or behaviour with which they disagree and which will make them angry later.

It may seem odd that people who have anger problems may also have difficulty asserting themselves, but the two are not incompatible. Since they have low self-esteem, some people are more likely to accept a situation than complain or try and make changes. Their anger builds up inside because (1) they feel angry with themselves for not standing up for themselves; and (2) because they feel angry with other people whom they perceive as taking advantage of them. These feelings slowly increase until, for some individuals, they explode unpredictably.

Being assertive is different from being aggressive or passive. People who are aggressive tend to be overly forceful when communicating with others, whilst people who are passive tend to be submissive. Their underlying needs are not met, thus leaving them with feelings of resentment and/or anger. To be assertive is to be able to express how you feel in a direct and honest manner without hurting or putting down others (as in aggression) or feeling hurt or put down yourself (as in passive behaviour).

Table 10.2 provides a list of assertive attributes completed by a man who had difficulty telling people what he really wanted or felt. The table can be reviewed with the client in order to help them identify particular strengths and weaknesses. The chart can be used pre-treatment, during treatment, and post-treatment to measure progress and outcome. (This is presented on the Companion Website in Table 10.2a for the self-report version and in Table 10.2b, which provides an informant report version.)

Table 10.2 Measure of assertion

How well can you…	Never	Rarely	Sometimes	Mostly	Always	Don't know
1. Stand up for yourself if you feel someone is taking advantage of you	✓					
2. Make alternative suggestions to the ideas of others				✓		
3. Say 'No' to other people		✓				
4. Tell someone you disagree with them			✓			
5. Resist being pressured to going along with something you don't want to	✓					
6. Request an explanation if someone is not being clear			✓			
7. Express your feelings of dissatisfaction		✓				
8. Tell someone they have made a mistake	✓					
9. Face up to difficult or challenging situations		✓				

Treatment sessions should initially be psychoeducational and enable the individual to understand the difference between assertiveness and aggression. Assertiveness involves standing up for oneself, whilst being calm and courteous at the same time. It requires acting in one's best interests but without inducing anger or aggression in others. Both assertiveness and aggression can involve feeling angry, but being assertive requires the ability to express anger or distress without hurting or angering others. For example, someone who is being assertive may communicate their anger but without threatening the other person, or insulting them, or being punishing and sarcastic. The way to convey this to the client is to encourage them to think about the outcome they wish to achieve. What do they really want out of the interaction? Then show them the way to get it using the steps outlined earlier in the ADHD formula; that is, tell the person how they feel, tell the person what they want, tell the person the outcome. Express this calmly and state it factually and explicitly. Then ask the client to determine the outcome of not asserting themselves. This means they are unlikely to get what they really want and achieve the desired outcome.

The manner of expression is important. Clients should be encouraged to express themselves using the first person, because 'I' messages are assertive and communicate feelings, for example, 'I feel very angry at the moment'. In contrast, 'You' messages are more likely to be perceived as aggressive and punishing, for example, 'You make me feel very angry'.

The tone and manner of expression can be role-played in sessions. The therapist should also look out for opportunities during treatment to acknowledge and positively reinforce assertive behaviour. In such situations and in role-plays, attention should be drawn to functional characteristics of speech and body language that impress assertion as opposed to aggression. These include:

1. Take a step back – do not stand too close as invading another person's personal space could be perceived as threatening and induce a 'fight-or-flight' response. This is likely to escalate a situation and maximise the possibility that it will have a negative outcome, as the recipient is likely to respond in an angry way, which in turn will increase the client's anger.
2. Maintain eye contact and a firm facial expression – this allows the other person to see that the client is serious about what they are saying. Help the client to practise facial expressions and avoid 'menacing looks' by getting them to practise in a mirror. Get them to do this in sessions and at home.
3. Maintain voice volume and pace at a steady level – no shouting or whispering. Raising the volume and increasing the speed of speech may feel threatening to the other person, thus increasing the likelihood that they will become angry and the situation may escalate. If the other person is already angry, using a normal volume of voice may also assist them in calming down. In contrast, speaking very quietly or not at all may irritate the other person by appearing 'passive-aggressive' and/or denying the individual the opportunity to be heard and understood.
4. Use the ADHD formula outlined above.

CONCLUSIONS

This chapter has highlighted the nature of anger and its adaptive functions. It has identified how people with ADHD may respond to anger and sensitive areas for them. Anger management skills crucially require the ability to identify anger signals within a CBT framework and raising awareness of antecedents, behaviours and consequences of anger. The chapter also discusses the difference between insults and criticisms and presents techniques for coping with each. Finally, the issue of assertiveness, as distinct from aggression, is explored with strategies for increasing assertive behaviour. It is important for the therapist to be aware of previous anger-inducing experiences with services that may block the development of a therapeutic alliance. Furthermore, it is also necessary for the therapist to ensure their own safety when addressing topics which may arouse anger in their client.

11

LOW MOOD AND DEPRESSION

Depression is a common comorbid condition in adults with ADHD. In ADHD clinical samples, 16–31% of adults have major depression (Biederman et al., 1993; Murphy & Barkley, 1996). In addition, 19–37% of adults with ADHD have dysthymia, a more mild but persistent form of depression with low mood as a core feature. Therefore, dips in mood are very likely to be experienced by ADHD clients and it is well worth exploring mood-related symptoms with individuals when assessing for ADHD. It is also helpful to establish whether these have been experienced in the past and, if so, teach the client techniques to prevent their low mood from spiralling into a more entrenched depressed mood in the future.

People with depression have symptoms of low mood, loss of energy and motivation, and a sense of hopelessness about the future. When these symptoms are comorbid with ADHD, the person also has additional symptoms, such as greater concentration problems and feelings of lethargy. Although they feel restless inside, their lack of motivation and energy means their natural optimism and creativity is 'trapped' in a negative cycle of depressive rumination.

In a study of individuals diagnosed with ADHD for the first time in adulthood and comparing severity of depression in different age groups by decade (Bramham et al., 2005b), a positive association was found between age and depression ratings. This means that the later a person received a diagnosis, the greater their severity of depressive symptoms. Thus, clinicians need to be sensitive to the possibility of underlying depressive symptoms in adults diagnosed with ADHD, especially when this diagnosis is made well into adulthood. Qualitative research investigating the experience of obtaining a diagnosis of ADHD and treatment found an increased likelihood that following diagnosis, treatment and improvement in ADHD symptoms, people with ADHD are more likely to engage in depressive rumination (Young et al., in submission). Even mild depression should be taken seriously and treated as a priority, especially since ADHD individuals are more likely to attempt suicide in the context of a depressive illness (Weiss et al., 1985). If they have thoughts of suicide, they may impulsively act out their ideation.

There are several possible explanations for why individuals with ADHD may be at greater risk of depression. For example, they are more likely to have experienced adverse events early in childhood. It is likely that parents of ADHD children are not without their problems. It is not easy being a parent at the best of times and parenting an ADHD child who challenges authority, breaks rules and disrupts stable family life is difficult to manage. Additionally, many parents have undiagnosed ADHD, meaning that they themselves may be disorganised and chaotic in their parenting style, and unable to provide the appropriate structure and stability for their children. At school as well as home, a child with ADHD is likely to have been overly criticised. Scholastic underachievement is usually not initially recognised to be associated with ADHD symptoms but construed by others as 'laziness'. Relationship difficulties seem to be a consistent problem; as children, they may have had difficulty developing supportive relationships and become unpopular with peers; as adults they have difficulty maintaining friendships and lack intimate relationships. They may have low self-esteem. It is no great surprise that these experiences predispose an individual to feel low and develop depression at some period in their life.

People with ADHD can find that, along with low mood, they become particularly irritable and intolerant. They may feel guilty about the hurtful things they say and do on impulse to people they love and care for. Attentional deficits can also be exacerbated, leading the person to be even less likely to complete tasks and depriving them from feeling a sense of achievement. People can become distracted from constructive activities and preoccupied by their own internal negative automatic thoughts, which characterise depression. This leads to disturbed sleep with insomnia and early waking. The internal conflict between feelings of restlessness and lack of motivation can be a source of discomfort and emotional exhaustion. Seeing the world through dark glasses and observing hopelessness all around leads some people to cope by increasing their alcohol intake or taking drugs. Such coping mechanisms are only temporarily effective. Alcohol 'drowns their sorrows' and drugs give brief relief (and possibly temporary symptom improvement, depending on the substance of preference). However, the short-term aftermath is a hangover and symptoms of withdrawal, including low mood. In the longer term, these strategies have the expensive price tag of psychological and physical dependence. These issues are discussed in Chapter 13.

Mood regulation is a considerable problem for adults with ADHD and their capacity to regulate mood worsens when depressed or low in mood due to an increase in emotional lability. Individuals may find that they become tearful quickly and without apparent reason. They are also much more likely to be 'touchy', or 'snappy'. Indeed, in clients with ADHD, low mood is often displayed as anger and understood by others as bad temperament. This may reflect a need to hide their feelings of despair and futility from others.

Emotional lability has been misdiagnosed in people with ADHD as bipolar disorder. Mania is characterised by excitability, over-talkativeness, racing thoughts, euphoria and increased energy. All of these symptoms are exhibited by adults with ADHD and it can sometimes be difficult to tease the disorders apart phenomenologically. One way of differentiating between them is to establish rate of onset of the elated mood and its persistency. Mood swings in ADHD can occur very rapidly and dissipate quickly, for example within an hour or a day, whereas manic episodes are more likely to have a prodromal stage, to increase gradually and be more persistent over time, for example weeks or months. The age of onset is also a useful indicator as the majority of bipolar illnesses do not emerge until late adolescence or early adulthood, whereas ADHD has onset in early childhood. It is unusual for a child of 7 years or under to be diagnosed with bipolar disorder.

When clinicians are faced with individuals with comorbid ADHD and severe depression, it is recommended that the depression is treated with antidepressant medication *and* psychological interventions. Traditional psychostimulants (e.g. methylphenidate) have been shown to be of benefit for depression and therefore may act as a dual intervention. However, a side effect of this treatment is that it may induce anxiety (Vance, Luk, Costin, Tonge & Pantelis, 1999). Norepinephrine reuptake inhibitors, such as Atomoxetine, have been shown to treat ADHD (Pliszka, 2003), but these can also be used as an antidepressant and may be a treatment of choice for individuals with both diagnoses.

Suggestions for psychological treatment of people with ADHD and comorbid mood problems are presented in this chapter. A cognitive model of depression can be adapted for individuals with ADHD with an intervention that addresses depressive and ADHD thinking styles. The chapter will examine common negative thinking and thinking errors of ADHD adults. Cognitive and behavioural interventions are suggested that include challenging negative thoughts and activity scheduling.

THE COGNITIVE MODEL OF DEPRESSION

Beck's (1976) well-established cognitive model of depression can be adapted to describe the experience of adults with ADHD who exhibit depressive symptoms. Individuals with ADHD are likely to be able to elaborate on multiple early negative life experiences. They have usually a history of being criticised by parents and teachers who have told them that they are lazy, stupid or unable to learn. In comparison with their peers, there may even be objective evidence, for example test marks, which may have made them feel less able than others and lead them to internalise the idea of their reduced status. Through this typical ADHD childhood experience, individuals are likely to have generated schemas about themselves that are related to feelings of inferiority. In our experience, a common schema is that the individual is 'different' from others in some unique way and that others are more able, successful, likeable, etc. Such schemata lead to the formation of dysfunctional assumptions. These are usually 'if... then' statements and they serve to maintain a sense of low self-value and self-worth. For example, 'If I don't play the clown and entertain people, then they won't want to spend time with me'; 'If I don't get a new account this week, my boss will think I'm no good and fire me'. These assumptions are not available at a conscious level, but are likely to have influenced the manner in which ADHD individuals interact with others and the expectations they place on themselves. These expectations are often unrealistic and overly high, causing them to be perfectionistic and pedantic in their attempts to achieve them. This is stressful and in order to reduce the stress, some people with ADHD choose to settle for undemanding activities in which they are more likely to achieve success. However, deep down they know that they are underachieving, that they lack the confidence to stretch themselves and reach their potential, which causes them to feel unhappy and deeply dissatisfied. For others their schemas mean that they accept criticism uncritically from others and they may become enmeshed in an abusive relationship.

Due to both their inattentive and impulsive symptoms, ADHD individuals are more likely to incur critical life events, such as losing their job (either because they walk out on impulse or are fired), getting divorced or being involved in accidents, etc. When such events occur, this precipitates the activation of previously developed dysfunctional schemata and leads to an increase in negative automatic thoughts about themselves (see Figure 11.1 adapted from Beck, 1976; also on the Companion Website in a format for use in session as Figure 11.1a). Unlike earlier, at this stage in the process the individual assumptions are conscious and the individual may be aware of the multiple negative thoughts about themselves racing through their head. These thoughts may be so rapid and so severe that the individual feels completely overwhelmed and metaphorically beaten by them. An inability to modulate cognitions and emotions means the individual may develop symptoms such as labile mood swings of low mood and anger; hopelessness and a sense of loss of control about the future; distraction and preoccupation; and a loss of the creative resources, interest and energy that are usually readily accessible to the individual. It is not easy for a person with ADHD to stay on task at the best of times, but especially when their own thoughts and feelings become 'internal distracters' or an additional hurdle or obstacle to overcome. If low mood spirals further into depression, the person may become withdrawn, indecisive and give up completely. In turn, this will confirm an underlying schema and the dysfunctional assumptions that are held about themselves are activated. This in turn reinforces the behaviour and keeps the person engaged in a vicious cycle of depression.

However, there appears to be a positive aspect to the ADHD personality that may protect individuals from spiralling into clinical depression – this is 'resilience' and the ability to cognitively reframe social problems and disappointments. Indeed, from interviewing individuals with ADHD, it appears that a common characteristic is their ability to bounce back and try again. Lability in mood means their mood state is changing (sometimes rapidly) and these fluctuations may 'kickstart' their creativity and zest for life. An alternative explanation may be that they are unable to resist the impulse to have another go when others may conclude that an option is unviable.

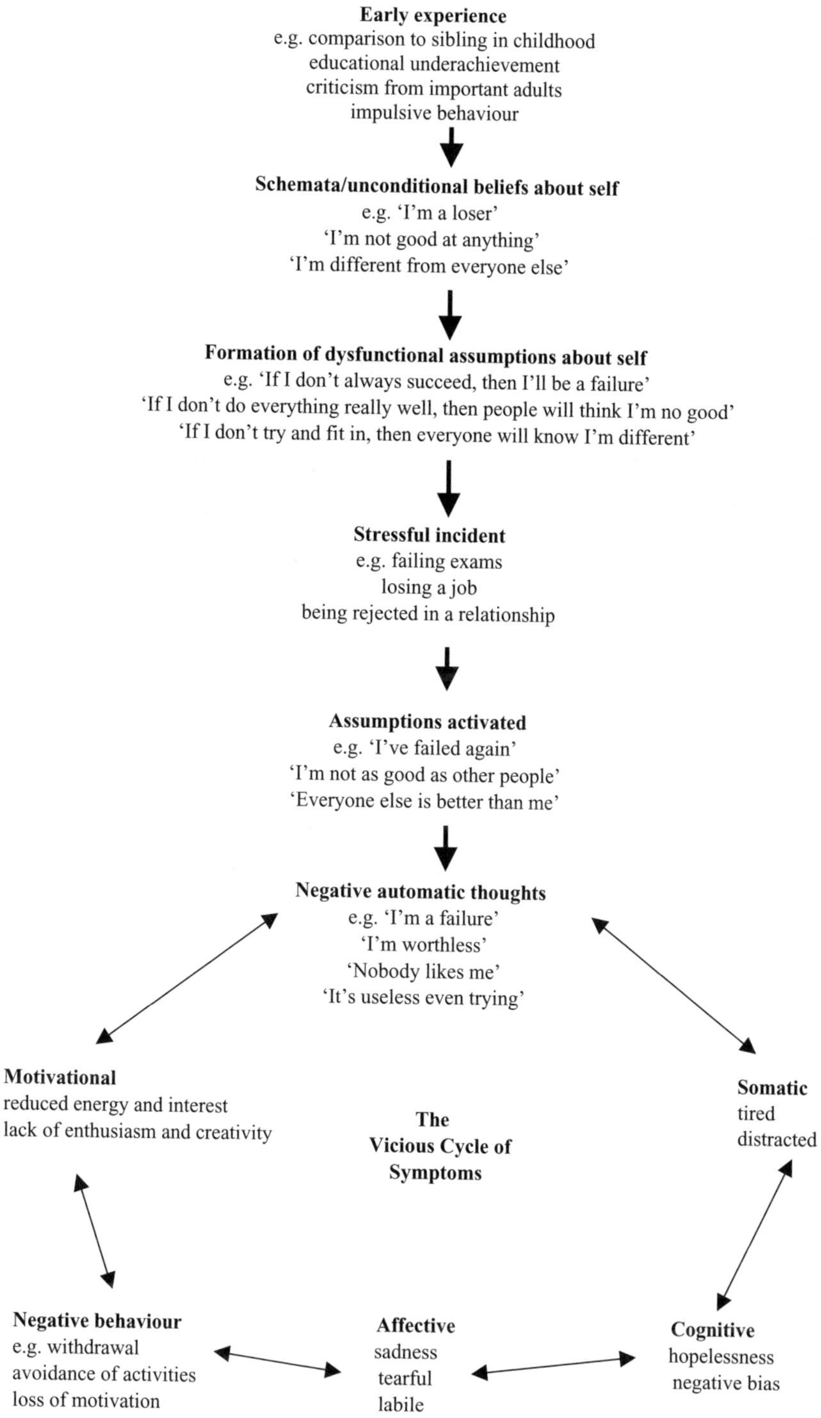

Early experience
e.g. comparison to sibling in childhood
educational underachievement
criticism from important adults
impulsive behaviour

↓

Schemata/unconditional beliefs about self
e.g. 'I'm a loser'
'I'm not good at anything'
'I'm different from everyone else'

↓

Formation of dysfunctional assumptions about self
e.g. 'If I don't always succeed, then I'll be a failure'
'If I don't do everything really well, then people will think I'm no good'
'If I don't try and fit in, then everyone will know I'm different'

↓

Stressful incident
e.g. failing exams
losing a job
being rejected in a relationship

↓

Assumptions activated
e.g. 'I've failed again'
'I'm not as good as other people'
'Everyone else is better than me'

↓

Negative automatic thoughts
e.g. 'I'm a failure'
'I'm worthless'
'Nobody likes me'
'It's useless even trying'

Motivational
reduced energy and interest
lack of enthusiasm and creativity

**The
Vicious Cycle of
Symptoms**

Somatic
tired
distracted

Negative behaviour
e.g. withdrawal
avoidance of activities
loss of motivation

Affective
sadness
tearful
labile

Cognitive
hopelessness
negative bias

Figure 11.1 Cognitive model of depression in ADHD
Adapted from Beck (1976). *Cognitive Therapy and the Emotional Disorders*. International University Press.

Attentional problems may also feed resilience by limiting the ability to reason about the implications of negative consequences and predict or anticipate future problems. A word of warning, however, as whilst in some individuals this characteristic may serve as a protective factor, in others it may predispose to depression as it leads them to experience a higher number of negative events or failures. These may aggregate to reach a critical mass when resilience can no longer spring them back to positivity and they are left with a legacy of failures and regrets which appear insurmountable.

ADHD NEGATIVE THINKING STYLES

Negative thinking styles directly relate to mood. When their mood fluctuates, as is common in people with ADHD, their cognitions fluctuate and this can cause the person to feel confused, uncertain and distressed. Additionally, depressed ADHD individuals are more likely to be snappy or irritable, which is likely to increase the frequency of negative social encounters. This may lead to social withdrawal in order to reduce feelings of irritation, by avoiding people or situations they perceive will make them feel this way. However, this may mean they conceptualise themselves as an 'unlikeable' person. The 'cognitive triad' is a focus on negative aspects of the self, the world and the future (Beck, 1963). It is easy to see how this position may develop when a person has an underlying schema that they are stupid and useless (self), others find them lazy and irritable (the world), and that tomorrow is bleak and unchangeable (the future). Perhaps it is this latter aspect that prevents people with ADHD completely capitulating to clinical depression, as fundamentally they see the world as a challenge that may be changeable. They see a better outcome is possible because they sense that they underachieve their potential. This means that they believe they have potential even if they do not appreciate the full extent of this. Such beliefs are 'food' for cognitive challenges and alternative thinking, which can be achieved by developing the ADHD individual's natural interest and curiosity for novel tasks. Their talents must be identified and exploited.

The ADHD thinking style is driven by speed. People with ADHD involuntarily react both behaviourally and cognitively. People describe themselves frequently being distracted by thoughts that 'come from nowhere' and flit from one idea to the next, when they are trying to focus on one thing. When these thoughts are negative, they are particularly distressing. The characteristics of negative thoughts are that they are:

- *automatic* – they just pop into your head and are not generated consciously
- *distorted* – they only take into account the negative
- *unhelpful* – they keep the vicious cycle of low mood going
- *plausible* – they are not questioned, because they seem 'true'
- *involuntary* – they do not happen through choice and are hard to switch off

Individuals with ADHD are more likely to accept the plausibility of negative automatic thoughts (NATs) because they have difficulty thinking about consequences and evaluating thoughts, so they often erroneously accept negative thoughts as the truth. Psychoeducation regarding the nature of NATs is important in any therapy for depression. However, this will be particularly important for individuals with ADHD as their familiarity with such thoughts may be exceptionally strong. People with ADHD are passionate people and when they feel low they will feel passionately low. It is not easy to learn to identify NATs and this will take practice and guidance in sessions.

People with ADHD have often been seeking an explanation of their negative life experiences and problems. The cognitive model is something that they understand and recognise. By seeing the model outlined in Figure 11.1 and completing the categories with their own experience, clients will take important steps towards making sense of any confusion and inner turmoil. Although recognition, insight and understanding of past problems and current needs may seem like 'turning on a light', the problem remains, for example feelings of inadequacy and anxiety that they will fail to meet their own expectations and those of others. These concerns underpin their self-assumptions and core beliefs that they are inferior human beings. Thinking errors may additionally relate to the tendency of ADHD adults to make rapid, erroneous attributions due to their inability to 'stop' and engage in a process of consequential thinking. This haphazard 'hit and miss' approach to life means that ADHD adults do not develop the ability to reason in a rational stage-by-stage process. The most common thinking error for people with ADHD is the tendency to jump to conclusions, which stems from their poor impulse control. For example, Pete, a client with ADHD thought his manager did not like him. One day he was asked to go to speak to his manager, and he jumped to the conclusion that he was going to be fired from his job. Acting on this notion, he went into the general office, shouted at his manager, resigned and walked out. This was in the absence of any information suggesting that he was going to be fired. He later learned that he was about to be promoted. Thinking errors common to people with ADHD are presented in Table 11.1 (also on the Companion Website).

The therapist may perform an exercise jointly (see Table 11.2) with their client in order to teach them how to identify and evaluate thinking errors before going on to encourage them to identify their own (i.e. without the support of the therapist). A blank version is included on the Companion Website. However, the categories are not mutually exclusive and there may be more than one error of thinking present. It does not really matter if the client identifies the categories correctly, the point is to get the client to recognise that they are making thinking errors. If they stop and evaluate their own thoughts, they may not make the same errors.

CHALLENGING NEGATIVE THOUGHTS

Individuals with ADHD need greater practice and rehearsal of challenging negative thoughts due to their attentional problems and difficulty in grasping concepts. They are also more likely to give up impulsively and quickly decide that they cannot do it.

Table 11.1   Typical thinking errors of people with ADHD

Type of error	
Jumping to conclusions	Negative interpretations in the absence of facts *Example: Predicting the future or reading someone's mind*
All or nothing	There seems to be no middle ground and everything can be categorised as 'black' or 'white' *Example: I can't concentrate at all*
Overgeneralising	Drawing extreme conclusions from a single event *Example: I am always tactless and offend people when I speak to them*
Catastrophising	Exaggerating and overestimating outcomes *Example: I have missed a deadline and therefore am going to be sacked*
Personalising	Taking the blame for everything that goes wrong or is unpleasant, believing that everything people do or say is a personal reaction to you *Example: It's all my fault*
Negative focus	Ignoring or misinterpreting positive aspects due to learned helplessness. Always assuming the worst *Example: The glass is half empty rather than half full*
Shoulds and oughts	A sense of failure to meet standards or expectations, without consideration of whether these are reasonable or realistic *Example: I should always get it right*

It is therefore crucial to make homework very manageable. Early failure will reinforce the negative schema and lead to disengagement. Adaptations need to be made to improve the likelihood of clients completing thought records, for example, by getting them to quickly telephone an answerphone to record the thought or by saying

Table 11.2   Thinking errors exercise

What are the following thinking errors?
1. I did that badly and have completely ruined it all. Answer: Catastrophising
2. I upset her by blurting out gossip. I'm a terrible person. Answer: Personalising
3. I should have finished everything I planned to do. Answer: Shoulds and oughts
4. Everything goes wrong. Answer: All or nothing
5. He didn't shake my hand. I definitely won't get the job. Answer: Jumping to conclusions
6. She didn't return my call. All women find me unattractive. Answer: Overgeneralising

it into a recording device (the latter facility is often incorporated into mobile phones which means this is likely to be an easily accessible resource).

Just as thoughts can exacerbate low mood, they can also be exploited to improve moods. Explaining how the vicious spiral can be reversed can be a strong motivator and give a sense of hope. Recognising that different more negative thoughts in the same situation can lead to the experience of positive feelings and result in positive behaviours can improve mood. This is a difficult skill to master as the client must learn to impose control over a lability they have long believed they cannot control.

The client should be encouraged to look at alternative interpretations or alternative outcomes, for example replace thoughts such as 'I can't cope' with 'this is difficult, but I can manage if I take it a step at a time'. However, people with ADHD are likely to find considering alternatives to original thinking difficult due to their executive functioning problems and relative inflexibility. This seems ironic given that they often have strong creative talent. The issue here is that they have the ability to generate lots of original ideas but do not do so spontaneously as they either stick rigidly to one aspect for some time and do not consider alternative ideas or solutions at all, or they give up and move on to a completely different topic leaving a task incomplete or a problem unresolved. This rigidity needs to be overcome by teaching the client to relax and let new ideas flow. Brainstorming techniques are helpful and might include asking the client to:

1. Think of many different solutions to the problem, even silly ones.
2. Disregard all solutions that are not pragmatic.
3. Consider the outcome of remaining solutions and rate how useful they may be on a scale of 0 = useless to 10 = very helpful: problem likely to be resolved.
4. Select a solution.

Aside from the brainstorming techniques outlined above (and presented for client use on the Companion Website in Table 11.2b), it can be useful in sessions to develop with the client a set of standard questions which they ask themselves to help them challenge the belief that they cannot cope with their negative thinking, generate alternative thinking or commence a creative thinking process (see, for example, Table 11.3). Table 11.5 provides examples of challenging the negative thoughts of people with ADHD. (Both tables are presented on the Companion Website.)

Table 11.3   Exercise – challenging negative thinking

1. What is the evidence that you can't cope? Write down the times when you have successfully coped in the past.
2. Imagine your friend came to you with this problem – what would you tell them? Would you view it in the same way, that is, believing that there are no solutions?
3. What is the worst that could happen? Am I overestimating the likelihood of this happening?

Table 11.4 Replacing negative thoughts

Exercise

Think of a negative thought:
'I cannot complete this form – it's too difficult and long.'
Now counteract it with a positive self-statement:
'I have managed to finish many more forms in the past and some were even longer.'

One positive aspect of working with people with ADHD is that once they have procured the skills of brainstorming and perspective taking, they seem to quickly develop these skills and adopt them in their daily lives. This most likely reflects the fact that these techniques tap into their creativity and ingenuity and, once they have learned the skill of alternative thinking, they have no difficulty applying the process. The key is learning to stop their automatic acceptance of an original thought or idea and engage in a process of consequential or alternative thinking. The therapist may have to prompt many times to do this. It may be helpful to encourage the client to write out the prompting questions outlined in the exercise in Table 11.4 and carry them on a card. The Companion Website contains this list in a format that can be copied for this purpose. The client could, at a more fundamental level, be encouraged to interrupt automatic responding by linking the process with a visual image, e.g. new idea, red flash, 'stop' sign.

Once negative thoughts have been determined and the thinking process halted, the client may be helped by learning to replace a negative thought with a more positive one. This may be motivating as well as rewarding. It can be helpful to make up a list of possible negative and positive thoughts. This involves dividing a sheet of paper into two columns and writing a list of negative thoughts down one side of the page and then a list of positive self-statements on the other side. Make sure that items are not 'global' abstract thoughts or schemas but refer to thoughts about that moment in time. With careful prompting, the therapist must ensure that positive thoughts and outcomes far outweigh the negative outcomes. If the page is folded over to show only the positive side, this provides a list of self-generated positive statements that may be usefully applied in treatment. Examples of negative thoughts and cognitive challenges are presented in Table 11.5.

ACTIVITY SCHEDULING

As discussed previously, individuals with ADHD often feel overwhelmed by what are perceived to be insurmountable problems and therefore give up very early or easily. It can be difficult to know where to start, especially if motivation is low and the task is not of particular interest. This can make the client feel worse, because they are even less likely to achieve tasks and lose attention before they are completed. When this happens, the system needs to be 'kick started'. Activity makes people feel better and more alert, and motivates further activity; that is, the more you do, the more you feel like doing. This can be counterintuitive, however, as many people do not perform activities

Table 11.5 Examples of negative thoughts and challenges

Negative thoughts	Challenges
I am not as capable as other people.	I am not good at everything. Like everybody I am good at some things and not so good at others.
There is no way I can complete that task. What is the point in trying?	If I don't try, I won't know. If I break it down into smaller sections I will be able to complete it. Trying in itself will broaden my experience and skill. Nobody is expecting me to do it all in one go.
I'm bound to miss something out or make a mistake.	Everybody makes mistakes, even people without ADHD. I know how to check what I have done for mistakes and I can ask others to help me. Sometimes it is good to make mistakes because that is the best way to learn.
I end up talking about rubbish and nobody wants to listen to me.	I have opinions, thoughts and feelings. A lot of people find it very difficult to talk in public and I may put them at their ease. I can make sure I talk about things which interest them.
Everybody hates me and thinks I'm a moody person.	There are people who like me for who I am. Everyone is allowed to have their down moments.
People without ADHD are happier than me.	I don't know this for a fact. Some people may be and others may be very unhappy. Just because somebody appears to be in control, doesn't mean they are more satisfied.
It would be best if I avoided people, because I end up being rude and offending people.	If I stay away I don't give myself a chance. There are many more occasions when I get on well with people than occasions when I offend them.
My mood swings around so much – I may start crying in front of everyone.	It is acceptable to be upset sometimes. When I see others crying, I am understanding and do not think any worse of the person. It would not be the end of the world. What is wrong with showing emotion?
I'm hopeless at everything and always have been. I've been trying all my life to sort myself out and have got nowhere.	There are many things that I can do very well. I have made great improvements in many areas of my life and this aspect is not any more important.

because they 'do not feel like it'. The client should be encouraged to understand the behaviour-motivation lag, whereby starting an activity (even when they do not want to at first) can make them feel like doing it when they have finished. However, an attention deficit means that people have difficulty finishing tasks at the best of times, let alone when they feel low in mood. So tasks need to be broken down into smaller stages, with the client aiming to start at a pre-determined point of a task and finish it. By learning to apply this methodology, clients who feel unmotivated and are low in mood may find that not only do they complete their target but in the course of time they may develop motivation to complete many other parts, if not complete the whole task.

Table 11.6   Making a task list

1	*Tasks that must be done*
	collecting the children from school
	going shopping
	renewing the bus pass
2	*Tasks that client wants to do*
	watching new film at cinema
	going to hairdressers
	meeting friend
3	**Rewards**
	reading magazine
	going for a run
	watching television

The first task for the therapist is to engage the client in a process of categorising what has to be done. The way to do this is to make a list of tasks that are compulsory, important and necessary, and finally desirable (see Table 11.6; also on the Companion Website). This will be intuitively interesting to the client as they will see spread before them a frame or plan that structures achievement. People with ADHD are generally active and so activity schedules and plans are unlikely to be rejected. However, because clients can be chaotic and disorganised in their general approach to life, using such plans and outlines will be unusual. If they have tried and failed to use similar techniques, this is probably for one of two reasons: (1) either they have not broken tasks down into sufficiently small steps, or (2) because they have not incorporated a reward system into their schedule.

By definition, a reward is something that is pleasurable to the individual and will lift mood. However, if a person is very depressed, their avoidance of tasks or social withdrawal may represent a 'reward' to the individual and reinforce their depressed state. In such cases, the therapist must guide the client to select rewards that will act as positive reinforcers. Of course, rewards will vary between individuals. One man's meat is another man's poison! If the client is feeling particularly low it can be hard to think of things that give pleasure so it can be helpful to encourage the client to think about what they would suggest to somebody else. If they find it difficult to define 'rewards' they would like now, ask the client about activities and/or treats that used to give them pleasure. Identify small rewards as well as large rewards. A reward could be taking a bath, watching a television programme, going for a swim, going to the cinema, going to the gym, meeting a friend, going for a walk, making a telephone call to a friend, a piece of cake, listening to music, a holiday… there are endless possibilities.

Once the tasks and rewards have been established, the client can be guided to plan ahead by making up a Diary Activity Plan, which divides each day into hours (see Table 5.2 on Companion Website). The client should be encouraged to avoid the temptation of doing too much in one go. Schedule activities in small amounts so they become manageable. Initially, the planning phase may seem a daunting task for someone with ADHD so the client should be encouraged to reward themselves once the planning is completed. The schedule should include regular breaks, for example, stop for a drink or go for a quick walk. The timing of breaks should be determined by their concentration span. This may need to be determined by trial and error, however, they should ensure that the schedule is not all reward for little achievement. The rest of the time can be filled in, from morning to evening, with the activities identified previously in the Task List (see Table 11.7 – also in handout format on the Companion Website). People with ADHD have a difficulty with 'delayed gratification', that is, they find it difficult to wait for a reward, so long periods should not be scheduled between rewards. Completion of tasks or structured activity must be paired with reward, which may be brief periods of relaxation or alternatively high stimulation. Rewards that involve some form of activity can be particularly stimulating, such as physical exercise, as this will help alleviate feelings of restlessness.

The aim is to create a system whereby frequent rewards are incorporated to reward completion of tasks that have been put off or avoided. Rewards can be matched according to task demand and complexity, for example if the client is working on a task requiring a lot of thought and sustained concentration (such as completing a report) then schedule in frequent short breaks for a drink and/or snack. When the report has been completed, say at the end of the day, a bigger reward can be scheduled, such as going out to the cinema or going for a run. The goal is to maximise activity levels and increase the level of satisfaction and feeling of achievement.

Clients should be reminded of the thoughts, feelings and behaviour cycle whilst completing tasks and increasing productivity. By being more active, the cycle can be reversed by using positive behaviour to improve mood. For the client, this will also increase a sense of control over their life and what they can achieve. The aim is to reduce an insurmountable mass of unstarted or half-finished tasks into a prioritised manageable list. A list that is completed and has an end. Once tasks are completed, the client should be encouraged to see this visually and increase feelings of satisfaction and achievement by ticking off items on their list or crossing them through. One client has told us that he used to use a highlighter pen to mark tasks done as he wanted to highlight achievement. He said it was a reward in itself to see a block of tasks in fluorescent yellow ink.

It is important to review what has been achieved at the end of each day and think about the days ahead. The client should be encouraged to focus on what they have managed to do and not to punish themselves for what they did not achieve – after all, they could have stayed in bed and done nothing. Some adjustments will inevitably need to be made to the plan, depending on how well the client has overestimated or underestimated the time it takes to complete tasks. As mentioned earlier, in the initial stages, it is better to schedule very short tasks into a longer period, in order to maximise the likelihood of success. If the plan has not been adhered to, then try to identify what went wrong and at what time. It will be useful to note this information in the Diary Activity Plan at the appropriate place. It could be, for example, that the client was able to stick to the plan in the morning but not after lunch, in which case the therapist should adapt the schedule to start the afternoon with a 'desirable' activity before moving to one from the 'must do' list. It is important to include tasks that give pleasure, and not just a list of chores.

Table 11.7   Example of a task list for activity scheduling

Tasks John must do

Complete tax return
Cut the grass
Buy my daughter a birthday present
Grocery shopping for the week
Household chores
Prepare invoices and statements for work completed
Visit a potential client and prepare an estimate
Finish current job fitting a water feature
Go to the bank
Return a movie to the hire shop

Tasks John wants to do

Go to the cinema
Finish reading book
Find out about joining the local gym
Visit a friend in hospital
Go to the opticians for an eye test
Find out about how to run in the next marathon

Rewards

Go running
Read the newspaper
Watch the football on television
Watch a movie
Meet a friend for a drink
Have a takeaway meal

An example of a diary activity plan is given in Table 11.8 (see blank version for use in sessions in Table 5.2 on Companion Website). This is a week's schedule for a client, John, who is a self-employed landscape gardener who lives on his own.

Before John made his Diary Activity Plan, he had to break down some of the items he wished to achieve (see Table 11.7). For example, in the 'must do' list he wrote 'household chores'. What John had to do was the vacuuming, tidying up, washing and ironing. These tasks needed to be listed out separately. Similarly some tasks required John to make telephone calls, for example finding out about the local gym and the marathon; enquiring about costs of materials required for his next job.

John could work for a two hour span before he lost concentration, so his Diary Activity Plan was organised around this time span to optimise completion of tasks. In the regular allotted breaks, John either ate lunch or dinner or during the 15 minute breaks he had a cup of tea or coffee or wandered outside. He usually relaxed during the longer breaks and read the newspaper or watched something on television.

Table 11.8 Diary Activity Plan

Week beginning…

	Monday	Tuesday	Wednesday	Thursday	Friday	Saturday	Sunday
9–10 am	Work	Work	Tax form	Invoicing and statements	Cut grass	Sleep	Sleep
10–11 am	Work	Work	Tax form	Invoicing and statements	Cut grass	Read book	Vacuuming
	Break	Break	Break	Break	Break	Break	Break
11.15–12 am	Work	Work	Tax form	Phone calls	Paperwork and correspondence	Travel to shops	Ironing
12–1 pm	Work	Work	Go out for run	Hoovering	Write and post letters	Shop for present	Ironing
1–2 pm	Lunch	Lunch	Lunch	Lunch	Lunch	Lunch	Lunch
2–3 pm	Work	Work	Tidy up house	Prepare estimate	Travel to shops	Visit gym	Go out for run
3.15–4 pm	Work	Work	Post tax form and travel to client	Post estimate Travel to hospital	Banking	Travel home	Watch football on TV
	Break	Break	Break	Break	Break	Break	Break
4.15–5 pm	Work	Work	Visit new client	Hospital visit	Opticians	Read book	Watch football on TV
5–6 pm	Travel home	Travel home	Travel home	Travel home	Travel home	Go out for a walk	Read book
6–7 pm	Break	Break	Break	Break	Break	Break	Break
7–12 pm	Takeaway	Football on TV	TV	Watch movie	Go to cinema	Out with friend	Visit family

An example of John's schedule is provided in Table 11.8. The text in bold represents break and reward periods.

CONCLUSIONS

This chapter has discussed the reasons why many individuals with ADHD may also experience comorbid low mood or depression. It has elaborated the traditional cognitive model in order to elucidate how particular features of ADHD can exacerbate low mood and/or typical depression. There may be a potential risk period following the diagnosis and treatment of ADHD symptoms, when the individual appears to engage in depressive ruminations and analysis of the past. Examples of thought patterns and thinking errors are provided along with exercises for the client and therapist to perform in sessions. Suggestions for activity scheduling are explained with a particular emphasis on how short-term rewards are crucial in maintaining motivation in depressed individuals with ADHD.

12

SLEEP PROBLEMS

Many people with ADHD report difficulties with their sleep but the nature of the relationship between ADHD and sleep disorders is unclear. Sleep disorders themselves can cause underfunctioning of the prefrontal cortex and lead to symptoms such as short attention span and impulsivity in people without ADHD. It is therefore likely that sleep problems can exacerbate existing ADHD cognitive deficits. Sleep difficulties may arise from a comorbid disorder that coincides with ADHD, such as depression, anxiety or substance misuse. It is also possible that some sleep problems are experienced as a symptom of the ADHD syndrome, as ADHD is characterised by poor regulation of the arousal system, leading to attentional difficulties and overactivity. Thus, some individuals report feeling too restless to fall asleep, as though they are constantly 'on the go' and cannot relax. These sleep problems may be related to disturbances of the arousal system, so the neurobiological basis of ADHD is also responsible for producing disturbances in sleep.

There is evidence to suggest that there is a specific relationship between attentional problems and sleep disorders due to the close linkage between brain systems involved in regulation of the domains of sleep/arousal and those involved in the regulation of attention and affect (Owens, 2005). Sleep (during the night) and attention/alertness (during the day) can be conceptualised as being opposite extremes of the same continuum. Disturbance in attention and alertness in the daytime may impact on sleep at night, and vice versa. It may be that a problem with regulating the arousal system renders individuals with ADHD unable to achieve both full alertness and deep sleep, and only allows them to function in grades of semi-alertness throughout the day and night.

Restlessness is one of the core symptoms of ADHD and this may prevent individuals from relaxing and/or achieving adequate sleep. Children with ADHD have been shown to exhibit higher levels of nocturnal activity (as measured by upper and lower limb movements at night) than healthy controls (Konofal, Lecendreux, Bouvard & Mouren-Simeoni, 2001). However, this activity has not been shown to

214 ADHD IN ADULTS

affect sleep continuity in a significant way, in other words, it did not cause them to wake up. Nevertheless, adult clients have commonly reported experiencing difficulties with ceaseless mental activity and this problem may well persist into the night and prevent them from sleeping. This can have a knock-on effect on their ability to attend in the day when they may be more prone to 'day-dream' due to sleep deprivation. In addition, ADHD individuals' difficulties with organisation and prioritisation can often leave them trying to complete tasks very late at night, which encroaches on their sleep time. When they do go to bed, they may be preoccupied with their unfinished tasks. A further explanation may relate to sleep problems being a side effect of the medication that is being used to treat ADHD symptoms, as this is often a cerebral stimulant, which may cause the individual to have difficulty falling asleep.

This chapter will describe the sleep disorders that are commonly experienced by people with ADHD, including insomnia, sleep apnoea, nightmares, narcolepsy and restless legs. In order to treat sleep problems, it is necessary to provide clients with psychoeducational information regarding the process and function of sleep, and the ways in which this can be disrupted. Strategies for monitoring and managing sleep problems are outlined in the chapter. The relationship between mood and sleep is also considered, as affective disturbances may be maintaining difficulties getting to sleep and staying asleep.

SLEEP DISORDERS

There is evidence from studies of ADHD in children that they are more likely to suffer from insomnia, snoring, restless legs and daytime sleepiness than children without ADHD (Owens, 2005). It is not yet clear to what extent these problems persist into adulthood as very little research has been conducted. This section will describe how sleep difficulties may affect adults with ADHD and the characteristics of each of the following disorders: insomnia, apnoea, nightmares, narcolepsy, and restless legs syndrome.

Insomnia

Clients with ADHD usually report sleep problems that fall in to one or more of three categories (Brown & McMullen, 2001):

1. Difficulty getting to sleep – not being able to fall asleep and lying awake for several hours.
2. Not being able to wake up in the morning – finding it impossible to gain enough momentum to get themselves out of bed.
3. Difficulty remaining alert during the day – feeling sleepy, particularly when there is little stimulation.

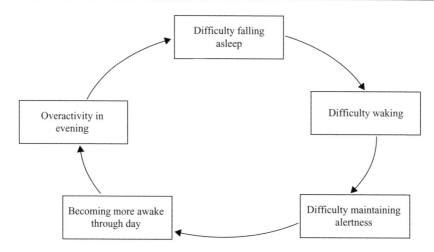

Figure 12.1 Dysfunctional sleep cycle

Many individuals with ADHD experience all three sleep problems (getting to sleep, waking up, maintaining alertness) because these are interrelated. They have difficulty in getting to sleep because they are wide awake in the evenings and tend to do stimulating activities, such as working or socialising intensively. They may find it difficult getting to sleep, eventually sleep fitfully, then find it hard to wake up in the morning as they are still tired. Since they have not had enough sleep during the night, they feel drowsy and find it difficult to remain alert during the day. However, as the day wears on they gradually feel more awake and are ready to become more active. The achievements made in the evening when they believe they are more alert seem to negatively reinforce this schedule. In time, this cycle of negative reinforcement becomes a dysfunctional pattern, in other words, a sleep disorder (see Figure 12.1, which is also provided on the Companion Website in handout format).

People with ADHD often describe difficulties in falling asleep and staying asleep. Their problems can include any one or more of the following: delay in falling asleep, insufficient duration of sleep, frequent awakenings, early final awakening. However, most clients who complain of insomnia will *overestimate* how long it takes them to fall asleep and *underestimate* how long they have actually been asleep.

Some people with ADHD may find that they become more restless later in the day and as a result find themselves becoming involved in activities in the evening that are incompatible with sleep such as sport, playing computer games or surfing the internet. Overactivity in the evenings for other people with ADHD can be related to their finding it easier to concentrate in the evening, perhaps because it is quieter and the opportunity for distraction is minimised, for example when their children have gone to bed. Also some evening activity can become necessary for individuals with

ADHD as their tendency to procrastinate throughout the day means that they have to make up time and complete tasks by working late at night. Others describe gradually feeling sluggish in the morning but become increasingly alert and energised as the day progresses. For example, Jane, a mature student, felt that she only had the motivation to get her assignments completed the day before a deadline and usually ended up staying up extremely late to finish her work.

Problems waking up in the morning are often related to not getting enough sleep earlier in the night. Many individuals with ADHD describe finding it extremely difficult to settle to sleep until well past midnight, even when they need to get up early for work or college. This problem, therefore, may be a delayed reaction to a late onset of sleep. Some 'night owls' can adapt their schedule to their sleep-wake cycle and may be in a position to organise themselves so their day begins later than most if necessary. This will work particularly well for self-employed individuals, although this could feed into a lack of structure and cause more time management difficulties through the day. Those who cannot be so flexible find themselves trying to function on insufficient sleep. They end up feeling 'groggy' and irritable, particularly in the morning. This can lead to an exacerbation of ADHD-related cognitive deficits due to tiredness. Of course, lateness and fatigue will negatively influence an individual's progress in education and work. This sleep problem can also cause problems for families if morning responsibilities are not being shared appropriately, for example partners of clients have reported feeling very resentful if they are left to get the children up and ready for school, whilst the ADHD partner continues to sleep through the morning. For example, James was a self-employed carpet-layer and he had always had a problem with getting up in the morning. As a consequence, he often only scheduled his first appointment of the day at 12.00 noon, and in order to get jobs finished, would have to work until 8.00 pm or beyond. This meant that he spent very little time with his young children as they were usually in bed when he arrived home and he was in bed when they were getting ready in the morning. The majority of the childcare was left to his partner.

Most people with ADHD have difficulty with sustaining attention. However, some people with ADHD also have difficulty in maintaining a sufficient level of arousal or alertness when they are not performing stimulating mental tasks or physical activity. They may feel drowsy and find themselves yawning persistently. They may fall asleep in lectures or meetings, in some cases despite having an adequate night's sleep. Again, this can have a huge impact on their education, career and social relationships. For example, Simon was made redundant when his firm went bankrupt. He quickly ran out of money and was extremely worried about being able to last until his next social security cheque. He often lay awake at night thinking about what might happen to him in the future. As a result, he was unable to sleep and during the day found himself feeling sleepy and yawning all the time. He managed to get several interviews, but was never offered the posts because he was told he seemed disinterested and lethargic.

Sleep Apnoea

Sleep apnoea is a disorder of interrupted breathing during sleep. A common form is *obstructive* sleep apnoea where the windpipe collapses during breathing when the muscles relax during sleep. The brain responds by awakening the person to open the windpipe, usually resulting in a snort or gasp. This can happen hundreds of times a night. Sleep apnoea is associated with obesity or loss of muscle tone and can result in loud snoring. It is often associated with excessive daytime sleepiness, fatigue and altered attention, particularly vigilance (Mazza, Pepin, Naegele, Plante, Deschaux & Levy, 2005).

In a study of children with sleep disorders and/or ADHD, Chervin, Dillon, Bassetti, Ganoczy and Pituch (1997) found that habitual snoring was more common among children with ADHD and that in general snoring was associated with higher levels of inattention and hyperactivity. They suggest that sleep-related breathing disorders could be a cause of ADHD symptoms and that these difficulties would improve if their sleep disorder was treated. Improvements in ADHD symptoms have been reported for three adults with ADHD who had their sleep apnoea treated (Naseem, Chaudhary & Collop, 2001).

Nightmares/Night Terrors

Night terrors are extreme and animated versions of nightmares. The sleeper experiences a sense of terrible danger and may physically and vocally appear distressed and try to defend themselves. Terrors can differ from nightmares in that they are less likely to be remembered. This can be particularly frightening for the individual as they may wake in the night with palpitations and other symptoms similar to a panic attack, and yet not recognise the triggers. This may lead to a catastrophic interpretation in terms of their health, for example, that they are having a heart attack. For children, it has been noted that some medications, particularly dexamphetamine-based preparations, can increase the frequency of nightmares (Efron, Jarman & Barker, 1997). For adult clients, nightmares seem to be more likely in the context of daytime anxieties where distress or preoccupations can adversely affect their sleep and content of their dreams.

Narcolepsy

People with narcolepsy fall asleep at various times of the day, even if they have had a normal amount of night-time sleep. Narcoleptics skip the first four stages of sleep and plunge straight into REM sleep (REM sleep is explained in the following section on psychoeducation). These attacks last from several seconds to more than 20 minutes. People with narcolepsy may also experience cataplexy (loss of muscle control during emotional situations), hallucinations and temporary paralysis when they awaken.

Adults and children with ADHD have been shown to be significantly more sleepy during the day. However, it is unclear to what extent individuals with ADHD suffer from true narcolepsy or whether their attentional difficulties may lead them to daydream and drift into a sleep-like state.

Restless Legs Syndrome

Restless Legs Syndrome (RLS) is a disorder that causes unpleasant crawling, prickling or tingling sensations in the legs and feet and an urge to move them for relief. RLS can lead to constant leg movement during the day and repeated awakening during the night. In a study of adults with RLS, Wagner, Walters and Fisher (2004) found that over a quarter exhibited ADHD symptoms. It is not clear whether discomfort from RLS leads to poor sleep quality, which thus affects concentration and hyperactivity, or alternatively whether RLS and ADHD are part of a symptom complex with dopaminergic deficiency being involved in both disorders.

PSYCHOEDUCATION

It is important for individuals to gain an understanding about the process and functions of sleep in order for them to identify where their sleep problems arise, and consequently how to improve their sleep. The sleep cycle is a good starting point as it allows the client to recognise that sleep is not just one steady state but goes through phases, and actually that sometimes it is normal to wake through the night. Reviewing the functions of sleep with a client can be a useful exercise in order to identify any misconceptions about what happens if they do not obtain sufficient sleep or their sleep lacks quality. In addition, the causes of sleep problems should be explained to a client as they may quickly recognise a pattern to their sleep difficulties and be able to help generate suitable strategies for improving their sleep.

The Sleep Cycle

In order to improve sleep disorders, it can be useful for people with ADHD to understand the characteristics and cycles of normal sleep. It was once thought that sleep was a passive process, in which the brain 'shut down' and nothing happened, but it is now established that sleep is a highly active state. Sleep goes in cycles, moving quickly into deep restorative sleep, then coming back up towards wakefulness, then back down again. This cyclical pattern is thought to exist for evolutionary reasons, as it can be dangerous, because of increased vulnerability, to 'shut down' completely. The intermittent return to a state from which it is easy to wake therefore serves an important function that enables the individual to enter a state of semi-vigilance from which they may wake if they perceive danger.

There are two different states of sleep: non-REM sleep and REM sleep. REM stands for rapid eye movement as the eyes move rapidly during this stage of sleep, but

Table 12.1   Stages of sleep

Stage	Description
Stage 1	This stage is characterised by drowsiness and 'half sleep', with a pattern of moderately alert but relaxed brain waves. This is when drifting in and out of sleep occurs for about 5–10 minutes but it is possible to be woken up easily
Stage 2	Brain waves slow down from about eight per second to five per second and eye movements stop. The heart rate slows down and body temperature drops
Stage 3	Extremely slow *delta* waves begin to appear, interspersed with some small quicker waves
Stage 4	During this stage the brain produces delta waves almost exclusively. It is very difficult to wake someone during stages 3 and 4, which together are called *deep sleep*. There is no eye movement or muscle activity
REM	REM sleep is associated with shorter brain waves. This occurs after the sleeper has moved back through a reversal of stages 4 to 3, to 2, to 1. In REM sleep, breathing, pulse rate and eye muscles fluctuate erratically and the muscles of the body, apart from those involved in breathing and circulation, become paralysed

not during non-REM sleep. During sleep, an individual passes down through four phases of non REM-sleep then back through them in reverse order before entering REM sleep (see Table 12.1). Each stage can be characterised by different patterns of brain activity as measured by EEG recordings. Table 12.1 is also on the Companion Website in handout format for use in sessions.

Non-REM sleep is associated with slower electrophysiological waves than during waking; that is, the electrical activity of the brain becomes less pronounced. As the muscles of the body become relaxed, the person enters a deep sleep from which it is difficult to be roused. If someone is woken during this time, they may report fragmented and/or static visual images. It is during non-REM sleep that sleepwalking and night terrors are most likely to occur.

After stage four, the sleeper goes back through stages three and two until they reach stage one again. This phase is sometimes referred to as 'stage one emergent' but more commonly called 'REM' sleep. When the sleeper switches to REM sleep from non-REM sleep, their breathing becomes more rapid, irregular and shallow, their eyes jerk rapidly in various directions and limb muscles become temporarily paralysed. Heart rate and blood pressure rise. REM sleep is also associated with shorter electrophysiological waves. The respiratory system, pulse and eye muscles fluctuate erratically. In addition, the muscles of the body, apart from those involved in breathing and circulation, become paralysed. A sleeper woken during REM sleep will have an 80% chance of recalling a dream.

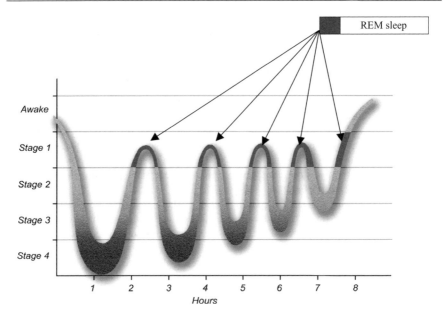

Figure 12.2 The sleep cycle

These sleep stages progress in a cycle down to deep sleep and back up to stage one and into REM sleep, then the cycle starts over again going back into a deeper sleep (see Figure 12.2, which is also presented in the Companion Website in handout format for use in sessions).

Adults typically go through four or five cycles of sleep, each taking about 90 minutes. Each cycle becomes gradually less deep, such that most of the deeper stage four sleep occurs in the earlier half of the night. Almost 50% of total sleep time is spent in Stage 2 sleep, about 20% in REM sleep and the remaining 30% in the other stages. However, infants spend about half their sleep time in REM sleep and typically sleep for 16 hours a day. Sleep requirements decrease through childhood although adolescents still need over 9 hours per night. This is because considerable growth occurs during this period. Most adults need approximately 7–8 hours of sleep per night, although this varies from individual to individual. People who sleep more or less than this amount may be at increased risk of illnesses, as sleep is unable to carry out its usual functions, such as restoration of the immune system.

Functions of Sleep

Sleeping takes up such a significant proportion of our lives and yet it is still not clear why it is so necessary. The functions of sleep can be surmised from what is affected when someone has not had adequate sleep. Sleep deprivation has an effect on the nervous system, the immune system and cell growth and repair. Without sleep, neurons may become depleted in energy or over polluted with the by-products of normal cellular activity. They need sleep to repair themselves in order to perform effectively during the day. In addition, sleep may allow the brain to encode and store new information. Deep sleep coincides with the release of growth hormone in children and young adults. There is also an increased production and reduced breakdown of proteins during sleep. These are the body's building blocks needed for cell growth and repair. Sleep deprivation can impair judgement, reaction times (e.g. in a driving simulator) and can magnify the effects of alcohol. In extreme cases, it can lead to hallucinations and mood swings.

Sleep may have increased importance in ADHD because many individuals have heightened activity levels during the day, and hence may require even more sleep than non-ADHD people to fully recover their energy expended during the day.

Causes of Sleep Problems

Many different factors can influence sleep, including psychological, behavioural, environmental or biological factors. Psychological factors include ADHD-related symptoms, such as restlessness, as well as other mood disorders. Behavioural difficulties, particularly maladaptive sleeping patterns, can affect sleep during the night. Although they are often very obvious, external triggers from the environment can be causal in sleep difficulties because they wake the individual up. Biological factors may be particularly relevant for people with ADHD as not only their medication can influence their quality of sleep but also other lifestyle characteristics may play a role. The different factors are explained in Table 12.2 (also provided on the Companion Website in handout format).

TREATMENT OF SLEEP DISORDERS

Intervention with sleep disorders initially requires close monitoring of the problem in order to obtain a baseline from which to measure change. This should include consideration of the multiple factors that may affect sleep, such as activity levels, diet, caffeine, alcohol, medication, etc. It is also important to explore fully the person's expectations of sleep, for example by determining how much they believe they need and what happens to them when they do not achieve this. Much of the literature regarding insomnia suggests that people with sleep difficulties expect more sleep than is necessary, for example, assuming that if they do not have eight hours of sleep, then they will be unable to perform the next day. Sleep needs vary between individuals and also reduce with age. It may be that a 40-year-old client believes that they should aim to sleep as much as they did when they were 18 years old. The therapist, therefore, can educate the client about this issue and assist them in establishing their optimal amount of sleep.

Table 12.2   Factors which may affect sleep in adults with ADHD

Psychological/behavioural factors

Restlessness/Ceaseless mental activity
This core ADHD symptom may affect normal sleep patterns because the individual still feels 'on the go' at bedtime and finds it very difficult to settle and relax

Worrying specifically about sleep
Worries about getting enough sleep or being tired in the morning if sleep is not achieved may adversely affect the likelihood of falling asleep

Incompatible bedtime activities
For example, playing computer games whilst sitting in bed can make the individual more alert and less likely to go to sleep easily. Working in the bedroom can also have a similar effect, i.e. it distracts the individual from the function of the room, which is to sleep and rest

Chronic anxiety and/or depression
Ruminating about issues, such as the day's events or low self-worth, may keep individuals awake as they become more alert due to an increase in mental activity

Disturbance of activity-rest cycles
Irregular sleep patterns may arise from irregular bedtimes and waking times. For people with ADHD, this may occur as a result of disorganisation causing them to leave tasks until the last minute and stay up late to complete them. Other influences include changing from night- to day-shifts or jet-lag

Oversleeping during the daytime
A common problem for individuals with ADHD is not getting up in the morning and lying in bed until lunchtime or beyond. This has an effect on their ability to sleep at night. Similarly, napping during the day may provide a short-term fix but does not facilitate a good night's sleep

Nocturnal panics
People with ADHD often procrastinate and leave things until the last minute. This can leave them panicking late at night about the tasks they have not achieved for the deadline the following day. They may then either choose to stay up all night working on the activity, or decide to flout the deadline, which may then affect their sleep through worry or nightmares

Environmental factors

Unpredictable sensory stimulation (noise, light, etc.)
Given their distractibility, people with ADHD are more sensitive to external noises when they are trying to get to sleep. For example, voices outside their window, noise from the traffic, other people switching lights on and off outside their room or even when they have fallen asleep with the television on

Significant signals
Due to their distractibility, ADHD individuals may be more sensitive to predictable significant signals, such as daylight in the morning, or children waking. Children with ADHD are more likely to have sleep disorders, which obviously affect their parents' sleep quality

Intense sensory stimulation
For example, high or low temperatures may unduly affect sleep, as can humidity, etc.

Table 12.2   (*continued*)

Biological factors

Stimulant medication
For some adults with ADHD, cerebral stimulant medications such as methylphenidate (Ritalin, Concerta) may improve ADHD symptoms and reverse restlessness. However, for many individuals, stimulant medication may also keep them awake

Side effects of medication for health problems or psychiatric disorders
Other treatments, such as antidepressants, may affect sleep

Excessive caffeine intake
Some ADHD individuals choose to consume large amounts of caffeine during the day either to self-medicate their ADHD symptoms, or to stay awake or more alert. Given that caffeine has a long half-life (i.e. it remains in the system for several hours), intake of caffeine in the late afternoon or early evening may disrupt sleep

Heavy meals shortly before bedtime
Digesting food is not conducive for sleep as the body is more active. Many people with ADHD find that they forget to eat during the day, possibly due to their medication suppressing their appetite, and then feel incredibly hungry in the evening and eat just before they go to bed

Vigorous physical exercise shortly before bedtime
Due to their hyperactivity, some people with ADHD find that at the end of the day they need to 'burn off' excess energy, for example by going for a run or playing squash. Such physical activity serves to wake the body up and may make it less possible for them to sleep adequately immediately afterwards. Nevertheless, exercise earlier in the day is often beneficial for sleep

Physical health problems
Comorbid health problems, particularly pain, may prevent individuals with ADHD falling asleep and maintaining sleep. For example, they may suffer from chronic toothache because they have not organised their life sufficiently to go to the dentist for several weeks

Need for urination
Late night drinking may lead to an individual waking up with a need to urinate during the night

Respiratory difficulties
Problems such as obstructive sleep apnoea can lead to disturbed sleep and cognitive deficits, which may masquerade as ADHD-like symptoms, or exacerbate pre-existing attentional difficulties

---

Methods of managing sleep difficulties can be practically based by monitoring sleep problems and changing behavioural patterns and/or include a more cognitive focus, the latter technique being more effective if mood factors are influencing the quality of sleep. Both of these approaches are described in the following sections.

Monitoring Sleep Difficulties

The first stage in treating sleep problems is to carefully monitor sleep in order to identify features that may be contributing to sleep difficulties. The sleep diary shown in Table 12.3 (and

Table 12.3 Sleep diary

Night of week	Did you sleep during the day? If so, for how long?	How much caffeine did you drink and when?	How much alcohol did you drink and when?	What was the last thing you ate and when?	What time did you take your medication?	How were you feeling before you went to bed?	What were you doing before you went to bed?	Time you went to bed	Time you went to sleep approx	Times you woke up in the night and for how long	Time you woke up in the morning	Total hours of sleep	Quality of sleep (0–10)
Mon	No sleep	Coffee at 10.30 pm	Whisky at 1.15 before bed	Pasta at 1.00 am	Tablet at 6 pm	Stressed	Finishing assignment	1.30 am	3.45 am	5.10– 5.55	8.15 am	4 1/2	4
Tues	Nap at 2.00– 3.30 pm	Tea at 6.00 pm	Bottle of wine, brandy	Curry at 10.30 pm	Forgot	Agitated	Out with friends	1.00 am	2.45 am	4.30, 5.10, 6.00	9.30 am	6 3/4	3
Wed	No sleep	Coffee at 11.00 pm	None	Toasted sandwich 10 pm	Tablet at 9 pm	Worried about course	Trying to read for seminar tomorrow	11.45 pm	3.00 am	4.00, 4.30, 5.00,	6.30 am	3 1/2	2
Thurs	No sleep	Tea at 4.30 pm	None	Shepherds pie at 6.30 pm	Tablet at 4 pm	Tired	Watching soap operas	10.15 pm	10.30 pm	None	10.30 am	12	8
Fri	Nap at 3.00 in lecture	Coffee at 4 pm	2 bottles of wine	Takeaway pizza at 1 am	Forgot	Drunk	Chatting to friends	3.00 am	3.05 am	6.00	6.00 am	3	2
Sat	Napping all afternoon	None	None	Soup at 6 pm	Tablet at 5 pm	Low	Watching DVD	11.00 pm	2.00 am	3.15– 4.30	10.00 am	6 3/4	4
Sun	None	Coffee at 1 am	Bottle of wine	Sandwich at 1 am	Tablet at 11 pm	Stressed	Preparing presentation for Monday	3.20 am	6.30 am	None	7.00 am	30 mins	0

also on the Companion Website in a format for use in sessions) provides a strategy for recording those features of sleep that are necessary to investigate prior to intervention. Ironically, the process of monitoring may exacerbate sleep difficulties as they are the subject of focus. Thus, the monitoring process must be applied over a period of several days or weeks in order to obtain a reliable baseline. Table 12.3 shows the sleep diary of Jane, a mature student at university. Jane had deadlines for course work and exams pending. She was having problems organising her work. Some nights she worked late into the night and she was feeling very anxious about passing her exams.

The sleep diary records information relating to 13 areas of interest as follows:-

1. *Sleep during the day.* Extra sleep during the day can affect sleep at night-time and disrupt circadian rhythms. Therefore napping during the day should be avoided wherever possible.
2. *Caffeine intake.* Caffeine stimulates the central nervous system, and leads to increased heart rate and alertness. Most people who consume caffeine experience a temporary increase in energy and elevation in mood. Sensitivity to caffeine can vary and depends to some extent on body mass (i.e. a smaller person would require less caffeine to produce the same effect as a larger person). However, caffeine sensitivity is particularly affected by caffeine use, so people who drink caffeine regularly develop reduced sensitivity to caffeine. Nevertheless, caffeine has a long half-life and remains in someone's system for up to 16 hours after consumption before being passed through urine. Therefore, even drinking a cup of coffee in the afternoon can affect sleep patterns later in the evening when the noticeable effects have worn off. People who are experiencing sleep difficulties may increase their caffeine intake during the day to keep them alert. This in turn has a delayed effect on their sleep.
3. *Alcohol intake.* Although alcohol can be used by some individuals as a 'nightcap' to help them go to sleep, this can actually perpetuate sleep difficulties. Alcohol can induce drowsiness, but paradoxically prevents the individual from entering the deeper more restorative stages of sleep. Thus, people who have been drinking alcohol and then slept all night may still complain of being tired in the morning as the majority of their sleep may have been in sleep stages 1 and 2 where brain waves are slowing down, rather than the more restorative stages 3 and 4 (see Table 12.1).
4. *Food intake.* Different types of food can affect sleep in various ways. Heavy food, which is protein-rich or high in sugar, can lead to increases in overall levels of alertness and can also activate the digestive system for longer. However, food that is high in carbohydrates but low in protein and sugar (e.g. cereals, pasta), can stimulate the release of neurotransmitters, which induce relaxation, such as serotonin and melatonin.
5. *Medication.* Both prescribed and non-prescribed drugs can have side effects of sleep difficulties. Cerebral stimulants are the mainstay treatment for ADHD and they work on the reticular activation system, which is involved in arousal. Sometimes people with ADHD find that if they have taken their medication later in the day, they have difficulty getting to sleep, possibly because the drug is still acting on their level of arousal.

6. *Affective state.* Happiness, excitement, sadness, stress, anxiety can all play a role in preventing sleep. The individual should try and record their feelings and associated thoughts in order to identify what might be keeping them awake, such as recurrent worries. This issue is dealt with later in this chapter.

7. *Activity before bed.* It is important for the body to be cued that it is time to slow down and then sleep. Activities that counteract this process should be avoided, such as exercise, mentally stimulating work or stress-inducing conversations. People with ADHD are likely to be active throughout the day and the evening is no exception. If they are busy performing last minute tasks right up until their bedtime, this may affect their sleep. It is preferable to use activities to 'wind down', such as listening to relaxing music, having a caffeine-free drink and reading a magazine.

8. *Time in bed.* The basic boundaries of sleep are important to record as an ADHD individual may lack routine and their bedtime may vary according to the day's activities and whether they suddenly remember to do something just before they go to bed. Having a fixed bedtime helps to induce a regular pattern of sleep and can reduce difficulties falling asleep. For example, if someone frequently does not go to bed until after 2 am and then tries to 'catch-up' on some sleep by going to bed at 9.30 pm, they may find it difficult to fall asleep.

9. *Time fallen asleep.* Although this is difficult to record directly, people generally have a sense of roughly when they have fallen asleep because they do not remember seeing their alarm clock after a certain time.

10. *Waking times during night.* People with ADHD may be more likely to get out of bed due to feelings of restlessness, and (impulsively) engage in activities such as watching television and playing computer games. These provide stimulation and make it more difficult to return back naturally to sleep. However, other people may lie awake and have restless thoughts that stop them from going back to sleep.

11. *Waking time in morning.* The individual may not have a consistent pattern of when to sleep and when to wake, so this can lead to them oversleeping or waking too early. Early morning waking and then lying awake ruminating can be associated with low mood and depression. However, sometimes individuals feel that if they have been awake for a great deal of the night, they are too tired to get up in the morning so lie in bed.

12. *Total hours of sleep.* This is a useful quantative way of measuring any improvement (or deterioration) in sleep. It will also allow the therapist to explore any expectations of the number of hours of sleep an individual believes they should be getting per night. As described above, sometimes expectations can be too high and some normalisation of what is usual can help an individual realise that they are maybe even sleeping too much.

13. *Quality of sleep.* The client should rate the quality of each night's sleep on a Likert scale from 0 (worst possible night's sleep) to 10 (fully relaxed and refreshed in the morning). This area is where clients may have most complaints. Conversely, this is the area where the client is most likely to see improvements during therapy.

The example provided in Table 12.3 illustrates how Jane's napping during the day affected how late she went to bed in the evening and the amount of time she slept at night. Caffeine and alcohol consumption also affected the time she was able to fall asleep and the quality of sleep she gained. For example, on Friday when she was out late drinking wine with friends, she only managed three hours with very poor quality sleep. Eating late at night also seemed to affect her sleep. However, her sleep quantity and quality were strongly related to her activity before going to bed, such as last-minute preparation of coursework, and the anxieties this caused. The night when she had the most and best quality of sleep was Thursday when she went to bed early but then she overslept. This shows how important it can be to have regular times to go to bed and get up in the morning so that a sleep-wake rhythm can be achieved.

MANAGING SLEEP DIFFICULTIES

If the client takes longer than 30 minutes to fall asleep on most nights, then the first step is to review bedtime routines. 'Sleep hygiene' refers to arranging environmental and behavioural factors that are conducive to sleep. For people with insomnia, the bed and its surroundings can become a signal for being unable to fall asleep and for the worry and frustration associated with that state. It is possible to 'undo' this association so that the body learns to sleep in bed and view sleep as rewarding.

In order to achieve this, all activities in the bedroom should be stopped except sleep and intimacy. Visual or physical contact with the bed should be avoided except when going to sleep. For example, people should avoid activities in the bedroom such as working, reading, watching television or playing computer games. Sometimes rearranging the furniture can help by creating a new condition that is not associated with insomnia.

Paradoxically, sleep difficulties can often best be managed by making adjustments during the day to activities and consumption of food, cigarettes and alcohol. Preparing for going to bed is also crucial for the individual to develop a routine so that their body is expecting sleep from regular cues. Whilst in bed, the client should aim to be relaxed, even if they are awake, and they should get out of bed if they feel uncomfortable or unable to sleep. Strategies to cue waking up can complete an intervention as sometimes the individual may be anxious about going to sleep in case they do not wake up on time. Table 12.4 provides a selection of behavioural strategies which may be tried at appropriate times. The Companion Website includes a version of the strategies which clients may find helpful.

In order to improve the sleep of Jane, the mature student (described in Table 12.3), the therapist suggested avoiding all sleeping during the day. She also developed a routine whereby she did not drink any tea or coffee after 4 pm, she ate her evening meal at 7 pm and did not drink any alcohol during the week. At 11 pm, she changed into her nightclothes, brushed her teeth then sat for 30 minutes in the living room listening to relaxing music and reading a magazine. Then she went to bed at 11.30 pm. For the

Table 12.4 Behavioural sleep strategies

During the day

Avoid taking naps and do not lie down
When the client is feeling tired, it can be tempting for them to 'cat nap'. Whilst this is a
quick fix with a short-term gain (and therefore appealing to individuals with ADHD), it is
likely to disrupt sleep in the night. If the client feels particularly tired during the day, they
may take rests without lying down, or alternatively try to distract themselves by becoming
involved in a more energising task

Relax by reading/listening to music if necessary
Instead of sleeping during the day, the client should be encouraged to read or listen to
music (but not in the bedroom). If they perform these activities when feeling tired, they
may become conditionally paired with this feeling, and thus induce this state in the evening
when the individual needs to sleep

Make a list of the activities for the following day
This prevents mental rehearsal at night when the client is attempting to get to sleep but
trying not to forget certain things they need to do the next day

Eating and drinking
The client should avoid heavy meals just before going to bed as this can cause increased
alertness. Spicy and acidic foods may cause indigestion, which will affect sleep. However,
light snacks that are high in carbohydrates but low in sugar can be helpful before going to
bed. Also, drinking too much liquid in the few hours before bed may mean that sleep is
disturbed by a need to go the toilet in the night, so clients should limit their liquid intake in
the later part of the evening

Smoking
Nicotine is a stimulant, which acts in a similar way to caffeine and stimulant medication,
and therefore should be avoided just before bedtime. Smokers may therefore have reduced
REM sleep and only sleep very lightly. Some heavy smokers may wake up a few hours after
going to sleep due to nicotine withdrawal. It is advisable for people to avoid smoking if they
wake up in the night

Alcohol
The effects of alcohol on sleep are counterintuitive. Although alcohol can make drinkers
feel drowsy, it actually prevents people from achieving REM and deeper sleep. Alcohol
induces only a light sleep and therefore the restorative processes cannot occur, and
individuals may be woken up more easily. Alcohol consumption should be avoided or kept
to a minimum when treating a sleep disorder

Before sleep

Maintain a consistent bedtime
Irregularities in bedtimes for people with ADHD are often determined by what is
happening around them. For example, starting to watch a film late at night, being invited
to go for late-night drinks. This should be minimised where possible during the sleep
intervention as having a consistent bedtime allows a routine to develop where sleep is
expected at a certain time

Changing bedtime to when normally get to sleep.
For example, if a client is only getting four hours of sleep per night, then they should only be
allowed four hours in bed but this can be gradually increased by 15–30 minutes per night

Table 12.4   (*continued*)

Follow a routine
An hour or more before going to bed, the client should allow a 'winding down' period, which can be organised into a routine. For example, reading enjoyable magazines or books, listening to music, having a bath

Get ready for bed
This should be done before the client gets tired or commences the winding down routine in order to avoid waking themselves up by the routine. For example, brushing teeth and washing or showering can wake up the individual as these activities are also associated with the morning

Only get into bed when tired
The aim is to associate the bedroom with rapid onset of sleep

In bed

Avoid activities incompatible with sleeping
For example, watching TV or listening to the radio, eating, reading in bed should all be avoided. The bed must be associated with sleep and intimacy, and nothing else

Do not lie awake for long periods
If the client is unable to fall asleep within 30 minutes, they should get out of bed, move to another room and only return to bed when they are ready to fall asleep. They should make sure the room is not at a noticeably different temperature from that of the bedroom. If they return to bed and still cannot sleep, this stage should be repeated. The goal is to minimise the amount of time spent in bed ruminating about lack of sleep

Awakening

Regular alarm
The client should be encouraged to try and wake with an alarm and rise at the same time each day, even at weekends

Two alarm clocks
It may be helpful to set two alarm clocks. The client can take their medication when woken by the first clock in order to improve their concentration and focus for their morning routine. The client should also set a second alarm clock at a time when their medication is likely to have begun acting. This could be positioned at a distance that requires them to leave the bed to turn it off

Hide alarm clock
Exposure to bright light or sunshine soon after waking can help the client wake naturally and feel more refreshed from their sleep. This could be done using lamps, which are on timers. A partner who wakes earlier than the individual can help by throwing open the curtains. This can help regulate the body's natural clock

first few nights, Jane found that she still could not sleep, so she was advised to return to the living room and continue reading, or just sat still, before returning to bed. She set her alarm for 7.30 am every morning and took her medication and listened to the radio before a second alarm roused her at 8.00 am when she got out of bed. The total number of hours asleep gradually increased to a more regular 7–8 hours per night and her quality of sleep improved. She also reported feeling less worried about the amount of sleep she was getting as this had been preoccupying her thoughts during the day.

SLEEP AND RUMINATION

Ironically, people with ADHD often report lying awake restlessly worrying about not being able to sleep. Worry and chronic anxiety can affect the amount and quality of sleep at all stages of the process:

- Before falling asleep – worrying thoughts can cause and maintain insomnia
- During sleep – day time stress and chronic anxiety can be associated with restless 'tossing and turning' or even nightmares
- After awakening – worrying thoughts and anxiety can occur after nightmare/ night terrors and prevent sleep. Also when individuals with ADHD experience low mood, their sleep may be affected and this can lead to reduced quality of sleep through the night accompanied by early waking. However, they may also find it extremely difficult to get up and face the day.

For individuals with ADHD, mood disturbance can also be exacerbated by a lack of sleep, whereby irritability, 'frayed nerves' and snappiness can lead to social problems. These difficulties can be self-perpetuating if others begin responding in a negative way towards the individual and cause them to feel more negative about themselves. The sleep hygiene techniques described above can be particularly useful for treating comorbid low mood and anxiety.

As for other affective symptoms, a cycle between thoughts, feelings and behaviours can maintain sleep difficulties. For example, a client who is unable to fall asleep may start thinking that they will not be able to perform the following day because they will be too tired, they then become anxious and frustrated about not being able to sleep, which means that they are less likely to sleep. They may then get up and try and carry out tasks, which they hope will prevent them from underachieving during the following day, but this makes them more alert and even less likely to be able to sleep during the night.

Examples of the thoughts, feelings and behaviours that mediate sleeplessness are provided below:

- Thoughts:
  'If I don't get seven or eight hours sleep, I haven't had enough sleep'
  'If I don't sleep, I won't be able to get up'
  'I won't be able to concentrate tomorrow and will forget things'
  'Lying in bed with eyes closed is more restful than sitting up'

- Feelings:
  Anxiety, frustration, worry

- Behaviours:
  Unable to fall asleep
  Surfing the net

Have a night cap
Get up and pace around
Get up and do activities in case by tomorrow they have been forgotten
Get up and look for something that may have been lost.

For example, the client Jane reported that when she woke up in the morning, she was already planning how she could fit extra sleep into her day in order to catch up on sleep missed during the night. Before she got into bed in the evening, she would be concerned that she would not fall asleep and then would frequently check her alarm clock and calculate the maximum number of hours more she could sleep before she had to get up.

Behavioural strategies to overcome sleep problems were outlined previously in Table 12.4. If these problems are associated with ruminative thinking, then it may also be helpful for the client to engage in the anxiety reduction techniques provided in Chapter 9. They may also be low in mood and benefit from work focusing on this issue, as suggested in Chapter 11. However, there are also several simple techniques which can be useful when working with clients who have specific concerns about their ability to sleep, which target the thoughts, feelings and behaviours described above (see Table 12.5, which is also presented on the Companion Website).

Table 12.5   Mood-related sleep strategies

Thoughts
Have designated 'worry time' well before winding down. Worries can be written down so they do not need to be rehearsed or remembered until the following day. Calming self-talk may also be useful by rehearsing statements such as 'A few hours sleep is better than no hours sleep'

Feelings
Relaxation techniques can help to reduce anxious feelings. For example, the client could imagine having their thoughts switched off or perform one of several simple techniques:

1. Counting from one to ten steadily but pausing after one of the numbers, e.g.
   1 (pause) 2 – 3 – 4 – 5 – 6 – 7 – 8 – 9 – 10
   1 – 2 (pause) 3 – 4 – 5 – 6 – 7 – 8 – 9 – 10
2. Progressive muscle relaxation (see Chapter 9)
3. Deep breathing
4. Guided imagery/distraction – imagine a pleasant scene: what can you see? what can you hear? what can you smell? what can you feel?

Behaviour
Behavioural strategies have been outlined previously in Table 12.4. If anxiety is driving the sleep problem, then the 'thought' and 'feeling' components should additionally be targeted.

CONCLUSIONS

The techniques described above can be helpful for people with ADHD regardless of whether sleep is their main complaint or their sleep problems are associated with other symptoms. Gaining an understanding of the nature of a sleep disorder and careful monitoring of the difficulties using a Sleep Diary will provide useful clues as to how best to intervene. Strategies can be implemented through the day, before bedtime, through the night and in the morning. Routines may be particularly useful for people with ADHD, who are often very active late at night trying to catch up with tasks they have not completed during the day. Change is usually monitored by the client spontaneously, who will quickly notice any improvement in the quantity and quality of sleep. However, it is also useful to repeat the exercise of monitoring sleep shown in Table 12.3 in order to objectively demonstrate improvements and the changes that underpin them.

13

SUBSTANCE MISUSE

When people with ADHD are being assessed by clinicians for the first time, it is recommended that the assessment includes a comprehensive screen for past and current history of substance misuse. In cases of serious drug misuse and/or dependency, the client should be treated by the appropriate service (e.g. drug rehabilitation service) prior to treatment for their ADHD.

People with ADHD often experience a different route into substance misuse than others. Use or abuse of substances (including nicotine, alcohol, cannabis, amphetamines and cocaine) is more common in adolescents and adults with ADHD than in the general population because they may have misused substances in order to self-medicate. In such cases, adolescents and young adults report a contraindicative effect of certain substances altering their functioning, for example, when taking amphetamines they may find that they do not experience the same hyped-up excitement as other people and report that they are better able to focus and concentrate. They may smoke a considerably greater number of cigarettes as nicotine, like amphetamine, is a dopamine agonist, which induces secretion of dopamine in the brain. This can have a similar effect to psychostimulant medication and can improve their ADHD symptoms. Other substances, such as alcohol and cannabis, tend not to have the same reinforcement in terms of symptom reduction but are used by ADHD adults in order to dampen down feelings of agitation to help them feel calmer.

When health professionals work with ADHD clients who have addictions they often voice concern about the prescription of psychostimulant medication to treat ADHD. This causes anxiety regarding the potential for abuse, for example: that it will be taken irregularly and in large doses; crushing, snorting and injecting it intravenously for its euphoric properties; taking it to stay awake for long periods of time; to lose weight; or sold for the recreational need of others. Whilst it is obviously difficult to generalise and caution must be taken, studies have suggested that treatment with stimulant medication for childhood ADHD does not increase the likelihood that

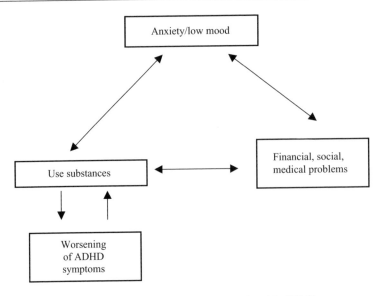

Figure 13.1   Context of substance misuse for people with ADHD

young people will misuse substances in later life (Brasset-Grundy & Butler, 2004a; Wilens, Faraone, Biederman & Gunawardene, 2003).

Substance misuse rarely occurs in isolation from other difficulties or stress affecting the individual. Figure 13.1 shows how many of the features often associated with ADHD that have been discussed in previous chapters can play a role in substance misuse.

People who become addicted to substances find themselves going through a vicious cycle, wherein emotional lability and/or low mood exacerbates ADHD symptoms and vice versa. Both problems may independently or cumulatively increase the risk that a person will use substances to bring (temporary) relief of their symptoms and/or fluctuating emotions. In turn, and with increasing use of substances, this may lead to financial and social problems, and/or medical complications. Such problems may overwhelm an individual who does not necessarily have adaptive coping strategies, causing them to feel anxious and/or low in mood. This state can exacerbate symptoms causing the individual to seek relief for their discomfort and engage in the cycle again.

This chapter will review each potential substance of abuse likely to be favoured by people with ADHD. Ways in which the therapist can best support and treat the ADHD client who is engaging in substance misuse will be introduced, drawing strongly on psychoeducation and motivational interviewing techniques to encourage the individual to engage in a process of change. Specific psychological management techniques are proposed for treatment and inclusion in a relapse prevention plan. A comprehensive treatment plan that would be required for individuals who have chronic and long-term substance misuse problems is not outlined comprehensively here as this would require specialist rehabilitation. However, the chapter does provide a brief intervention to motivate change in individuals who engage in intermittent use of drugs and alcohol.

SUBSTANCES USED BY ADHD INDIVIDUALS

Nicotine

Nicotine is primarily derived from smoking cigarettes and tobacco, although some individuals use nicotine patches or gum when they are trying to quit smoking. Many individuals with ADHD smoke over 20 cigarettes per day and find it extremely difficult to give up. Nicotine is one of the most addictive substances of misuse. It is a cerebral stimulant drug and hence provides some effect in reducing ADHD symptoms through its impact on the dopamine system. For individuals without ADHD, it has been shown to enhance sustained, divided and focused attention (Kassel, 1997). Indeed, there has even been research that suggests that nicotine patches may be an effective treatment of symptomatic ADHD (Levin et al., 1996). The health risks incurred from the long-term consequences of smoking are now well established in medical research and include cancer, lung and heart disease. However, ADHD smokers may be exposed to greater risk than their non-ADHD peers due to their inattentive problems. This is not from a health perspective, but from a risk perspective. For example, ADHD clients are easily distracted/or forgetful; they may not fully extinguish a cigarette; they may put their cigarette near flammable material or leave matches within the reach of small curious children.

Alcohol

Alcohol is the most commonly misused drug in the world and yet it is frequently not acknowledged as a potential substance of misuse, most likely reflecting its social acceptance in many cultures. However, alcohol has a sedative effect and people with ADHD report using alcohol to calm themselves down, which reduces feelings of agitation and restlessness. In social situations, they may use alcohol to overcome social inhibitions or social anxiety, arising from a history of social gaffs and/or poor impulse control. However, due to their poor impulse control, people with ADHD may find it difficult to regulate their alcohol intake; they may drink quickly and to excess. When intoxicated, individuals with ADHD will be even less likely than usual to regulate their mood, increasing the risk that they will become reckless and engage in risk-taking behaviour such as dangerous driving or criminal acts. Whilst the sensation of intoxication can provide initial rewards in terms of apparent symptom relief, a contraindicative side effect is that it may exacerbate underlying cognitive deficits associated with ADHD. Heavy alcohol use has been associated with executive dysfunction and poor short-term learning and memory, particularly in the visual domain in a general population study (Powell, 2004). Other health risks include chronic liver failure, kidney disease and gastrointestinal problems, in addition to acute alcohol poisoning leading to accidental death.

Tranquilizers

As with alcohol, tranquilizers are often used for their sedative effects in order to calm the individual. Benzodiazepines, which are prescribed for anxiety, are readily available in many homes and Tamazepam has been reported to be the most frequently abused. Barbiturates are now rarely used in the UK. ADHD individuals with sleep difficulties may be prescribed tranquilising medication, which is highly addictive (see Chapter 12 for psychological treatment to help reduce sleep problems).

Solvents (e.g. butane gas, lighter fluid, glue)

Solvent use is more common in young children and adolescents, possibly due to their relative availability to these age groups (Uzun & Kendirli, 2005). Matsumoto, Kamijo, Yamaguchi, Iseki and Hirayasu (2005) found that inhalant abusers have a higher incidence of childhood ADHD than methamphetamine abusers. Inhalation initially gives rise to a pleasurable reaction, but frequent use leads to problems such as poor coordination, confusion and hallucinations. Adolescents who use inhalants are more likely to go on to develop substance abuse problems with alcohol and opiates (Wu, Pilowsky & Schlenger, 2005). The long-term health implications include neurotoxicity, in addition to alterations in gastrointestinal, respiratory and cardiovascular functioning.

Cannabis

If young people are going to use illegal drugs, then cannabis seems to be the drug of choice. Anecdotal reports from clients suggest that they started to use cannabis as teenagers and have continued to use it into middle age and beyond. They report that it 'takes the edge' off their ADHD symptoms; particularly their feelings of restlessness and inability to relax. They report feeling that cannabis induces a sense of control and well-being by smoking small amounts of cannabis throughout the day to reduce symptoms yet maintain an adequate degree of day-to-day functioning. This is in contrast to alcohol misuse, which may impair functioning. The major disadvantage of cannabis for people with ADHD is that it exacerbates existing cognitive deficits associated with ADHD, for example it has an adverse effect on attention, working memory and time estimation. Excessive use may induce feelings of paranoia and deterioration in mental state.

Stimulants (amphetamines, cocaine, crack, etc.)

Psychostimulant use in individuals without ADHD can produce an elevation of mood and a sense of increased energy with reduction in appetite and sleep. However, lower doses may 'normalise' the behaviour of people with ADHD as this group of drugs impacts on the dopaminergic system, leading to improved attention and a reduction in impulse control difficulties. Some individuals with ADHD report having used amphetamines regularly for years prior to their diagnosis and receiving prescribed treatment with psychostimulants. Nevertheless, notwithstanding the huge variability in quality and purity of the substance, the disadvantages of self-medicating (either consciously or unconsciously) by using recreational drugs are that high doses of stimulants can make people feel anxious or irritable. In addition, street stimulants can be highly addictive and people can develop dependency very quickly. Withdrawal and cravings can lead to changes in their behaviour, such that they may change from being talkative and overly friendly to agitated and irritable. In some cases, clients have reported feeling deeply disturbed by feelings of paranoia, for example visual or auditory hallucinations, in the context of heavy stimulant use. In such cases, individuals will require close and regular monitoring if they are to be prescribed psychostimulant medication, preferably on an inpatient basis.

Hallucinogens

Hallucinogens include ecstasy and LSD. These drugs may be used by people with ADHD in their quest for stimulation and sensation seeking. Ecstasy is associated with a sense of euphoria, well-being, increased activity and a reduced need for sleep. Dehydration is a very common side effect and it is extremely important that users consistently drink fluids such as water. However, ecstasy is commonly used recreationally at 'raves' or clubs, where fluid intake may be excessive alcohol. High doses can result in paranoid psychosis, depression, anxiety and suicidal ideas. Ecstasy is also associated with a rapid development of tolerance.

LSD is another hallucinogen. This drug creates the effect of visual distortion, disturbance in sense of time and increased sensitivities to colours and sound. These sensations may be attractive to people with ADHD, who are experimental in nature and not afraid to take risks. However, users are particularly sensitive to their environment and a threatening atmosphere can create a 'bad trip'. Adverse effects include later flashbacks and panic attacks.

Opiates (heroin, methadone, codeine, etc.)

Some adults with ADHD have experimented with harder drugs such as heroin. Regular use of such drugs results in a higher tolerance to opiates leading to dependency and addiction. Dependence withdrawal occurs 8–12 hours after the last dose, leading to symptoms of intense craving for the drug, restlessness, irritability, increased bowel activity, nausea and vomiting. Withdrawal and craving, combined with an impulsive temperament, may increase the likelihood of individuals committing opportunistic theft and violence to fund their habit. The prescription of oral methadone is the commonest approach to the management of opiate withdrawal. If individuals present with this level of dependency, then it is strongly recommended that the person is referred for detoxification. Only after this has been successfully completed and the person has been drug free for a period of at least six months should psychological treatment for ADHD be commenced. Prior to this, it would be difficult to determine whether symptoms relate to drug misuse or ADHD.

PSYCHOEDUCATION

Psychoeducation is a vital component of the process of change. It is important that clients make informed decisions and are empowered to make choices. This is achieved by the therapist outlining the model of the stages of substance misuse. It applies techniques to assess the position of the client within the model, and evaluates the risk of their behaviour.

The Five Stages of Substance Use

Substance use can usually be categorised into one of five different stages of use. Individuals may use several substances, each in different stages. Table 13.1 shows the different stages and describes the function or motivation each stage serves to an individual with ADHD (this is also included on the Companion Website in handout format).

A characteristic of ADHD is sensation-seeking behaviour and a need for stimulation. The first stage of experimenting with drugs can fulfill these needs as they provide personal gratification in the form of thrills and excitement. For example, a client, Craig, described how he first began abusing solvents when truanting from school. This arose partly because, by not attending school, he had more unstructured time on his hands; he became bored and wanted thrills and excitement. He thought he could achieve this by trying new experiences. He made friends with a group of

Table 13.1   The five stages of substance use

Stage of use	Motivation for use
1. Experimental	Curiosity; pleasure seeking; risk taking; sensation seeking; poor impulse control
2. Social	Need to be liked; affected by peer group social influence; social attitude; depends on availability
3. Instrumental	Used purposefully to create certain behaviours such as seeking 'highs' or using to 'cope' with stress and negative feelings
4. Habitual	The 'need' to use becomes more regular and frequent
5. Dependent	The substance is constantly 'needed' and misuse is regarded as 'normal' despite negative consequences

adolescents who spent time at the local park, drinking alcohol and sniffing glue. He also started to steal items from shops. People with ADHD are unlikely to consider the risks attached to taking a mind-altering substance because they do not think about the potential consequences. Aside from damaging his health, Craig ran the risk of being caught and prosecuted, but he did not consider this possibility.

The second stage of substance use, the social stage, may be particularly relevant for people with ADHD as they may perceive this to be a way of making friends and increasing their popularity. Drug misuse may be a means of integration with peers, as opposed to being an outsider. The ADHD individual may believe that if they take drugs, they will be accepted by their peer group (even if this is a deviant peer group), which is a position to which they have long aspired. For example, Craig looked older than his friends and got away with buying alcohol when he was 15 years old. For a brief period he found he was very popular with his new friends who requested him to purchase drink on their behalf. He believed he was accepted socially and spent time with these friends in the park drinking to excess. When his new friends became old enough to buy their own alcohol, they were no longer interested in Craig.

Once the individual enters the instrumental stage, the drug provides 'positive reinforcement'. This means the individual feels rewarded by their experience of taking the drug itself and this increases the likelihood that they will take it again. For example, many young people take ecstasy to stay up and dance all night. They have a great time and do not feel tired, so the next time they go out late, they take ecstasy again. This begins to become a problem when the person believes that they cannot have a good time or enjoy themselves without taking the drug. Ironically, for individuals with ADHD, the positive reinforcement may be that they are better able to concentrate and complete tasks. Their social skills may improve as they engage better in social situations by resisting the urge to flit about in company or frequently change the topic of conversation. For example, after trying speed (amphetamines), Craig felt more confident and believed he was more capable in social interactions. He believed he was wittier and that he engaged in a more meaningful way with his new friends.

However, when a person feels the need to use substances on a daily basis in order to fulfill routine functions, they move to the 'habitual stage'. This can be a costly habit and, for some individuals, this may be the trigger to engage in criminal behaviour in order to fund the addiction. This may commence in a small way, and one that may not always be considered as 'criminal', such as taking money from their mother's purse. However, in time, these behaviours may escalate and include petty crimes of theft or shoplifting. As a young man, Craig used to make excuses and postpone paying his rent to allow him to buy more cannabis and speed as he believed he could not function without it. As the debts stacked up, he borrowed money from his friends, parents and girlfriend, intending to repay them on his next payday, but he never managed to achieve this.

The state of 'dependency' arises when an individual continues to use substances in spite of negative consequences and they feel they cannot manage without it. For example, Craig found that he was not able to get up in the morning to go to work after a night of clubbing and poly-drug use. He avoided seeing his girlfriend because she became angry with him for wasting his money and being irritable.

Table 13.2 provides a checklist that allows the therapist and the client to identify problems the client may be experiencing due to their drug use. Items that are endorsed

Table 13.2 Problems associated with substance misuse

As a result of taking…do you ?	Circle Y / N
Engage in verbally aggressive behaviour	(Y)/ N
Engage in physically aggressive or violent behaviour	(Y)/ N
Often feel irritable	(Y)/ N
Often feel temperamental	Y /(N)
Often feel frustrated	Y /(N)
Feel depressed/unhappy	(Y)/ N
Feel anxious	Y /(N)
Feel inadequate	(Y)/ N
Lack self-control	(Y)/ N
Have difficulty communicating with people (i.e. you feel people misunderstand you)	(Y)/ N
Fall out with people	Y /(N)
Not look after yourself well, e.g. personal hygiene, pride in appearance	Y /(N)
Engage in delinquent and/or criminal behaviour	(Y)/ N
Have difficulty studying or working	Y /(N)
Engage in unsafe sex	(Y)/ N
Self-harm (ideas or behaviour)	Y /(N)
Have greater concentration problems	Y /(N)
Have greater memory problems	(Y)/ N
Lack motivation to do anything	(Y)/ N
Have loss of appetite	Y /(N)
Have feelings of paranoia	(Y)/ N
Have unusual experiences, e.g. visual hallucinations, 'flashbacks'	Y /(N)
Engage in reckless or risky behaviour	(Y)/ N
Experience employment problems	Y /(N)
Lack in confidence	(Y)/ N
Feel dissatisfied with life	(Y)/ N
TOTAL SCORE	15

Table 13.3   Substance, stage and motivation

Substance	Stage of use	Reason for use	Consequence of use
Alcohol	Habitual	I can't cope in social situations without it	I have hangovers and feel low
Nicotine	Dependent	I can't concentrate without it	I have breathing difficulties
Cannabis	Habitual	It has a calming effect. It allows me to get through the day	I feel edgy and paranoid
Cocaine	Social	I become more entertaining and have more energy	I need more each time I use it
LSD	Experimental	I like the sensation of having a trip. It's exciting	I have panic attacks
Speed	Instrumental	It calms me down	I feel rough when it wears off

should be used as a basis for further discussion and exploration in sessions. A blank copy is provided in the Companion Website for use in sessions. In time physiological tolerance to substances means the individual must increase their dose to obtain the same effect or stimulation. Dependency is characterised by a state when the drug/alcohol becomes a priority for the individual and no longer causes the desired effect but withdrawal causes undesired effects. Short-term benefits (e.g. the ability to concentrate) are replaced by an increasingly greater need for the drug.

A drug of preference is often augmented by the use of alternative or additional substances, such as an alcoholic 'chaser' drinking strong lager with spirits or poly-drug use. In such circumstances, the individual may find themselves operating at different stages in the cycle (outlined in Table 13.3) for different substances. Thus, when a client with ADHD is misusing substances, it is very important to identify the substances they use, the stage of use for each substance and tease apart the purpose each serves and the consequences of use. Table 13.3 shows an example of how the therapist and client can achieve this to identify potential areas requiring intensive treatment (see Companion Website for a copy suitable to be used in sessions).

An exercise to help the client identify both their goals for improvement and their current vulnerabilities is to ask them to imagine a person with a drug addiction and rate this person's behaviour in the risk domains. They should then imagine a person without an addiction and predict this person's behaviour in the same domains. See Table 13.4 for an example of the exercise completed by Craig (see Companion Website for a blank version for use in sessions).

Craig was asked to look at the ratings for each person and think about what they told him. He decided that the better outcome was for the non-user and this allowed him

Table 13.4 Risk domain exercise

Imagine you are observing two different people, one is a dependent substance user and one is an ordinary person who does not use substances – say a successful man/woman in full-time work with a family. What are they like? How likely are they to have the following problems? Rate them on a scale of 0–4.

0 Not at all likely	1	2	3	4 Highly likely

	Substance user	Non-substance user
Engage in verbally aggressive behaviour	3	1
Engage in physically aggressive or violent behaviour	4	1
Often feel irritable	4	0
Often feel temperamental	4	1
Often feel frustrated	4	2
Feel depressed/unhappy	4	0
Feel anxious	3	1
Feel inadequate	3	1
Lack self-control	4	0
Have difficulty communicating with people	3	0
Fall out with people	2	1
Not look after self well	3	0
Engage in delinquent and/or criminal behaviour	3	0
Have difficulty studying or working	3	1
Engage in unsafe sex	3	1
Self-harm (ideas or behaviour)	4	2
Have greater concentration problems	3	1
Have greater memory problems	4	1
Lack motivation to do anything	4	0
Have loss of appetite	4	1
Have feelings of paranoia	4	1
Have unusual experiences, e.g. visual hallucinations, 'flashbacks'	4	2
Engage in reckless or risky behaviour	4	1
TOTAL PROBLEM SCORE	81	19

Look at the ratings for each person. What does it tell you? Who would you rather be?

to reflect on his own drug use and where this was leading him. This process was an influential factor in his decision to stop taking drugs and make changes in his life.

MOTIVATIONAL INTERVIEWING

Encouraging an individual to make important change in their life involves the individual acknowledging that they are dissatisfied with aspects of their life and accepting that alternative possibilities are achievable. In order to do this, the therapist must encourage the individual to think about change as a process. This can be likened to a journey that requires organisation and preparation. In these sessions the client will learn about the stages of the journey, in other words the stages of change and the reasons for making the journey. It is hoped that they will recognise that their goal is to achieve a better quality of life.

Making Change

The readiness of the individual to tackle their addictions will depend on many factors, both environmental (e.g. all their friends being drug users; having to walk past a venue every day where dealers offer them drugs) and psychological (e.g. having insight into their problem; believing that they can function adequately without the substance). Research has shown that people with substance misuse problems can be classified as being at various points on a 'transtheoretical model of change' (Miller & Rollnick, 2002; Prochaska and DiClemente, 1982). In this model, individuals move systematically through a series of five stages in the course of resolving their problems: pre-contemplation; contemplation; preparation; action; and maintenance.

Motivational interviewing is a technique based on the transtheoretical model of change. It is designed to help individuals explore and resolve ambivalence to change and is particularly useful in helping people in the contemplation stage of change, where the task of the therapist is to help 'tip the balance' from ambivalence to favouring change. Motivational interviewing engages the client in an empathetically supportive but strategically directed conversation about their substance misuse and has received empirical support in the treatment of alcohol and drug abuse (Van Horn & Bux, 2001).

Table 13.5 summarises these stages, which are also provided in handout format on the Companion Website. The stages are likely to be recognised by the client, particularly with respect to where they get 'stuck' in the process and prevented from moving forward. This is helpful to determine obstacles to progression.

An alternative to the maintenance stage is relapse, when the individual begins another cycle. Most people experience slips or relapses and have to go through the cycle of change again before successfully maintaining change.

It is important to remember that these stages can be 'cyclical' with the client oscillating between stages (and this may occur for some time). For example, the client may revert back a step and waver between earlier stages by engaging in a stage of 'action' but then relapse and misuse substances again. This may mean that they revert to a stage of preparation or even contemplation before progressing further in the cycle. Being able to stop misusing substances takes time, courage and motivation before a person can be successful. It is far from easy, and working through the process of stages will involve the support and encouragement from family and friends as well as the therapist.

Table 13.5 Five stages of seeking help

Stage 1: Pre-contemplative stage

The core feature of the pre-contemplative stage is that the problem of substance misuse is not acknowledged and using is considered to be more important than the problems it causes. Individuals in this phase do not consider changing their behaviour as they do not accept that they have a problem. For people with ADHD, it can be difficult to move out of a pre-contemplative stage to a contemplative stage, as this involves a process of self-reflection and also because their thoughts are often racing ahead so they are unable to stop and consider their situation or needs

Stage 2: Contemplative stage

At this stage the individual begins to acknowledge that they have a problem and considers making change but finds reasons to justify continued use and/or does not consider themselves able to change. This stage is characterised by ambivalence

Stage 3: Determination stage (sometimes referred to as the 'preparation' or 'decision-making' phase)

The individual makes a decision to change the problem behaviour. At this stage the individual has the intention to take action to stop substance misuse but may be uncertain about how to follow this through

Stage 4: Action stage

In the action stage, the individual will stop substance misuse and exhibit a change in their belief system regarding substance misuse. The individual begins to modify the problem behaviour

Stage 5: Maintenance stage

After successfully negotiating the action phase, individuals move to maintenance or sustained change, during which the individual is actively working towards continuing to stop substance use over a period of months and years

It is important to introduce the concept of change to the client. This may seem obvious, but to an individual who has physiological and/or psychological dependency, plus poor impulse control, this may seem far from an 'obvious' phenomenon. To encourage 'change', the client and therapist need to identify the clients' future goals, for example what they desire, and what they will plan to achieve. In Chapter 11, the importance of breaking down goals into smaller achievable steps was introduced, such as for the goal to get a job, an action plan may be to buy daily newspapers, go to the job centre, register with employment agencies, make enquiries about voluntary work, find out about local training courses organised by the job centre or further education courses, etc. The substance misusing client must determine not only how to motivate themselves and achieve these steps, but how to do so without using alcohol or drugs. This often means working with the client to improve their self-efficacy and raise their self-esteem. This will involve determining the social support structures around the individual (including those that may be undesirable and negative), what problems may be encountered in achieving the goals and how they may be overcome. Table 13.6 provides a structure to help the client identify reasons to engage in a process of change, who is likely to assist, as well as identify potential pitfalls. The table shows the information completed by Craig (see Companion Website for a format for use in sessions).

Table 13.6   The problem of change

Why do you want to stop? I want to stop using because:
Using speed is making me feel edgy and low
I don't get anything done any more
I've lost my job

What do you want? My main goals for making this change are:
I've been evicted from my flat and I need to find a new one
To improve my relationship with Sarah

What can you do about it? This is what I plan to do to achieve my goals:

Action	When?
Look in local newspaper	Thursdays
Register with local estate agents	Saturday
Arrange a special date with Sarah	Saturday
Don't go where the dealers hang out	All week

Who can you get to help you? Other people could help me with change:

Person	Possible ways
Mum	Can store furniture, put me up in short-term
Sarah	Doing things together away from places where there are drugs
Steve + Jan	Arrange an evening with Sarah's friends
Dave	Go to the gym

What might stop you succeeding? I anticipate possible obstacles to change:

Possible obstacles	How to respond
Going to a club or party where there are drugs	Leave. Tell Sarah or a friend how I feel
Sarah not trusting me	Reassure her as best I can and stay off drugs. Ask her to help
Bad credit reference	Save up and offer to pay cash in advance

---

I will know that my plan is working when I see these results:
Move into a new flat
No rent arrears
Manage my money
Relationship seems better with Sarah and we see each other on a more regular basis

---

It should always be acknowledged that one of the main reasons why individuals continue to use substances is that they perceive it holds some advantage for them, despite the disadvantages. Miller and Rollnick (2002) highlight that the nature of a client's ambivalence can be complex, and can comprise a set of pros and cons for each of the options available. Thus, in order to explore ambivalence to change, the client should be asked to discuss the positive and negative aspects of their substance misuse and generate a list of advantages and disadvantages for continuing to use the substance. Hence, Craig completed a 'decisional balance sheet' in the form of a 4×4 matrix (see Table 13.7; a blank version of the table is provided on the Companion Website),

Table 13.7   Decisional balance sheet

Continuing to use amphetamines	Making a change and giving up amphetamines
Benefits	*Benefits*
Stops me from drinking	I'll save money
I like it	Less trouble with the police
I lose my temper less often	I'll be able to concentrate
I feel relaxed	More positive influence on my brother
I've got new friends I take it with	I'll get more motivation
Costs	*Costs*
It's hard to get up for work in the morning	I might lose my drug taking friends
I can't concentrate	
I feel uptight and anxious	
I think people are looking at me	
Sarah said she would leave me	
My mother won't let me stay with her	

which incorporated the costs and benefits of continuing to use substances, and of making a change. It is imperative that the client thinks carefully about the impact of the substance on their health, personal functioning, interpersonal relationships, ability to study or work, and behaviour. Indeed, the therapist must guide the client and ensure they recognise that the costs often outweigh the benefits. In Craig's example, with guidance he generated many more reasons to discontinue taking amphetamines than continuing. Whilst these techniques may appear somewhat repetitive, when introducing the concept of change repetition of the advantages is an important positive reinforcer that should be employed in sessions.

Miller and Rollnick (2002) argue it is not a simple matter of the number of positive versus negative factors that influence motivation, but the importance of each of the factors. In some cases, the client will insist on emphasising the positive qualities of using a substance and resist acknowledging the negative qualities. This may result in them identifying just as many reasons to use it as not to use it. In such cases, the client should be invited to weight their reasons in terms of importance. This is illustrated in Table 13.8 when Craig was asked to assign an importance score (0–5) to each of the advantages and disadvantages for continuing to take amphetamines (see Companion Website for blank version for use in sessions). Craig assigned a total importance rating of 15 to the benefits of taking amphetamines and a total importance rating of 25 to the costs. He gave a weighting of 21 to the benefits of giving up amphetamines and only 4 to the cost of giving up. Thus, the outcome clearly illustrated that the disadvantages far outweighed the advantages both in terms of the number of positives and negatives, and their weighted importance.

Table 13.8 Weighted advantages/disadvantages worksheet

0	1	2	3	4	5
Not important at all					*Extremely important*

Continuing to take amphetamines		*Making a change and giving up amphetamines*	
Benefits	*Weight*	*Benefits*	*Weight*
Stops me from drinking	5	I'll save money	5
I like it	5	Less trouble with the police	4
I lose my temper less often	3	I'll be able to concentrate	4
I feel relaxed	1	More positive influence on	4
I've got new friends I take it with	1	my brother	
		I'll get more motivation	4
TOTAL WEIGHTED SCORE	15	TOTAL WEIGHTED SCORE	21
Costs	*Weight*	*Costs*	*Weight*
It's hard to get up for work in the morning	4	I might lose drug-taking friends	4
I can't concentrate	4		
I feel uptight and anxious	5		
I think people are looking at me	4		
Sarah said she would leave me	5		
My mother won't let me stay with her	3		
TOTAL WEIGHTED SCORE	25	TOTAL WEIGHTED SCORE	4

MANAGEMENT STRATEGIES

Bellack and DiClimente (1999) recommend that once a client is engaged in treatment they should be taught the skills necessary to become and remain abstinent. At this stage, therapy sessions should include behavioural skills for refusing substances, with emphasis on simple behavioural elements, such as making eye contact, not smiling and saying 'no' clearly. Role-play is helpful in the treatment sessions, as the overt rehearsal of skills has generally been shown to enhance treatment effects (e.g. Kazdin and Mascitelli, 1982). The aim is for the client to learn a few specific skills that may be used automatically, thereby minimising cognitive load for decision making during stressful interactions.

Once the client has engaged in the action stage, they will be supported to maintain this position and develop the skills to resist temptation. This involves clients developing the confidence to apply successful strategies to overcome physical and psychological cravings. This may be achieved by employing methods such as distraction and imagery; challenging and controlling dysfunctional beliefs; self-empowerment through the ability to embrace the concept of 'choice'; increasing self-esteem; the application of self-reinforcement techniques; activity scheduling; and motivating social support, rewards and positive feedback.

Controlling Physical Cravings and Urges

A craving is when someone really 'wants' something and an urge is where they 'do' something. For example, cravings for certain foods can occur, because you want to eat them; but you may have urges to eat certain foods because you feel you 'must' eat them. People who have urges feel uncomfortable unless they are able to relieve the sense of wanting something. Physical cravings and urges are linked with negative mood and/or low self-esteem. It is helpful to use distraction techniques to manage cravings, such as talking to someone, listening to music. Urges can be relieved by replacing what is wanted with something else that is less harmful. For example, methadone is commonly provided in place of heroin for people on drug rehabilitation programmes; nicotine patches can be an effective substitute for cigarettes; chewing gum and drinking fizzy drinks may also help alleviate urges to misuse drugs and alcohol. The client may have already identified techniques that work; Table 13.9 shows the distraction and replacement techniques that Craig identified as having worked for him in the past. He also added to the list some possible techniques that he could try out (see Companion Website for a version for use in sessions).

The distraction techniques outlined in Table 13.10 may prompt ideas for the client to try out. The Companion Website includes this table in handout format and as a flashcard, which the client may keep in a wallet and use to remind themselves of a technique they can apply when needed. For example, a cognitive method to help the client cope with cravings is to teach them to say to themselves 'stop!' Train them to employ visual imagery to do this by imagining a stop sign or a brick wall. They should then focus on their surroundings and describe items in the room in minute detail. Once they have become less tense and more relaxed, encourage the client to conjure up an image in their head. They may wish to think of a positive image, for example a place where they have felt safe

Table 13.9 Distraction and replacement techniques

Substance: amphetamines	
Distraction techniques that work for you	Replacement techniques to manage urges
go to the gym	drinking caffeinated tea/coffee
play guitar	chew nicotine gum
talk to Sarah and ask for her help	take a caffeine tablet
go for a run	have a glucose energy drink

Table 13.10 Distraction techniques

Focus on the external environment to distract thoughts from internal cravings – concentrate
  on the trees, the grass, the people, the shops, etc.
Engage in some form of mental activity, e.g. mental arithmetic, crossword puzzles, reading
Talk to someone who is unconnected to the substance
Physical exercise, get out and about, e.g. take a brisk walk, visit a friend, go for a drive to
  escape cravings
Perform household tasks to keep busy
Spend some time playing games, such as cards, computer games, board games, etc

and happy once before, such as the seaside, and focus on little details, e.g. the
sound of the gulls, the lapping of the waves, the sand between their toes, etc.
Alternately, they may wish to use a *negative image*, for example imagine what it
would be like to lose the house, family, friends, health, hurting the people they
love and having them feel angry towards them, etc. It may help to refer back to
the exercise in Table 13.4 when the client imagined a substance user and compared their life with that of a non-user, and incorporate aspects of the exercise
into the imaginal mode.

Dysfunctional Beliefs

Dysfunctional and addictive beliefs are very unhelpful and contribute greatly
to the generation of perceived uncontrollable urges for substances. Figure 13.2

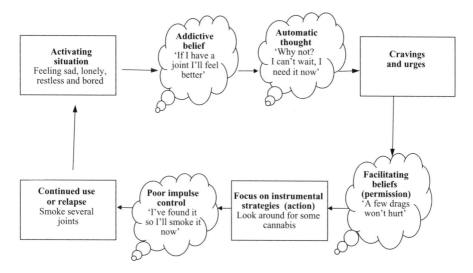

Figure 13.2 The sequence of thoughts and beliefs during cravings and urges

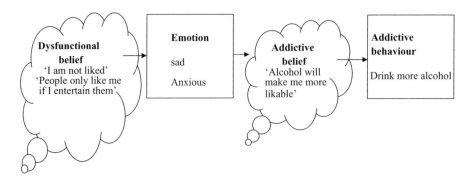

Figure 13.3   Dysfunctional beliefs that can maintain substance misuse

demonstrates the negative cyclical relationship between such thoughts, cravings and urges.

This figure can be used in treatment with the client by asking them to complete thoughts and behaviours as appropriate using the blank copy on the Companion Website. This will identify thoughts and beliefs that may be cognitively challenged at relevant points in the process. *Dysfunctional beliefs* play an important role in the maintenance of substance misuse. For example, a client, Katherine, believed that she was only liked when she was being sociable and witty. Katherine formed the dysfunctional belief that drinking alcohol made her more amusing. This reinforced the urge to drink and created an *addictive belief* that alcohol made her more likeable. The relationship between Katherine's dysfunctional beliefs and addictive behaviour is shown in Figure 13.3. A blank version is provided on the Companion Website for use in sessions.

Table 13.11 gives examples of other addictive beliefs commonly expressed by ADHD clients.

Choice and Self-esteem

Individuals who have travelled far in the hierarchy of substance misuse may lose sight of the concept of choice and will. Clients should be asked to think back to a time when they made the choice not to use and had a positive outcome and positive self-esteem. They should then describe how they felt. The therapist should explore what they can do to help themselves get back to this stage again. They should focus on the good qualities such as positive feelings, experiences and behaviours that have occurred during their effort to stop misusing substances. This technique can be particularly empowering for people with ADHD who find themselves at the mercy of their impulses and incorrectly believe their lack of self-control means they lack choice. This belief is a thinking error.

Table 13.11   Addictive beliefs

Taking drugs…	_Example of addictive belief_
Improves concentration	I can't focus without it
Reduces inner restlessness	I can't feel calm without it
Improves confidence	I can't perform without it
Increases in social functioning	I'll be witty and seem dull without it
Improves self-efficacy	I can't achieve without it
Increases pleasure and excitement	Life is boring without it
Increases energy and motivation	It is the only thing that motivates me
Relieves boredom	The situation won't be so bad if I have it beforehand
Relieves tension, anxiety, and depression	I can't cope without it – it's the only thing that makes me feel better about myself
Maintains psychological and emotional balance	I'll go to pieces without it
Improves social skills	I communicate better and become more extroverted
Relieves craving	If craving is not appeased it will get worse
Justifies dependency	I am addicted so have no option

Self-reinforcement Techniques

Posters can be useful reminders of goals; that is, to reduce and quit using a substance. It may also be helpful to have an advantages/disadvantages table on the wall or a list of distraction techniques that the individual can use as a prompt when an urge or craving arises. A flashcard, kept in a wallet, for example, can be used to remind the individual of the advantages of stopping substance use. The client should carry the card at all times and read it when they feel weak and vulnerable (see Table 13.12). An example that can be used for this purpose is provided on the Companion Website.

It may be helpful to list on the flip side of the flashcard any coping strategies and techniques that have been determined in the course of treatment that will help the client get through the 'risk period' when they feel vulnerable.

Activity Scheduling

Activity scheduling involves making a structured plan to squeeze out risk periods when the client recognises they may be vulnerable to substance misuse. Pay particular attention to times when the client is most likely to be sensitive to cravings, urges and withdrawal. See Chapters 4 and 11 for further information about activity scheduling.

Table 13.12 Flashcards of self-reinforcement

I am in more control without it
I am less aggressive without it
I don't want to hurt my family or friends
I look healthier without it
I don't want it – I want it to stop NOW.

Social Support

It is essential that the client does not go it alone. It is really important that they are supported and that they engage the help of friends and family. There are also services that provide support and/or more formal treatment to help reduce excessive emotional reactions, modify self-defeating behaviour and help change beliefs and attitudes concerning the more problematic aspects of substance use. Some are local walk-in services where the client can obtain confidential support and advice. Others offer more formal rehabilitation for addiction. However, the client will require ongoing support not only outside of treatment but also following treatment, in order to plan and prevent relapse. Internet support groups have also become one source of such support.

Rewards and Positive Feedback

Rewards are a very important part of any treatment programme for people with ADHD. Immediate rewards for success include giving themselves a pat on the back, self-praise and/or a more tangible reward for periods where they have succeeded in reducing or rejecting using the substance. The client should inform others about their progress, so that they too can give support and encouragement. This will help to boost their confidence and self-esteem. Treats, rewards, showing off and telling others how well they have done will boost their confidence.

CONCLUSIONS

The process of change requires personal acceptance and once this has been achieved, abstinence and a healthier lifestyle may be maintained by applying specific treatment techniques. Substance misuse is complex and ADHD individuals with sustained long-term use at a level of dependency will require specialist intervention and rehabilitation. This chapter has provided a briefer intervention suitable for individuals who have perhaps long-term but intermittent use. Such individuals will be suitable for treatment using the motivational interviewing technique outlined in this chapter to wean them away from excessive use of drugs and alcohol as a social crutch and/or the risk of damaging their health with unprescribed drugs.

PART IV

THE FUTURE

14

PREPARING FOR THE FUTURE

This is the last chapter in the Young–Bramham Programme. By the time the final stages of treatment have been reached, the therapist is likely to feel that they have shared a journey of self-development with the client. The journey probably started with the words 'You have ADHD'. To the client, these words were not just a diagnosis, but a framework for self-understanding. The client is very likely to feel that they have undertaken an emotionally demanding process culminating in self-adjustment, adaptation and, finally, acceptance of their condition.

As a therapist, the journey's course has involved imparting new psychological techniques in order to develop or enhance the client's skills. The modular design of the Young–Bramham Programme has provided the structure to tailor the psychological intervention to the needs of the client. This began in Part I of the book, which described the background to the programme and provided advice about psychological assessment of the core symptoms of ADHD, in other words, inattention and memory problems, time management and problem-solving difficulties, and poor impulse control. Treatment modules to manage these problems were outlined in the second part of the book. Part III provided treatment modules providing interventions for the comorbid conditions and associated problems commonly experienced by people with ADHD.

This final module – preparing for the future – is extremely important as it entails a shift from problem-resolution towards a more positive position involving the optimisation of the client's strengths and their future application. It is important to be mindful, nevertheless, that the end of treatment is always difficult. This may be particularly so for ADHD individuals who have experienced a lifetime of telling their story yet feel that no one has listened or shown interest. The therapist who has conducted the Young–Bramham Programme has not only listened but also provided a programme suitable for the client's personal needs and development. This level of support or understanding may be new to the client and thus the ending of treatment must be carefully managed.

It is suggested that the final treatment sessions provide a pragmatic review of what has been learnt, but also acknowledge and processe the emotional journey undertaken by the client. This will involve thinking about the future, raising self-esteem, reviewing achievements and considering how to maximise these in the future to promote healthy mental functioning and instrumental success.

Consistent with the general format of the Young–Bramham Programme modules, the last module begins with a psychoeducational aspect in the form of a discussion regarding the heterogeneous progression of ADHD. There then follows discussion about what the client expects in the future, and a review of the progress made to date. The objective is to increase awareness of how ADHD may impact on individuals in the years ahead; making plans for the future; and how best to enlist support in future endeavours. It is important to emphasise the positive aspects of having ADHD such as creativity and resilience, and discuss how the client can apply these characteristics adaptively to achieve success in everyday challenges, as well as in medium and longer-term plans. In particular it is important to consider how expectations of the self may influence future outcomes and become self-fulfilling prophecies. Many people with ADHD have negative assumptions about themselves and an expectation of failure. Yet, through the reappraisal of their capabilities, people with ADHD can be encouraged to develop a greater sense of self-efficacy and purpose.

Thus, the latter sessions of the Young–Bramham Programme review the potential progression and sequelae of ADHD and summarise salient themes that have arisen in treatment. Cognitive behavioural techniques that have been effective in prior modules should be emphasised and reinforced. Raising self-esteem is an implicit theme in every module throughout the Young–Bramham Programme, but at the end of treatment this becomes more explicit with the introduction of specific techniques to draw attention to past successes and achievements and improve confidence in future performance and self-efficacy. Finally, the therapist should engage the client in a process of transferring the emotional and practical support provided in treatment sessions to outside resources. This may include enlisting the help of friends, family and sometimes the services of other professionals.

Hence, the termination of treatment involves a three-fold process:

1. To review the progression of ADHD and the clients' expectations of the future.
2. To review past achievements and successes during treatment with the objective of raising self-esteem.
3. To put in place methods to access social support outside of the therapeutic environment.

THE PROGRESSION OF ADHD

Different symptoms decline at different rates in ADHD. The course of the disorder usually involves hyperactivity diminishing first, followed by impulsivity. Inattention seems to be the most prominent symptom lasting into adulthood (Bramham et al., 2005a). However, even when they no longer have a full complement of symptoms or meet criteria for diagnosis, many clients remain partially symptomatic. This is known as 'ADHD in partial remission' and, for some, symptoms may continue into middle age. Thus, some individuals require pharmacological treatment well into adulthood. Others may only require pharmacological treatment if their residual symptoms continue to cause them functional problems in some settings or circumstances.

There are three primary factors that determine the extent to which symptoms will cause functional problems:

1. *Biological change* affects the symptoms directly, e.g. maturation of the brain.
2. *Environmental change*, e.g. the ability to change the environment around them so that problems arising from the symptoms are reduced.
3. *Psychological coping strategies*, e.g. by the individual recognising how symptoms affect them and the development of internal techniques to manage their symptoms and problems.

There is not much that the client can do to speed up biological change. Medication serves to relieve symptoms but does not treat the underlying cause of symptoms. An analogy is that spectacles help one to see better but do not change eyesight overall. Similarly, medication has been shown to improve concentration and impulse control (to varying degrees), but once the effects of medication have worn off, the symptoms rebound. Nevertheless, there are methods that one can apply to influence environmental and psychological factors, and many of these have been introduced in the Young–Bramham Programme modules.

Although most people gradually experience an improvement in some symptoms with maturation, some people find that, although their ADHD symptoms no longer cause them problems, they have difficulties due to the 'legacy' of ADHD. For example, some people experience mood-related difficulties due to low self-esteem. They may find that, despite improvement in their ADHD symptoms, they remain caught in a negative cycle of debasement and low self-expectations. They anticipate underachievement. Indeed, in spite of ADHD being a heterogeneous syndrome, many clients report consistently that they believe they are not achieving their potential. They feel that they have let themselves down and/or have let down others for whom they care. Low self-esteem and poor self-efficacy will undoubtedly hamper an individual's ability to succeed in our achievement-orientated society. In other words, because people with ADHD have tried and failed at so many projects in the past, they may begin to lose faith in themselves and believe that they will never achieve. In such cases, failure is repeatedly reinforced by further failure. Successes are often minimised, if recognised at all, and people with ADHD no longer believe in themselves. This is a negative cycle, where an individual fails because they expect to fail and thus becomes a self-fulfilling prophecy.

The sequelae of late diagnosis in adulthood are that the individual has lived and coped (either functionally or dysfunctionally) with their symptoms and associated problems for a very long time. Thus, adults with ADHD are likely to have a different range of problems compared with individuals who have been diagnosed and treated since childhood. Even when symptoms remit, internalised failure and learned helplessness may be interpersonally and socially 'ingrained'. The misattribution of the intent and behaviour of others, together with their own maladaptive behaviour, may have become part of a cycle that is difficult to break. Traditionally, the psychosocial adjustment process of 'graduating' from childhood ADHD has not been considered routinely. Yet, these individuals often feel that they are 'survivors' of a syndrome that has left them with significant personal, social and occupational consequences. This is anecdotally known as the 'hangover' of ADHD. Once no longer formally classified as suffering with ADHD, family and friends may be unsympathetic and attribute current difficulties to motivational and attitude problems, with little appreciation that these stem from a sense of insecurity and lack of confidence. Graduates of ADHD often need help re-appraising their place in life, their skills, capabilities and opportunities. Once they have identified what they want to do, they will need encouragement to put one foot in front of the other and take the first steps towards their goals.

RAISING SELF-ESTEEM

People with ADHD often enter treatment with a chronic sense of failure stemming from a mismatch between actual achievement and potential, and the belief that they have to work harder than others to achieve the same outcome (Ramsay & Rostain, 2005). They may have developed a coping style whereby they react to difficult situations with avoidance or procrastination, often hoping that problems will go away or sort themselves out. Through engaging in therapy, this may have become all the more apparent to them, resulting in them eliciting a more complete recognition of the severity of their problems and feeling regret about lost opportunities. It is therefore crucial when intervening with an individual with ADHD that the therapist remains consistently aware of self-esteem vulnerabilities.

Negative assumptions and expectations about the ability to succeed or simply cope in a given situation are likely to result in the client avoiding situations and exercises, particularly when they perceive these to be anxiety-provoking and unmanageable. One of the most difficult challenges faced by people with ADHD (as well as 'graduates' of ADHD) is to improve self-esteem as the negative experiences of adults with ADHD (whether symptomatic or not) are long-term and deep-rooted. This may sound rather bleak and indeed the future will not always be rosy for people following treatment as they are still likely to encounter various personal and social hurdles. Ironically, self-efficacy does not appear to be a problem and an underlying belief in their potential (albeit often unmet) most likely forms the basis of the resilient aspect of their personality (see Figure 1.1).

Thus, the experience of ADHD may be characterised as 'the good, the bad and the ugly'. So far the 'bad' and the 'ugly' experiences have been well described, but it is essential to focus on the positive features of ADHD and how these may influence the future prospects of the ADHD client. Indeed, people with ADHD have many strengths to draw on. They are often creative, artistic, witty and entertaining individuals. The most important way forward is to establish an area of expertise in which they can achieve by drawing on their specialised skills. This is often in the form of creative flair such as art, design and/or music, but may also be more practically based, for example computer skills. Such ADHD strengths can be considered as 'islands of excellence' that form the basis of a fundamental optimism and belief in themselves. Such characteristics are essential catalysts in the process of resilience outlined in the cognitive-behavioural model of ADHD presented in Chapter 1.

Resilience is the factor that helps individuals with ADHD stay the course. Indeed, the motto or rule of people who have ADHD is the adage 'if at first you don't succeed, try, try again'. People who do not try will never have the opportunity to succeed. A negative self-fulfilling prophecy may hold for a short while when life seems bad and nothing seems to work out, but then resilience kicks in. This may occur due to a rigid obstinacy to refuse to head towards despair and/or failure. On the other hand (and perhaps more likely), this may result from a process of alternative thinking generated from a natural creativity, optimism, and interest in new and challenging opportunities. The generation of multiple solutions and/or alternative possibilities to a problem can mean that an individual has access to multiple opportunities of success. Thus, people with ADHD are life's true entrepreneurs but in order to succeed they must find a way of defining their own structures and boundaries.

Low self-esteem has been discussed at length in the Young–Bramham Programme and the importance of improvement in self-esteem has been emphasised. However, a separate module has not been included to address this issue because improving self-esteem is so important that this concept has been integrated into each module of the programme. Raising self-esteem involves reviewing the client's lifetime achievements and drawing their attention to the achievements they have made in treatment and evaluating progress and success. The journey will start, however, with the *belief* that they can achieve. This means improving self-efficacy.

Review of Lifetime Achievements

In order to motivate the ADHD client to determine goals and strive to reach their potential in the future, it will be necessary to review past achievements and successes

Table 14.1   Top ten achievements

Exercise – list your top 10 achievements to date

1. Having Daniel and raising him as a single mother
2. Training as a nursery supervisor
3. Being featured in local newspaper for fundraising
4. Passing the driving test
5. Buying a car
6. Winning swimming competitions at school
7. Art work being exhibited in a school exhibition
8. Giving up smoking
9. Gradually renovating the house
10. Sitting exams at school and leaving with qualifications

to date. It is important to highlight the individual's strengths and emphasise what they do well. Often, people with ADHD are more familiar with their weaknesses and what they do less well. The 'top ten achievements' exercise in Table 14.1 may be used to draw clients' attention to previous achievements that they are proud of. This is shown for Rebecca, a 32-year-old client, who had a young son Daniel who was also diagnosed with ADHD. This example is included on the Companion Website in a format suitable for use in sessions.

The client should then be encouraged to determine goals for the future. Paperwork often provides external validation of success, so future targets to enrol or become involved with projects that will provide a tangible outcome are very helpful as these provide clear positive reinforcement. In sessions, Rebecca drew up a list of goals she wished to achieve in the future (see Table 14.2). This table is also provided on the Companion Website in a format for use in sessions.

Once Rebecca's goals had been identified, Rebecca was asked to suggest how she might achieve these goals, given what she had learned during the Young–Bramham Programme. This involved consideration of how each goal may need to be broken down into smaller achievable steps, as previously outlined in Chapter 5, on time management,

Table 14.2   Future goals

List five goals you wish to achieve in the next year

1. Become a qualified nursery teacher
2. Go to art classes
3. Buy a newer car
4. Refurbish the kitchen
5. Take up swimming again and obtain a life-saving certificate

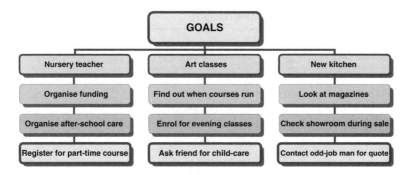

Figure 14.1   Steps towards goals

in Figure 5.1. Figure 14.1 shows the list of steps Rebecca determined she needed to complete to achieve three of her goals (see Figure 5.1 on Companion Website).

Completion of this exercise, 'steps towards goals', helped Rebecca prepare for disengagement of treatment as she shifted her focus from supportive therapy in planning and managing her time to self-management and planning for future goals. Additionally, the sessions provided her with a broader perspective; by looking both back and looking ahead. When reviewing previous achievements, the therapist emphasised how well Rebecca had coped in the past despite her many difficulties and encouraged future achievement based on what she had learnt during the course of treatment. Rebecca was also encouraged to include rewards for achievements at 'step' level in order to motivate her progress towards the desired goals. For Rebecca, it was not long before rewards she had given herself in the past (such as a cup of tea and a biscuit, time off-task, or a walk around the block), became less commonly applied in favour of more process-oriented rewards (such as going for a swim, researching local art classes). These latter rewards were more reinforcing as they made a much greater contribution towards achievement of goals.

Review of Successful Strategies

During the course of therapy, the client will have tried out various strategies to improve symptoms in several domains of function. These strategies will have been met with varying degrees of success. The therapist should review the techniques that have been implemented during the treatment and rate their utility. This, of course, may also include strategies that the client has developed themselves and which have yielded a positive (or negative) outcome. The exercise provided in Table 14.3 is designed to remind both the therapist and the client of which techniques have been tested and how well they worked. It will also provide the client with a list of helpful strategies for use when the intervention has been terminated. These strategies should be rated from 0 (not at all useful) to 10 (extremely useful). Table 14.3 shows the review generated

Table 14.3   Review of successful strategies

In order to improve my...	I can...	How useful is this strategy? 0–10
Attention	Make sure the room is quiet	8
	Use earplugs	6
	Switch off the phone	4
	Use a cue card	5
	Take regular breaks	7
Memory	Write a list of things I need to do	7
	Always keep my diary in my pocket	4
	Set an alarm on my mobile phone for appointments	9
Time management	Break down activities into steps	6
	Make a diary activity planner	8
	Work out rewards	5
Problem solving	Module not administered	
Impulsivity	Use the IMPULSE CONTROL method	7
	Use double-check questions	9
	Count backwards	3
Social relationships	Module not administered	
Anxiety	Module not administered	
Anger	Monitor how I'm feeling	4
	Use the ADHD formula	8
	Listen to criticism	5
	Keep voice volume low	5
Low mood	Module not administered	
Sleep	Stop sleeping in the day	5
	Regular bedtime	8
	Stop watching TV in bed	8
	Make a worry list	4
	Set two alarms	9
	Leave curtains open	7
Substance misuse	Use decisional balance sheets	7
	Use distraction and replacement techniques	5
	Challenge dysfunctional beliefs	6

by Graham, a client who had combined type ADHD, who presented with poor time-management skills, difficulties controlling his temper, moderate cannabis use and sleep difficulties. (Table 14.3 is also presented on the Companion Website.)

By working through the modules of the Young–Bramham Programme, it was possible for the therapist and Graham to review which strategies had been used to tackle each of his difficulties. For Graham, treatment began with a focus on his core symptoms including attention and memory difficulties, impulsivity and poor time management. Graham had found that practical techniques and external strategies seemed to work better than using internally driven strategies such as distraction. For anger management difficulties, he found the 'ADHD formula' particularly helpful, whereas applying volume control to his voice had been rather more difficult for him to achieve but surprisingly effective in experimental exercises. Several behavioural techniques had been effective in improving his sleep and a motivational interviewing approach to his substance misuse had helped him to reduce his cannabis use. Graham found that drawing up the list allowed him to systematically review what he had achieved during therapy as well as providing him with a list of a range of strategies that he could use in the future. Modules that were not completed were initially left blank for this exercise, although, in the course of the review, Graham found that there were aspects of what he had learnt that he could apply to make more general improvements both intrapersonally and interpersonally.

ACCESSING SUPPORT

A long-term problem for people with ADHD is that they have encountered numerous difficulties in developing and maintaining relationships. They find it difficult to pick up on subtle cues which should prompt them to alter their behaviour. Unfortunately, when interpersonal difficulties are pointed out, these are likely to be received negatively by an individual with ADHD, who is sensitive to criticism. By engaging in therapy, a client may be encountering for the first time a relationship in which they feel they have been constructively helped. In this way, self-esteem may be fostered. Ending this therapeutic relationship is therefore likely to be difficult and lead to an initial deflation in self-esteem accompanied by feelings of being unable to cope. It is therefore important to spend time preparing the individual for the end of treatment by devising a comprehensive 'relapse prevention' plan, which will arm the client with numerous coping options when therapy is discontinued. This has been achieved so far by reviewing what has worked during the intervention, what has facilitated success for them in the past and emphasising the positive features of ADHD. The final step is to discuss ways of enlisting help and support from family, friends and/or other professionals.

Support from Family and Friends

Throughout this book it has been emphasised how important it is for clients with ADHD to be educated about their disorder and thus be forewarned about the personal challenges they may face through their condition. The underlying premise for this is 'forewarned is forearmed'; that is, by being aware of and understanding their own difficulties, the client is better equipped to anticipate situations when they are likely to require extra help or support. A parallel reason for the importance of psychoeducation is for the client to be able to educate their family and friends about how they are likely to behave and react. Whilst ADHD should not be an excuse for inappropriate behaviour, it is useful that family and friends understand that, on occasions, such behaviour is not due to a lack of caring about the relationship on the part of the individual with ADHD.

By identifying specific ways in which family and friends can provide support, and also providing an explanation of why this is likely to help, the individual with ADHD and their supporters can both benefit from mutual gains. For example, prior to being diagnosed with ADHD, a client, Nick, was frequently criticised by his partner for not shouldering his share of the domestic chores. Nick insisted that this was not through laziness on his part, but through his lack of organisation, and he often requested that his partner made him a list of tasks. This request made his partner even more annoyed with the situation as she felt that he should be able to recognise what needed doing around the house without being told. Following being diagnosed with ADHD, Nick became more aware of his inattentive difficulties and consequently his need for structure. With this explanation, his partner was more able to understand the origin of his difficulties and started to make specific work lists for Nick's share of the housework. At weekends, Nick worked through the list and ticked off each chore as he completed it. The house became tidier and Nick had fewer arguments with his partner.

It is not unusual for family and friends who have known the person with ADHD for many years, to accommodate some of their difficulties, albeit in a begrudging way. However, it is not necessarily helpful always to make allowances. Family and friends are well placed to help the individual with ADHD look at a situation in a constructive way. They might remind the client of how they had coped with a similar difficulty in the past and help the client prepare for the future by talking about how it may be overcome and/or avoided.

One issue that clients often raise is that they are unsure of the extent to which others appreciate how much effort they have gone to in trying to do the right thing or trying to please them. Often, in spite of making a huge effort, the client does not achieve exactly what they hoped for. Even worse, their efforts end up causing upset or distress. In such circumstances, the client will feel angry (with themselves and others) and low in mood, which in turn can lead to further difficulties in achieving their quest for success. If family and friends are able to understand that individuals with ADHD do not derive pleasure from being late, behaving irresponsibly or acting inappropriately, then the client is likely to feel far better supported and more able to cope with the knock-backs they will inevitably encounter from people who do not share this understanding.

Whenever possible, family and friends are important to have on board in a treatment programme as they can help the client extend what they have learnt in the therapy sessions to outside of the sessions. They can continue to support the client when the therapy has ended. Additionally they may be helpful in monitoring the effects of treatment and give positive feedback. Such positive feedback will become part of a 'reward system' by providing positive reinforcement. Furthermore, they may recognise times when the client has forgotten to take their medication and prompt accordingly.

Professional Help

By the time most adults with ADHD seek treatment, it is unlikely that their ADHD symptoms are the only reason for seeking help. Many people with ADHD have a history of multiple presentations to health services both in childhood and adulthood (Young et al., 2003) so they may have become accustomed to a help-seeking model of coping with their problems. This needs to be transferred to a model that depends less on mental health services and more on self-help and/or accessing community support.

Of course, some individuals may require referral for more specialised treatment, such as detoxification or rehabilitation of addictions, or a more complex pharmacological regimen. Thus, in preparation for termination of therapy, it is recommended that the therapist discusses the range of services available, the grounds for re-referral, and states clearly how and when these services can be accessed. Waiting lists are an obvious flash point for people with ADHD. Clients need to recognise that, whilst it is clearly important for them to find out about waiting times and voice their concerns or complaints if they are waiting longer than they would wish, their desire for immediate gratification may cause them to appear unreasonable and/or confrontational. Additionally, responding to their requests may cause further delay in service provision.

Individuals with ADHD are also likely to have high expectations of the outcomes of treatment as they will be hoping for a panacea that requires minimal effort on their behalf but provides immediate gratification. When a treatment falls short of these expectations, the individual may feel that they have (once again) become a 'victim' of services' shortcomings and express their feelings in either general procrastination or by making explicit complaints about services and/or individual service providers. Such behaviours function as a projection or transference of their underlying feelings of anger, frustration and rejection. This propensity should be counter-transferred by reassuring clients about the future by preparing them to anticipate and cope with difficulties and challenges. By developing these skills, the client will (hopefully) be prevented from antagonising the people who may be best placed to help them.

Support Services

An important component of any relapse prevention plan is to determine sources of relevant available support (e.g. learning support, vocational counselling, social services, housing, etc.). Clients with ADHD may have difficulty knowing where to start in order to find out information about such support provision, so the therapist may need to prepare a list of available local resources such as the internet, local libraries, local council offices, etc.

Resources that may benefit clients with ADHD who are studying include learning support and assignment/examination dispensations. These may be particularly relevant for clients with comorbid dyslexia. Similar support structures may be available in the workplace of large organisations. Clients with employment problems may gain benefit from vocational counselling services. In sessions, the therapist can prepare the client for this by drawing up a list of likes and dislikes from previous jobs and determine a skills repertoire. This will help the client to reflect on what they would like to do and where they would excel.

Before attempting to access local support services, clients need to make contact and find out what the service can offer. However, individuals with ADHD may expect immediate responses to their requests and if these are not forthcoming they may become irritated and dismissive of the support service provided. This may fuel underlying negative dysfunctional assumptions that nobody really cares about them. They are likely to give up trying to get help. In particular, adults with ADHD can be particularly infuriated by services who have no knowledge of the disorder. Thus, the therapist may need to revise sections of the social relationships module and role-play appropriate responses to requests for information that may irritate them and/or cause long delays.

Support Groups

Today there are numerous modes of ADHD support groups available, ranging from face-to-face contact meetings to internet chat lines and networks. Gaining support from others with the disorder is beneficial for many reasons. Indeed, the most important, yet most obvious, reason for joining support groups is to access peer support. People with ADHD are more likely to be able to understand the experience of their peers and find it both reassuring and empowering to offer advice to others. It is often a relief for clients to meet people who share similar histories and experiences. It can also be useful to share strategies for coping with ADHD symptoms. People with ADHD have often developed specific expertise to accommodate their difficulties and can provide advice regarding adaptive compensatory strategies to others.

Some people report feeling nervous in the first instance about joining a group that requires face-to-face contact. They worry that they will not have anything to say or be too embarrassed to speak. Also, people may be fearful that they may not be able to concentrate. However, when running the Young–Bramham Programme in group workshop format, these apprehensions seem to rapidly dissipate in the face of shared understanding and experiences. One outcome is that the groups often become mutually supportive between sessions and group members are able to swap their contact details if they wish. In some cases, some clients have linked up as 'buddies' to help support each other on a more regular basis.

CONCLUSIONS

This chapter has described the final module of the Young–Bramham Programme. In these sessions, the client will review the past and look towards the future. For those in symptom remission, the legacy of ADHD may outlive the disorder in the form of low self-esteem and anticipated failure. The Young–Bramham Programme has outlined modules and techniques to address these problems. The natural ebullience and resilience of the ADHD client will considerably further the endeavours of the therapist. People with ADHD are engaging to work with, in spite of a tendency to procrastinate. They have great potential to make positive change and when this occurs it is a rewarding experience for both the client and therapist alike.

REFERENCES

American Psychiatric Association. (1994). *Diagnostic and statistical manual of mental disorders* (4th edn). Washington DC: APA.

Anderson, J.C., Williams, S., McGee, R. & Silva, P.A. (1987). DSM-III-R disorders in preadolescent children: prevalence in a large sample from the general population. *Archives of General Psychiatry*, 44, 69–76.

Asherson, P., Kuntsi, J. & Taylor, E. (2005). Unravelling the complexity of attention-deficit hyperactivity disorder: a behavioural genomic approach. *British Journal of Psychiatry*, 187, 103–105.

Baddeley, A (1986). *Working memory*. Oxford: Clarendon/Oxford University Press.

Baddeley, A. & Wilson, B. (1988). Frontal amnesia and dysexecutive syndrome. *Brain and Cognition*, 7, 212–230.

Barkley, R.A. (1998). *Attention Deficit Hyperactivity Disorder. A handbook for diagnosis and treatment*. New York: The Guilford Press.

Barkley, R.A. (2002). Major life activity and health outcomes associated with attention deficit/hyperactivity disorder. *Journal of Clinical Psychiatry*, 63, 10–15.

Barkley, R.A. & Biederman, J. (1997). Towards a broader definition of the age-of-onset criterion for attention-deficit hyperactivity disorder. *Journal of American Academy of Child and Adolescent Psychiatry*, 36(9), 1204–1210.

Barkley, R.A., Guevremont, D.C., Anastropoulos, A.D., DePaul, G.J. & Shelton, T.L. (1993). Driving-related risks and outcomes of attention deficit hyperactivity disorder in adolescents and young adults: a 3–5 year follow-up study. *Pediatrics*, 92, 212–218.

Bauermeister, J. (1992). Factor analyses of teacher ratings of attention-deficit hyperactivity and oppositional defiant symptoms in children aged four through thirteen years. *Journal of Clinical Child Psychology*, 21, 27–34.

Beck, A.T. (1963). Thinking and depression. I. Idiosyncratic content and cognitive distortions. *Archives of General Psychiatry*, 14, 324–333.

Beck, A.T. (1976). *Cognitive therapy and the emotional disorders*. New York: International Universities Press.

Bellack, A.S. & DiClimente, C.C. (1999). Treating substance abuse among patients with schizophrenia. *Psychiatric Services*, 50(1), 75–80.

Biederman, J., Faraone, S.V., Keenan, K., Steingard, R. & Tsuang, M.T. (1991). Familial association between attention deficit disorder and anxiety disorder. *American Journal of Psychiatry*, 148, 251–256.

Biederman, J., Faraone, S.V., Spencer, T., Wilens, T., Norman, D., Lapey, K.A., Mick, E., Lehman, B.K. & Doyle, A. (1993). Patterns of psychiatric comorbidity, cognition, and psychosocial functioning in adults with attention deficit hyperactivity disorder. *American Journal of Pyschiatry*, 150, 1792–1798.

Biederman, J., Faraone, S.V., Mick, E., Spencer, T., Wilens, T., Kiely, K., Guite, J., Ablon, J.S., Reed, E. & Warburton, R. (1995). High risk for attention deficit hyperactivity disorder among children of parents with childhood onset of the disorder: A pilot study. *American Journal of Psychiatry*, 152, 431–435.

Biederman, J., Faraone, S.V., Mick, E., Williamson, S., Wilens, T.E., Spencer, T.J., Weber, W., Jetton, J., Kraus, I., Pert, J. & Zallen, B. (1999). Clinical correlates of ADHD in females: findings from a large group of girls ascertained from pediatric and psychiatric referral sources. *Journal of the American Academy of Child and Adolescent Psychiatry*, 38, 966–975.

Biggs, S.H. (1995). Neuropsychological and psychoeducational testing in the evaluation of adults. In K. Nadeau (Ed.), *A comprehensive guide to attention deficit disorder in adults.* New York: Brunner/Mazel Publishers.

Bramham, J., Young, S.J., Morris, R.G., Asherson, P. & Toone, B.K. (2005a). Neuropsychological deficits in adults with ADHD: do they improve with age? Paper presented at the British Neuropsychiatry Association Conference, February.

Bramham, J., Young, S.J., Morris, R.G., Asherson, P. & Toone, B.K. (2005b). Behavioural symptoms and cognitive deficits in adults with ADHD: What changes with age? Paper presented at the Division of Clinical Psychology, British Psychological Society Conference, March.

Brassett-Grundy, A. & Butler, N. (2004a). *Prevalence and adult outcomes of Attention-Deficit/Hyperactivity Disorder.* London: Bedford Group for Lifecourse & Statistical Studies, Institute of Education, University of London.

Brassett-Grundy, A. & Butler, N. (2004b). *Attention-Deficit/Hyperactivity Disorder. An overview and review of the literature relating to the correlates and lifecourse outcomes for males and females.* London: Bedford Group for Lifecourse & Statistical Studies, Institute of Education, University of London.

Brown, T.E. (1996). *Brown Attention-Deficit Disorder Scales.* San Antonio, TX: Harcourt Brace.

Brown, T.E. & McMullen, W.J. (2001). Attention deficit disorders and sleep/arousal disturbance. *Annals of the New York Academy of Sciences*, 931, 271–286.

Burgess, P.W., Veitch, E., de Lacy Costello, A. & Shallice, T. (2000). The cognitive and neuroanatomical correlates of multitasking. *Neuropsychologia*, 38(6), 848–863.

Cairnes, E. & Cammock, T. (1978). Development of a more reliable version of the Matching Familiar Figures Test. *Developmental Psychology*, 14, 555–556.

Carlson, C.L., Tamm, L. & Gaub, M. (1997). Gender differences in children with ADHD, ODD, and co-occurring ADHD/ODD identified in a school population. *Journal of American Academy of Child and Adolescent Psychiatry*, 36(12), 1706–1714.

Castellanos, F.X., Giedd, J.N., Berquin, P.C., Walter, J.M., Sharp, W., Tran, T., Vaituzis, A.C., Blumenthal, J.D., Nelson, J., Bastain, T.M., Zijdenbos, A., Evans, A.C. & Rapoport, J.L. (2001). Quantitative brain magnetic resonance imaging in girls with attention-deficit/hyperactivity disorder. *Archives of General Psychiatry*, 58, 289–295.

Chervin, R.D., Dillon, J.E., Bassetti, C., Ganoczy, D.A. & Pituch, K.J. (1997). Symptoms of sleep disorders, inattention, and hyperactivity in children. *Sleep*, 20(12), 1185–1192.

Clark, D.M. (1986). A cognitive approach to panic. *Behaviour Research and Therapy*, 24, 461–470.

Cohen, P., Cohen, J., Kasen, S., Velez, C.N., Hartmark, C., Johnson, J., Rojas, M., Brooke, J. & Streuning, E.L. (1993). An epidemiological study of disorders in late childhood and adolescence – I. Age- and gender-specific prevalence. *Journal of Child Psychology and Psychiatry*, 34, 851–867.

Conners, C.K. (2000). *Conners' Rating Scales – Revised: technical manual.* New York: MHS.

Conners, C., Erhardt, D. & Sparrow, E. (1998). *The Conners Adult ADHD Rating Scale (CAARS).* Toronto: Multi-Health Systems Inc.

Coughlan, A.K. & Hollows, S.E. (1985). *The Adult Memory and Information Processing Battery (AMIPB).* Leeds: Psychology Department, St James's University Hospital.

Dalsgaard, S., Mortensen, P.B., Frydenberg, M. & Thomsen, P.H. (2002). Conduct problems, gender and adult psychiatric outcome of children with attention-deficit hyperactivity disorder. *British Journal of Psychiatry*, 181, 416–421.

Dalteg, A., Lindgren, M. & Levander, S. (1999). Retrospectively rated ADHD is linked to specific personality characteristics and deviant alcohol reaction. *The Journal of Forensic Psychiatry*, 10 (3), 623–634.

Danckaerts, M., Heptinstall, E., Chadwick, O. & Taylor, E. (1999). Self-report of Attention Deficit and Hyperactivity Disorder in adolescents. *Psychopathology*, 32, 81–92.

Deci, E.L., Koestner, R. & Ryan, R.M. (1999). A meta-analytic review of experiments examining the effects of extrinsic rewards on intrinsic motivation. *Psychological Bulletin*, 125(6), 627–668.

Denkla, M.B. (1996). Research on executive function in a neurodevelopmental context: application of clinical measures. *Developmental Neuropsychology*, 12, 5–15.

Disney, E.R., Elkins, I.J., McGue, M. & Iacono, W.G. (1999). Effects of ADHD, conduct disorder, and gender on substance use and abuse in adolescence. *American Journal of Psychiatry*, 156(10), 1515–1521.

Dowson, J.H., McLean, A., Bazanis, E., Toone, B., Young, S., Robbins, T.W. & Sahakian, B. (2004). Impaired spatial working memory in adults with attention-deficit/hyperactivity disorder: comparisons with performance in adults with borderline personality disorder and in control subjects. *Acta Psychiatrica Scandinavica,* 110(1), 45–54.

Duncan, C.C., Rumsey, J.M., Wilkniss, S.M., Denckla, M.B., Hamburger, S.D. & Odou-Potkin, M. (1994). Developmental dyslexia and attention dysfunction in adults: brain potential indices of information processing. *Psychophysiology*, 31(4), 386–401.

D'Zurilla, T.J. & Nezu, A.M. (1999). *Problem-solving therapy: A social competence approach to clinical intervention*. New York: Springer.

Ebbinghaus, H. (1885). *Memory: A contribution to experimental psychology*. New York: Teachers College, Columbia University.

Efron, D., Jarman, F. & Barker, M. (1997). Side effects of methylphenidate and dexamphetamine in children with attention deficit hyperactivity disorder: a double-blind, crossover trial. *Pediatrics*, 100(4), 662–666.

Elliott, R. (2002). The neuropsychological profile in primary depression. In J. Harrison & A. Owens (Eds.), *Cognitive deficits in brain disorders*. London: Taylor & Francis, pp. 273–293.

Ernst, M., Liebenauer, L.L., King, A.C., Fitzgerald, G.A., Cohen, R.M. & Zametkin, A.J. (1994). Reduced brain metabolism in hyperactive girls. *Journal of the American Academy of Child and Adolescent Psychiatry*, 33, 858–868.

Eyestone, L.L. & Howell, R.J. (1994). An epidemiological study of Attention-Deficit Hyperactivity Disorder and major depression in a male prison population. *Bulletin of the American Academy of Psychiatry and the Law*, 22(2), 181–193.

Faraone, S.V., Biederman, J. & Monuteaux, M.C. (2000a). Towards guidelines for pedigree selection in genetic studies of attention deficit hyperactivity disorder. *Genetic Epidemiology*, 18, 1–16.

Faraone, S.V., Biederman, J., Mick, E., Williamson, S., Wilens, T., Spencer, T., Weber, W., Jetton, J., Kraus, I., Pert, J. & Zallen, B. (2000b). Family study of girls with attention deficit hyperactivity disorder. *American Journal of Psychiatry*, 157, 1077–1083.

Fischer, M., Barkley, R.A., Fletcher, K.E. & Smallish, L. (1993). The stability of dimensions of behaviour in ADHD and normal children over an 8-year follow-up. *Journal of Abnormal Child Psychology*, 21, 315–337.

Fox, R.A. & Wade, E.J. (1998). Attention deficit hyperactivity disorder among adults with severe and profound mental retardation. *Research in Developmental Disabilities*, 19, 275–280.

Gaub, M. & Carlson, C.L. (1997). Gender differences in ADHD: a meta-analysis and clinical review. *Journal of the American Academy of Child and Adolescent Psychiatry*, 36, 1036–1045.

Gualtieri, T. & Hicks, R.E. (1985). An immunoreactive theory of selective male affliction. *Behavioral and Brain Sciences*, 8, 427–441.

Hallowell, E.M. (1995) Psychotherapy of adult Attention Deficit Disorder. In K. Nadeau (Ed.), *A comprehensive guide to Attention Deficit Disorder in adults*. New York: Brunner/Mazel Publishers.

Heptinstall, E. & Taylor, E. (2002). Sex differences and their significance. In S. Sandberg (Ed.), *Hyperactivity and attention disorders of childhood*. Cambridge: Cambridge University Press.

Hervey, A.S., Epstein, J.N. & Curry, J.F. (2004). Neuropsychology of adults with attention-deficit/hyperactivity disorder: a meta-analytic review. *Neuropsychology*, 18(3), 485–503.

Horrigan, J.P. (2001). Present and future pharmacotherapeutic options for adult attention deficit/hyperactivity disorder. *Expert Opinion in Pharmacotherapy*, 2(4), 573–586.

Hull, C. L. (1943). *Principles of behaviour*. New York: Appleton-Century-Crofts.

Jackson, B. & Farrugia, D. (1997). Diagnosis and treatment of adults with Attention Deficit Hyperactivity Disorder. *Journal of Counselling and Development*, 75, 312–319.

Jou, R., Handen, B. & Hardan, A. (2004). Psychostimulant treatment of adults with mental retardation and attention-deficit hyperactivity disorder. *Australasian Psychiatry*, 12(4), 376–379.

Kassel, J.D. (1997). Smoking and attention: A review and reformulation of the stimulus-filter hypothesis. *Clinical Psychology Review*, 17, 451–478.

Katz, L.J., Wood, D.S., Goldstein, G., Auchenbach, R.C. & Geckle, M. (1998). The utility of neuropsychological tests in evaluation of Attention-Deficit Hyperactivity Disorder (ADHD) versus depression in adults. *Assessment*, 5(1), 45–52.

Kaufman, A.S. & Kaufman, N.L. (1990). *Manual for the Kaufman Brief Intelligence Test*. Circle Pines, MN: American Guidance Service.

Kazdin, A.E. & Mascitelli, S. (1982). Covert and overt rehearsal and homework practice in developing assertiveness. *Journal of Consulting Clinical Psychology*, 50(2), 250–258.

Keller, M.B., Lavori, P.W., Wunder, J., Beardslee, W.R., Schwartz, C.E. & Roth, J. (1992). Chronic course of anxiety disorders in children and adolescents. *Journal of American Academy of Child and Adolescent Psychiatry*, 31, 595–599.

Konofal, E., Lecendreux, M., Bouvard, M.P. & Mouren-Simeoni, M.C. (2001). High levels of nocturnal activity in children with attention-deficit hyperactivity disorder: a video analysis. *Psychiatry and Clinical Neuroscience*, 55(2), 97–103.

Lazarus, R.S. & Folkman, S. (1984). *Stress, appraisal and coping*. New York: Springer Publishing.

Levin, E.D., Conners, C.K., Sparrow, E., Hinton, S.C., Erhardt, D., Meck, W.H., Rose, J.E. & March, J. (1996). Nicotine effects on adults with attention-deficit/hyperactivity disorder. *Psychopharmacology*, 123(1), 55–63.

Lezak, M.D., Howieson, D.B. & Loring, D.W. (2004). *Neuropsychological assessment (4th edn)*. Oxford: Oxford University Press.

Lovejoy, D.W., Ball, J.D., Keats, M., Stutts, M.L., Spain, E.H., Janda, L. & Janusz, J. (1999). Neuropsychological performance of adults with attention deficit hyperactivity disorder (ADHD): Diagnostic classification estimates for measures of frontal lobe/executive functioning. *Journal of the International Neuropsychological Society*, 5, 222–233.

MacLean, A., Dowson, J., Toone, B., Young, S., Bazanis, E., Robbins, T.W. & Sahakian, B.J. (2004). Characteristic neurocognitive profile associated with adult attention-deficit/hyperactivity disorder. *Psychological Medicine*, 34, 681–692.

Mannuzza, S., Klein, R.G., Bessler, A., Malloy, P. & LaPadula, M. (1993). Adult outcome of hyperactive boys. Educational achievement, occupational rank and psychiatric status. *Archives of General Psychiatry*, 50, 565–576.

Mannuzza, S., Klein, R.G., Bessler, A., Malloy, P. & LaPadula, M. (1998). Adult psychiatric status of hyperactive boys grown up. *American Journal of Psychiatry*, 155, 493–498.

Mannuzza, S., Klein, R.G., Klein, D.F., Bessler, A. & Shrout, P. (2002). Accuracy of adult recall of childhood attention deficit hyperactivity disorder. *American Journal of Psychiatry*, 159(11), 1882–1888.

Marsh, P.J. & Williams, L.M. (2004). An investigation of individual typologies of Attention-Deficit Hyperactivity Disorder using cluster analysis of DSM-IV criteria. *Personality and Individual Differences*, 36(5), 1187–1195.

Matsumoto, T., Kamijo, A., Yamaguchi, A., Iseki, E. & Hirayasu, Y. (2005). Childhood histories of attention-deficit hyperactivity disorders in Japanese methamphetamine and inhalant abusers: preliminary report. *Psychiatry Clinical Neuroscience*, 59(1), 102–105.

Mazza, S., Pepin, J.L., Naegele, B., Plante, J., Deschaux, C. & Levy, P. (2005). Most obstructive sleep apnoea patients exhibit vigilance and attention deficits on an extended battery of tests. *The European Respiratory Journal*, 25(1), 75–80.

Millstein, R.B., Wilens, T.E., Biederman J. & Spencer, T.J. (1997). Presenting ADHD symptoms and subtypes in clinically referred adults with ADHD. *Journal of Attention Disorders,* 2(3), 159–166.

Miller, W.R. & Rollnick, S. (2002). *Motivational interviewing: preparing people for change (2nd edn)*. New York: Guilford Press.

Milner, B. (1963). Effects of different brain lesions on card sorting. *Archives of Neurology*, 9, 90–100.

Moffitt, T.E. (1993). 'Life-course-persistent' and 'adolescence-limited' antisocial behavior: A developmental taxonomy. *Psychological Review*, 100, 674–701.

Morris, R.G., Downes, J.J., Sahakian, B.J., Evenden, J.L., Heald, A. & Robbins, T.W. (1988). Planning and spatial working memory in Parkinson's disease. *Journal of Neurology, Neurosurgery and Psychiatry*, 51, 757–766.

MTA Cooperative Group (1999). A 14 month randomized clinical trial of treatment strategies for attention-deficit/hyperactivity disorder. *Archives of General Psychiatry*, 56, 1073–1086.

Murphy, K.R. (1995). Empowering the adult with ADHD. In K. Nadeau (Ed.), *A Comprehensive Guide to Attention Deficit Disorder in Adults*. New York: Brunner/Mazel Publishers.

Murphy, K.R. (1998). Psychological treatment of adults with ADHD. In R.A. Barkley (Ed.), *Attention Deficit Hyperactivity Disorder. A handbook for diagnosis and treatment*. New York: The Guilford Press.

Murphy, K.R. & Barkley, R.A. (1996). Attention Deficit Hyperactivity Disorder in adults. *Comprehensive Psychiatry*, 37, 393–401.

Murphy, K.R. & Levert, S. (1995). *Out of the fog: treatment options and coping strategies for adult attention deficit disorder*. New York: Hyperion.

Murphy, K. & Schachar, R. (2000). Use of self-ratings in the assessment of symptoms of Attention Deficit Hyperactivity Disorder in adults. *American Journal of Psychiatry*, 157, 1156–1159.

Nadeau, K.G. (1995). *A comprehensive guide to attention deficit disorder in adults*. New York: Brunner/Mazel Publishers.

Naseem, S., Chaudhary, B. & Collop, N. (2001). Attention deficit hyperactivity disorder in adults and obstructive sleep apnea. *Chest*, 119(1), 294–296.

Nelson, H.E. (1992). *National Adult Reading Test (NART): test manual*. Windsor, Berks: NFER-Nelson.

Nelson, H.E. & Willison, J.R. (1991). *National Adult Reading Test (NART): test manual* (2nd edn). Windsor, Berks: NFER-Nelson.

Norman, D.A. & Shallice, T. (1986). Attention to action: willed and automatic control of behaviour. In R.J. Davidson, G.E. Schwartz & D. Shapiro (Eds.), *Consciousness and self-regulation: advances in research and theory*, vol. 4. New York: Plenum, pp. 1–18.

Owens, J.A. (2005). The ADHD and sleep conundrum: a review. *Journal of Developmental Behavioral Pediatrics*, 26(4), 312–322.

Parnes, S.J., Noller, R.B. & Biondi, A.M. (1977). *Guide to creative action: Revised edition of creative behavior guidebook*. New York: Charles Scribner's Sons.

Pauls, D.L. & Leckman, J.F. (1986). The inheritance of Gilles de la Tourette syndrome and associated behaviors: evidence for autosomal dominant transmission. *New England Journal of Medicine*, 315, 993–997.

Pliszka, S.R (1989). Effect of anxiety on cognition, behaviour, and stimulant response in ADHD. *Journal of American Academy of Child and Adolescent Psychiatry*, 28, 882–887.

Pliszka, S.R. (2003). Non-stimulant treatment of attention-deficit/hyperactivity disorder. *CNS Spectrums*, 8(4), 253–258.

Pliszka, S.R., Hatch, J.P., Borcherding, S.H. & Rogeness, G.A. (1993). Classical conditioning in children with attention deficit hyperactivity disorder (ADHD) and anxiety disorders: a test of Quay's model. *Journal of Abnormal Child Psychology*, 21, 411–423.

Powell, J. (2004). Effects of Medication on Cognitive Functioning. In L.H. Goldstein & J.E. McNeil (Eds.), *Clinical neuropsychology: A practical guide to assessment and management for clinicians*. Chichester: Wiley.

Powell, T. (2004). *Head injury*. Bicester: Speechmark.

Prior, M. & Sanson, A. (1986). Attention deficit disorder with hyperactivity: a critique. *Journal of Child Psychology and Psychiatry*, 27(3), 307–319.

Prochaska, J.O. & DiClemente, C.C. (1982). Transtheoretical therapy: Toward a more integrative model of change. *Psychotherapy: Theory, Research, and Practice*, 19, 276–288.

Quinlan, D.M. (2001). Assessment of Attention Deficit/Hyperactivity Disorder and Comorbidities. In T.E. Brown (Ed.) *Attention-deficit disorders and comorbidity in children, adolescents, and adults*. Washington DC: American Psychiatric Press.

Rabiner, D. & Cole, J.D. (2000). Early attention problems and children's reading achievement: a longitudinal investigation. The Conduct Problems Prevention Research group. *Journal of the American Academy of Child and Adolescent Psychiatry*, 39, 859–867.

Ramsay, J.R. & Rostain, A.L. (2005). Adapting psychotherapy to meet the needs of adults with attention-deficit/hyperactivity disorder. *Psychotherapy: Theory, Research, Practice, Training*, 42(1), 72–84.

Rasmussen, K., Almik, R. & Levander, S. (2001). Attention Deficit Hyperactivity Disorder, reading disability and personality disorders in a prison population. *Journal of the American Academy of Psychiatry and Law*, 296, 186–193.

Ratey, J.J., Greenberg, M.S., Bemporad, J.R. & Lindem, K.J. (1992) Unrecognised Attention-Deficit Hyperactivity Disorder in adults presenting for outpatient psychotherapy. *Journal of Child and Adolescent Psychopharmacology*, 2, 267–275.

Reitan, R.M. (1958). Validity of the Trail Making Test as an indicator of organic brain damage. *Perceptual and Motor Skills*, 8, 271–276.

Retz, W., Retz-Junginger, P., Hengesch, G., Schneider, M., Thome, J., Pajonk, F.G., Salahi-Disfan, A., Rees, O., Wender, P.H. & Rosler, M. (2004). Psychometric and psychopathological characterization of young male prison inmates with and without attention deficit/hyperactivity disorder. *European Archives of Psychiatry and Clinical Neuroscience*, 254, 201–208.

Riccio, C.A., Wolfe, M.E., Romine, C., Davis, B. & Sullivan, J.R. (2004). The Tower of London and neuropsychological assessment of ADHD in adults. *Archives of Clinical Neuropsychology*, 19(5), 661–671.

Robertson, I.H., Ward, T., Ridgeway, V. & Nimmo-Smith, I. (1994). *The Test of Everyday Attention*. Bury St Edmunds: Thames Valley Test.

Rosler, M., Retz, W., Retz-Junginger, P., Hengesch, G., Schneider, M., Supprian, T., Schwitzgebel, P., Pinhard, K., Dovi-Akue, N., Wender, P. & Thome, J. (2004). Prevalence of attention deficit/hyperactivity disorder (ADHD) and comorbid disorders in young male prison inmates. *European Archives of Psychiatry and Clinical Neuroscience*, 254, 365–371.

Ross, R.R., Fabiano, E.A. & Ross, R.D. (1986). *Reasoning and Rehabilitation: A handbook for teaching cognitive skills*. Ottawa, Canada: Center for Cognitive Development.

Roth, A. & Fonagy, P. (1996). *What works for whom?* New York: The Guilford Press.

Rubia, K., Oosterlaan, J., Sergeant, J.A., Brandeis, D. & Leeuwen, T. (1998). Inhibitory dysfunction in hyperactive boys. *Behavioural Brain Research*, 94, 25–32.

Rubia, K., Overmeyer, S., Taylor, E., Brammer, M., Williams, S.C.R., Simmons, A. & Bullmore, E.T. (1999). Hypofrontality in Attention Deficit Hyperactivity Disorder during higher-order motor control: A study with functional MRI. *American Journal of Psychiatry*, 156(6), 891–896.

Rubia, K., Overmeyer, S., Taylor, E., Brammer, M., Williams, S.C.R., Simmons, A., Andrew, C. & Bullmore, E.T. (2000). Functional frontalisation with age: mapping neurodevelopmental trajectories with fMRI. *Neuroscience and Biobehavioural Reviews*, 24, 13–19.

Rucklidge, J.J. & Tannock, R. (2001). Psychiatric, psychosocial, and cognitive functioning of female adolescents with ADHD. *Journal of American Academy of Child and Adolescent Psychiatry*, 40(5), 530–540.

Satterfield, T., Swanson, J., Schell, A. & Lee, F. (1994). Prediction of anti-social behaviour in attention-deficit hyperactivity disorder boys from aggression/defiance scores. *Journal of American Academy of Child and Adolescent Psychiatry*, 33 (2), 185–190.

Seager, M.C. & O'Brien, G. (2003). Attention deficit hyperactivity disorder: review of ADHD in learning disability: the Diagnostic Criteria for Psychiatric Disorders for Use with Adults with Learning Disabilities/Mental Retardation [DC-LD] criteria for diagnosis. *Journal of Intellectual Disabilities Research*, 47(Suppl. 1), 26–31.

Semrud-Clikeman, M., Biederman, J., Sprich-Buckminster, S., Lehman, B.K., Faraone, S.V. & Norman, D. (1992). Comorbidity between ADHD and learning disability: a review and report in a clinically referred sample. *Journal of American Academy of Child and Adolescent Psychiatry*, 33, 875–881.

Shaffer, D. (1994). Attention deficit hyperactivity disorder in adults. *American Journal of Psychiatry*, 151(5), 633–638.

Shallice, T. & Burgess, P.W. (1996). The domain of supervisory processes and temporal organization of behaviour. *Philosophical Transactions of the Royal Society London*, 351, 1405–1411.

Sharp, W.S., Walter, J., Marsh, W.L., Ritchie, G.F., Hamburger, S.D. & Castellanos, F.X. (1999). ADHD in girls: clinical comparability of a research sample. *Journal of the American Academy of Child and Adolescent Psychiatry*, 38(1), 40–47.

Shekim, W.O., Asarnow, R.F., Hess, E., Zaucha, K. & Wheller, N. (1990). A clinical and demographic profile of a sample of adults with Attention Deficit Hyperactivity Disorder, residual state. *Comprehensive Psychiatry*, 31, 416–425.

Smith, B.H., Pelham, W.W.E., Gnagy, E., Molina, B. & Evans, S. (2000). The reliability, validity, and unique contributions of self-report by adolescents receiving treatment for Attention-Deficit/Hyperactivity Disorder. *Journal of Consulting and Clinical Psychology*, 68, 489–499.

Sonuga-Barke, E.J., Taylor, E., Sembi, S. & Smith, J. (1992). Hyperactivity and delay aversion – I: The effect of delay on choice. *Journal of Child Psychology and Psychiatry*, 33(2), 387–398.

Spencer, T., Wilens, T.E., Biederman, J., Faraone, S.V., Ablon, S. & Lapey, K. (1995). A double blind, crossover comparison of methylphenidate and placebo in adults with childhood onset Attention Deficit Hyperactivity Disorder. *Archives of General Psychiatry*, 52, 434–443.

Spencer, T., Biederman, J., Wilens, T., Harding, M., O'Donnell, D. & Griffin, S. (1996). Pharmacotherapy of Attention Deficit Disorder across the life cycle. *Journal of the American Academy of Child and Adolescent Psychiatry*, 35, 409–432.

Spreen, O. & Strauss, E. (1998). *A compendium of neuropsychological tests*. New York: Oxford University Press.

Sprich-Buchminster, S., Biederman, J., Milberger, S., Faraone, S.V. & Lehman, B.K. (1993). Are perinatal complications relevant to the manifestation of ADD? Issues of comorbidity and familiarity. *Journal of American Academy of Child and Adolescent Psychiatry*, 32, 1032–1037.

Stevenson, C.S., Whitmont, S., Bornholt, L., Livesey, D. & Stevenson, R.J. (2002). A cognitive remediation programme for adults with Attention Deficit Hyperactivity Disorder. *Australian and New Zealand Journal of Psychiatry*, 36, 610–616.

Stroop, J.P. (1935). Studies of interference in serial verbal reactions. *Journal of Experimental Psychology*, 18, 643–662.

Taylor, E. (1994). Syndromes of attention deficit and overactivity. In Rutter, M., Taylor, E. & Hersov, L. (Eds.), *Child and Adolescent Psychiatry: Modern Approaches*. Oxford: Blackwell Scientific Publications, pp. 285–307.

Taylor, E., Chadwick, O., Heptinstall, E. & Danckaerts, M. (1996). Hyperactivity and conduct problems as risk factors for adolescent development. *Journal of American Academy of Child and Adolescent Psychiatry*, 35(9), 1213–1226.

Thapar, A., Harrington, R. & McGuffin, P. (2001) Examining the comorbidity of ADHD-related behaviours and conduct problems using a twin study design. *British Journal of Psychiatry*, 179, 224–229.

Thapar, A., Holmes, J., Poulton, K. & Harrington, R. (1999). Genetic basis of attention deficit and hyperactivity. *British Journal of Psychiatry*, 174, 105–111.

Trenerry, M.R., Crosson, B., DeBoe, J. & Leber, W.R. (1989). *Stroop Neuropsychological Screening Test Manual*. Odessa, FL: Psychological Assessment Resources.

Uzun, N. & Kendirli, Y. (2005). Clinical, social-demographic, neurophysiological and neuropsychiatric evaluation of children with volatile substance addiction. *Child: Care, Health and Development*, 31(4), 425–443.

Vance, A.L., Luk, E.S., Costin, J., Tonge, B.J. & Pantelis, C. (1999). Attention deficit hyperactivity disorder: anxiety phenomena in children treated with psychostimulant medication for 6 months or more. *Australian and New Zealand Journal of Psychiatry*, 33(3), 399–406.

Van der Linden, G., Young, S., Ryan, P. & Toone, B. (2000). Attention Deficit Hyperactivity Disorder in adults – experience of the first National Health Service clinic in the United Kingdom. *Journal of Mental Health*, 9(5), 527–553.

Van Horn, D.H. & Bux, D.A. (2001). A pilot test of motivational interviewing groups for dually diagnosed inpatients. *Journal of Substance Abuse Treatment*, 20(2), 191–195.

Wagner, M.L., Walters, A.S. & Fisher, B.C. (2004). Symptoms of attention-deficit/hyperactivity disorder in adults with restless legs syndrome. *Sleep*, 27(8), 1499–1504.

Ward, M.F., Wender, P.H. & Reimherr, F.W. (1993). The Wender Utah rating scale: an aid in the retrospective diagnosis of childhood Attention deficit Hyperactivity Disorder. *American Journal of Psychiatry*, 150, 885–890.

Wechsler, D. (1997a). *Wechsler Adult Intelligence Scale – III*. London: Psychological Corporation.

Wechsler, D. (1997b). *Wechsler Memory Scale – III*. London: Psychological Corporation.

Wechsler, D. (1999). *Wechsler Abbreviated Scale of Intelligence*. London: Psychological Corporation.

Wechsler, D. (2001). *Wechsler Test of Adult Reading (WTAR)*. London: Psychological Corporation.

Weinstein, C. (1994). Cognitive remediation strategies: An adjunct to psychotherapy of adults with attention deficit hyperactivity disorder. *Journal of Psychotherapy Practice and Research*, 3(1), 44–57.

Weiss, G. & Hechtman, L.T. (1993). *Hyperactive children grown up*. New York: The Guilford Press.

Weiss, M., Hechtman, L., Milroy, T. & Perlman, T. (1985). Psychiatric status of hyperactives as adults: a controlled perspective. 15 year follow up of 63 hyperactive children. *Journal of the American Academy of Child Psychiatry*, 24, 211–220.

Weiss, M., Hechtman, L. & Weiss, G. (1999). *ADHD in Adulthood: A Guide to Current Theory, Diagnosis and Treatment*. Baltimore, MD: The John Hopkins University Press.

Wender, P.H. (1998). Attention-deficit hyperactivity disorder in adults. *The Psychiatric Clinics of North America*, 21(4), 761–774.

Wender, P. (2000). *Attention Deficit Hyperactivity Disorder in children and adults*. New York: Oxford University Press.

Wender, P.H., Reimherr, F.W. & Wood, D.R. (1981). Attention deficit disorder ('minimal brain dysfunction') in adults: a replication study of diagnosis and drug treatment. *Archives of General Psychiatry*, 38, 449–456.

Wilens, T.E., McDermott, S.P., Biederman, J., Abrantes, A., Hahesy, A. & Spencer, T.J. (1999). Cognitive therapy in the treatment of adults with ADHD: a systematic chart review of 26 cases. *Journal of Cognitive Psychotherapy: an International Quarterly*, 13, 215–226.

Wilens, T.E., Spencer, T.J. & Biederman, J. (2002). A review of the pharmacotherapy of adults with attention deficit/hyperactivity disorder. *Journal of Attentional Disorders* 5(4), 189–202.

Wilens, T.E., Faraone, A.V., Biederman, J. & Gunawardene, S. (2003). Does stimulant therapy of attention-deficit/hyperactivity disorders beget later substance misuse? A meta-analytic review of the literature. *Pediatrics*, 111, 179–185.

Wilson, B.A., Alderman, N., Burgess, P.W., Emslie, H. & Evans, J.J. (1996). *Behavioural Assessment of the Dysexecutive Syndrome (BADS)*. Suffolk: Thames Valley Test Company, UK.

World Health Organization (1992). ICD-10 Classification of Mental and Behavioural Disorders. Geneva: WHO.

Wu, L.T., Pilowsky, D.J. & Schlenger, W.E. (2005). High prevalence of substance use disorders among adolescents who use marijuana and inhalants. *Drug and Alcohol Dependence*, 78(1), 23–32.

Young, S.J. (1999). *Attention Deficit Hyperactivity Disorder in adulthood*. DClinPsy Thesis. University College London, University of London.

Young, S. (2000). ADHD children grown up: an empirical review. *Counselling Psychology Quarterly*, 13, 191–200.

Young, S. (2002). A Model of psychotherapy for adults with ADHD. In S. Goldstein & A. Teeter (Eds.), *Clinical interventions for adult ADHD: A comprehensive approach*. London: Harcourt Academic Press.

Young, S. (2004). The YAQ-S AND YAQ-I: the development of self and informant questionnaires reporting on current adult ADHD symptomatology, comorbid and associated problems. *Personality and Individual Differences*, 36(5), 1211–1224.

Young, S. (2005). Coping strategies used by adults with ADHD. *Personality and Individual Differences*, 38(4), 809–816.

Young, S., Chadwick, O., Heptinstall, E., Taylor, E. & Sonuga-Barke, E.J. (2005b). The adolescent outcome of hyperactive girls. Self-reported interpersonal relationships and coping mechanisms. *European Journal of Child and Adolescent Psychiatry*, 14(5), 245–253.

Young, S., Channon, S. & Toone, B.K. (2000). Neuropsychological assessment of Attention Deficit Hyperactivity Disorder in adulthood. *Clinical Neuropsychological Assessment*, 1(4), 283–294.

Young, S. & Gudjonsson, G. (2005). Neuropsychological correlates of the YAQ-S self-reported ADHD symptomatology, emotional and social problems, and delinquent behaviour. *British Journal of Clinical Psychology*, 44, 47–57.

Young, S., Heptinstall, E., Sonuga-Barke, E.J.S., Chadwick, O. & Taylor, E. (2005a). The adolescent outcome of hyperactive girls: self-report of psychosocial status. *Journal of Child Psychology and Psychiatry*, 46(3), 255–262.

Young, S. & Newland, J. (2002). Attention Deficit Hyperactivity Disorder and mild learning difficulties: a case study. *British Journal of Learning Difficulties*, 30, 73–77.

Young, S.J. & Ross, R.R. (2007). *R&R2 for ADHD youths and adults. A prosocial competence training program.* Ottawa: Cognitive Centre of Canada.

Young, S. & Toone, B. (2000). The Assessment of Attention Deficit Hyperactivity Disorder in Adults: Clinical Issues. A report from the first NHS Clinic in the UK, *Counselling Psychology Quarterly,* 13 (3), 313–319.

Young, S., Toone, B. & Tyson, C. (2003). Comorbidity and psychosocial profile of adults with Attention Deficit Hyperactivity Disorder. *Personality and Individual Differences,* 35(4), 743–755.

Young, S., Bramham, J., Gray, K. & Rose, E. (in submission). The experience of receiving a diagnosis and treatment of ADHD in adulthood. A qualitative study of clinically referred patients using Interpretative Phenomenological Analysis.

Young, S. & Gudjonsson, G. (in press). ADHD symptomatology and its relationship with emotional, social and delinquency problems. *Psychology, Crime and Law.*

Young, S., Morris, R.G., Toone, B.K. & Tyson, C. (in submission). Problem solving in adults diagnosed with Attention Deficit Hyperactivity Disorder: a deficit in planning ability.

Young, S., Morris, R.G., Toone, B.K. & Tyson, C. (2006). Spatial working memory and strategy formation in adults diagnosed with Attention Deficit Hyperactivity Disorder. *Personality and Individual Differences,* 41, 653–661

Young, S., Morris, R.G., Bramham, J. & Tyson, C. (in press b). Inhibitory dysfunction on the Stroop in adults diagnosed with Attention Deficit Hyperactivity Disorder. *Personality and Individual Differences.*

INDEX